Treating Co-occurring Addictive and Mental Health Conditions

Treating Co-occurring Addictive and Mental Health Conditions

Foundations Recovery Network Workbook

FOUNDATIONS
RECOVERY NETWORK

NASHVILLE

Foundations Recovery Network (FRN) is a behavioral health organization whose mission is to be the leader in evidence-based, integrated treatment for co-occurring mental health and substance use disorders through clinical services, education, and research. Through its nationwide residential and outpatient treatment centers, FRN has helped thousands heal from addiction and mental health conditions and live sustainable lives in recovery.

Central Recovery Press (CRP) is committed to publishing exceptional materials addressing addiction treatment, recovery, and behavioral healthcare topics, including original and quality books, audio/visual communications, and web-based new media. Through a diverse selection of titles, we seek to contribute a broad range of unique resources for professionals, recovering individuals and their families, and the general public.

For more information, visit www.centralrecoverypress.com.

Publisher: Foundations Recovery Network
    1000 Healthpark Drive Building 3, Suite 400
    Brentwood, TN 37027
    foundationsrecoverynetwork.com

    Central Recovery Press
    3321 N. Buffalo Drive
    Las Vegas, NV 89129

21 20 19 18   3 4 5

ISBN: 978-0-9861645-0-7

Publisher's Note: This book contains general information about addiction, mental health disorders, and these two conditions as co-occurring disorders, as well as suggested treatments. This information is not medical advice, and should not be treated as such. Central Recovery Press makes no representations or warranties in relation to the information in this book; this book is not an alternative to medical advice from your doctor or other professional healthcare provider. If you have any specific questions about any medical matter you should consult your doctor or other professional healthcare provider. If you think you or someone close to you may be suffering from any medical condition, you should seek immediate medical attention. You should never delay seeking medical advice, disregard medical advice, or discontinue medical treatment because of information in this or any book.

Cover design by Megan Hassell
Interior design and layout by Deb Tremper, Six Penny Graphics

Contents

An Overview of the Foundations Recovery Network Treatment Model

Since 1995, Foundations Recovery Network (FRN) programs have been providing treatment for individuals suffering from addiction and mental health issues. Our treatment model has been developed by incorporating direct feedback from our residents, reviewing the results of long-term outcome studies, and extensive research of what is proven to be successful in treating individuals with co-occurring disorders. The FRN treatment model is comprised of integrated, evidence-based treatment that incorporates a community connection and is tailored to individuals with co-occurring disorders.

- **Treatment of the individual:** FRN programs use what is called a *patient-centered care approach* where *you* are the most important contributor to the assessment process and the development of the treatment plan and goals. Our staff will partner with you in exploring your options, creating your treatment plan to help you meet your goals, and providing you with encouragement and support throughout your treatment with us.

- **Treatment focusing on co-occurring issues:** Addiction and mental health issues commonly occur together, and they often share similar symptoms when untreated. This can sometimes make understanding which symptoms are from addiction and which are from mental health issues somewhat tricky. Our treatment approach works to integrate both addiction and mental health issues into a single treatment model to support you in identifying your unique treatment needs.

- **Integrated treatment:** In an integrated treatment approach, balanced attention to mind, body, and spirit through ongoing assessment allows the treatment process to be tailored to the needs of the whole person.

- **Evidence-based treatment:** The methods of treatment FRN uses have been researched and proven to provide improvement in co-occurring mental health and substance use disorders. FRN has shown a significantly higher recovery rate nationally in long-term outcome studies compared to other treatment programs.
- **Community connection:** The FRN model recognizes the importance of a supportive community. Your recovery community—in residential treatment, in outpatient treatment, or in a twelve-step or alternative recovery community—is a fundamental building block for recovery. We encourage you to consider relying on your community for honest feedback, support, and mentorship through the program.

Acknowledgments

We would like to acknowledge the following individuals for their notable contributions to the creation and development of this workbook:

Jessica Wilkinson

Krista Gilbert

Craig MacLaughlin

Anna McKenzie

Molly Gentry

Jennifer Angier

Kathleen Bigsby

Paige Bottom

Megan Hassell

Elizabeth Jameson

Siobhan Morse

Lee Pepper

Andrea Rutherford

Rob Waggener

INTRODUCTION
You're in Treatment, Now What?

Now that you are in treatment, you will have the opportunity to partner with a variety of professionals, including psychiatrists, psychologists, medical practitioners, nurses, clinical and family therapists, social workers, alcohol and drug counselors, a case manager or client care coordinator, and alumni program specialists. This team can be a powerful resource and support system for you as you begin to clarify your goals for recovery.

Ask for a list of people you will likely interact with during treatment or even have as part of your team. Each of these professionals are here to support you in meeting your needs and goals. Depending on the specific program you are in, there may be an opportunity to participate in an orientation workshop, where an introduction to tips for successful treatment is discussed. If you have any questions, your therapist and/or case manager can help you find the answers.

As you begin your recovery journey, we have found that there are some specific considerations for preparing yourself so that you may have the best possible experience with your treatment team. Please consider the following:

- Be intentionally open, honest, and truthful. Allow yourself to be vulnerable.
- Try to say things as you experience them. Avoid censoring yourself or making your problems appear smaller or greater than they are. Your team is getting to know you, too; letting them know how hard things are for you will benefit you both.
- Be willing to look at your hesitance to engage. If you have a problem with any member of your team or course of treatment, discuss it.
- Be open to your treatment team's communication with each other. This openness can be uncomfortable, but it significantly aids your treatment. Sometimes it can be comforting to have open, honest support.

- Growth and change is uncomfortable. Push yourself to engage and stay focused on today.
- Invite family members or significant others into your treatment. Your team can help the important people in your life understand more about the recovery process and gain tools to support your recovery journey.
- Keep a journal or record. A journal helps you clarify your thoughts and your feelings, and it is a great way to communicate if you are open to sharing this with your team.
- Be curious about yourself. Ask for assignments, do work between sessions, and ask questions. Learning about yourself allows you to move forward powerfully in your recovery.
- Remember your team of professionals can't "make you better" or "rescue you from yourself." Be an active participant on your team.
- Embrace letting go of "managing." Avoid falling into thinking you can hold onto parts of your illness and get better enough to be able to "manage" it again.

Who's Who: Professional and Natural Supports

Having both professional and natural supports provide better opportunities to learn about yourself and to meet your identified goals. Natural supports include your friends, family, and recovery community members. Professional supports have specific training and expertise, and use of their services usually involves some form of payment. These professional supports may include relationships with service providers, such as doctors, nurses, counselors, therapists, psychiatrists, residential staff, and care managers.

The nature of the relationship with a formal professional support does not allow for the same level of reciprocal interaction or personal mutual sharing as with natural supports.

Professional/Therapeutic Supports

The relationships between you and your treatment providers are based on meeting your goals. The relationships are not balanced, but weighted; they give, and you receive. They have skills, services, or abilities that you may be seeking. Every effort is made to reduce this imbalance of power by shifting the focus to a mutual task: your treatment. Your treatment providers will be invested in you in this mutually shared goal; however, it is important to recognize and admit that the relationship has limits.

These limits are commonly referred to as professional boundaries. Professional boundary limits are in place to prevent the following:

- Excessive self-disclosure by the professional (sharing unrelated personal experience not intended to benefit your recovery).
- Exchanged or accepted gifts.

- Dual or conflicting relationships (such as support group sponsorship or relationships inside or outside of the professional setting, such as friendships or business or sexual relationships).

Because treatment providers are in a position of power or authority, they are responsible for managing the issues of boundaries, even if you intentionally invite or seem to encourage boundary violations.

Your professional support team will be made up of professional and service supports necessary for your recovery. It may include some of the following specialists (this is not a comprehensive list):

- **Internist (MD/DO):** A physician who specializes in the prevention, detection, and treatment of illnesses in adults.
- **Medical Specialist (MD/DO):** A medical practitioner who engages in a medical specialty or particular branch of medical science.
- **Psychiatrist (MD/DO):** A physician who specializes in psychiatry and is certified in treating mental health disorders. All psychiatrists are trained in diagnostic evaluation and in psychotherapy. As part of their evaluation, psychiatrists may prescribe psychiatric medication, conduct physical examinations, and order and interpret laboratory tests.
- **Care Manager:** Refers to the facilitator of treatment plans. He or she coordinates the needs in all areas of your life, making sure appropriate medical, mental health, and community services are provided. A care manager (also called *case manager* or *client care coordinator*) helps you coordinate and manage your care when you are unable to do so yourself or when coordinating your own care would distract from your ability to fully engage in treatment.
- **Nurse Practitioner (NP):** An Advanced Practice Registered Nurse (APRN). Nurse practitioners hold national board certification in an area of specialty and are licensed or certified through the state nursing boards rather than medical boards. Nurse practitioners treat both physical and mental conditions through comprehensive history taking, physical exams, and ordering and interpreting diagnostic tests. They can then diagnose the disease and provide appropriate treatment, including prescribing medications.
- **Therapist/Counselor (LPC, LCSW, LMFT, LADAC):** Can be educated in a variety of disciplines and performs within the scope of individual licensure, such as psychotherapy, counseling, therapy, diagnosis, psychological testing, analysis, and treatment of mental health disorders.
- **Residential Counselor (RC):** Generally an unlicensed support person providing guidance and assistance to you if you are in a residential treatment setting. The primary role of the residential counselor is milieu safety supervision and in-the-moment skills training within a residential or supportive environment that is directed by a licensed staff.

- **Nutritionist (LD or RD):** A person who advises on matters of food and nutritional effects on health. Nutritionists are recognized healthcare professionals who have undergone post-secondary educational programs in the sciences and have studied nutrients and other components of food in depth. A dietician has met specified additional professional requirements.

- **Physician Assistant (PA):** Trained and licensed to practice medicine with limited supervision of a physician. A physician assistant is concerned with preventing, maintaining, and treating human illness and injury by providing a broad range of healthcare services that are traditionally performed by a physician. Physician assistants conduct physical exams, diagnose and treat illnesses, order and interpret tests, counsel on preventive healthcare, assist in surgery, and write prescriptions.

- **Addictionologist (MD/DO):** A physician who specializes in the prevention, detection, and treatment of illnesses and treatment of addiction issues, focusing on the whole body, as well as psychiatric concerns.

- **Nurse (LPN or RN):** A healthcare professional who, in collaboration with other members of a healthcare team, is responsible for performing a wide range of clinical and nonclinical functions necessary to the delivery of healthcare.

- **Psychologist (PhD or PsyD):** A clinical professional who works in a variety of contexts, including teaching, research, and therapeutic work with patients. In direct care, they function as therapists, performing analysis and counseling, and do not prescribe medications, as compared with psychiatrists, who typically provide medical interventions and drug therapies.

As important as natural supports are, professional supports have the training and expertise not available to you from natural supports. They are able to be objective and to assess, teach, guide, and challenge without the conflict of deep interpersonal dynamics. They are able to create an environment to foster experiential learning through interpersonal practice within a therapeutic setting, such as residential treatment, intensive outpatient groups, or supportive housing. The drawback is, however, that they are unable to truly fill the role of "community" for long-term and interdependent reciprocal practice in the way a true natural support or community is able to as a person progresses toward independence.[1]

Natural Supports or Recovery Community

Professional relationships are oftentimes limited. While your recovery is initially formed in these relationships, it must continue and progress in true, natural relationships in your recovery community that are not time- or service-based.

Natural supports fill a different role than to assess, teach, guide, and challenge objectively; the nature of the interpersonal relationships natural supports share with you are barriers to objectivity. Yet, the asset in these relationships is that they are mutual and flexible, and they offer challenges that are difficult, if not impossible, to therapeutically recreate.

Unlike professional relationships, most natural support relationships have a past, can participate in the present, and can anticipate for the future. Your recovery can be supported and maintained in these sustainable, open-ended natural relationships.

Therapeutic Approaches

When looking at what works or what doesn't, it is often important to consider a few points. Is this treatment approach or method researched, tested, and documented as effective? Has the research been tested over a significant length of time with consistent results? Is the research applicable to you and what you hope to gain in your treatment?

A number of treatment programs use integrated and evidence-based treatment approaches, resulting in improved outcomes for individuals with co-occurring addiction and mental health issues. Be sure to either do the research yourself or have a family member or friend look for those treatment programs that will provide you with the best chance of having a positive treatment experience. A few of the models you may encounter may include motivational interviewing, community-based treatment, psychological education interventions, family therapy, trauma grounding skills and reprocessing, eye movement desensitization and reprocessing (EMDR), systematic desensitization, and community support groups.

Motivational Interviewing

Motivational Interviewing is a collaborative, goal-oriented therapy that focuses particular attention on the language of change. It is designed to strengthen your motivation and movement toward change in order to meet your desired goals. Motivational Interviewing assists you in defining and accessing your strengths, skills, and abilities. Then, by partnering with your treatment team, you are able to move in the direction of health and recovery. By exploring any discrepancy between your identified goals and your current actions or inactions, you are able to move toward aligning your behavior, thoughts, and feelings in the direction of change.[2]

Community-Based Treatment

Your residential, outpatient, or recovery community is an aspect of what is proven through research to support successful recovery. We encourage you to develop connections and a system of support that will allow both practice and enhancement of problem-solving tools, as well as social skills. Whether recovery takes place in a residential community, an outpatient community, or your natural community, the navigation of the community structure and the people in it provide valuable opportunities for you to learn and grow in your recovery.[3]

Psychological Education Interventions

These interventions can be classes, workshops, or groups that provide information about topics and experiences that affect co-occurring conditions. They tend to promote interest, learning, and perhaps questions, which in turn can result in a better understanding of the illness. They can also create opportunities to explore new ideas or new ways to live in recovery.

- **Cognitive Behavioral Therapy (CBT)** is aimed at resolving symptoms of ineffective emotions, behaviors, and thoughts. CBT is useful for the treatment of a variety of symptoms, including mood, anxiety, personality, eating, substance use, post-traumatic stress, and psychotic disorders. Some treatment professionals are cognitively oriented and focus more on the way people think. Others are behaviorally oriented and focus more on actions. Sometimes interventions combine thinking and acting; this allows for exploration of both orientations of CBT therapy. CBT was developed with a focus on the "here and now" and on reducing symptoms. CBT is one of the most widely studied and accepted evidence-based treatments.[4]

- **Dialectical Behavior Therapy (DBT)** has been demonstrated to be generally effective in treating symptoms and behaviors associated with personality and mood disorders, including self-injury, trauma, and addiction. In founding DBT, Marsha M. Linehan, a psychology researcher, combined standard CBT for learning to regulate emotions with meditative practices to increase the ability to tolerate distress, as well as to improve one's measure of acceptance, reality-testing, and mindfulness toward achieving successful recovery.[5]

- **Rational Emotive Behavior Therapy (REBT)** focuses on resolving emotional and behavioral symptoms. REBT was created and developed by the American psychotherapist and psychologist Albert Ellis. Ellis worked to show how patients' views of reality, language, beliefs, meanings, and philosophies about the world, themselves, and others were shaped by life experience. REBT can help you clearly see connections between triggers for behaviors, consequences for behaviors, and your beliefs about the triggers. Becoming able to see the connection between actions, outcomes, and beliefs is a fundamental skill for recovery.[6]

- **Acceptance and Commitment Therapy (ACT)** looks functionally at what you say and the things you don't like about yourself. It then compares those things to observable daily activities and functioning to help you clarify your personal values and to take action on them. It helps you develop a self-concept from personal exploration. ACT has been shown to help reduce rigid self-judgments and help in brainstorming a larger variety of ways to cope.[7]

Family Therapy

Family therapy uses a range of counseling techniques, including individual therapy and group work. It encourages involvement with significant people in your life, including spouses, partners, parents, children, extended family, or other support figures. It helps families to explore and improve relationships through increasing insight, empathy, and communication.

- **Family Systems Therapy** approaches issues with a belief that regardless of the origin of the problem and regardless of whether you consider it an "individual" or "family" issue, involving families in solutions is beneficial. It tends to view change in terms of the systems of interaction between family members, rather than with you alone. Families are encouraged to be directly involved in treatment.[8]
- **Communication Therapy** is used to build communication skills, both individually and among systems or families. It helps you build knowledge and skills about how communication is affected by historical and social context, and it helps you to move beyond presentation of words or body language to a place where you are communicating within a meaningful exchange of understanding—in which both sides are sending and receiving information and connecting.
- **Multi-Systemic Therapy (MST)** emphasizes your treatment as an individual and the treatment/education of the family. The goal of family education and treatment is to better equip your natural supports to both recognize and encourage improvement of symptoms outside of treatment. An example of MST is your family member sharing some treatment experiences by coming to a family week while you are involved in your own treatment.
- **Genogram** is a pictorial display of your family relationships and medical history. It allows you to visualize hereditary patterns and psychological factors that stand out in your relationships. It can be used to identify repetitive patterns of behavior and to recognize relational tendencies.

Trauma Grounding Skills and Reprocessing

Trauma grounding skills and reprocessing are skills used to help soothe anxiety by connecting you to the "here and now." It can help reduce defensive responses, such as dissociation, flashbacks, and denial. Reducing these defensive responses helps you become able to participate in process therapy for trauma issues. Grounding can be as simple as allowing you to tell your story in a supportive environment that is actively empathetic, which validates and normalizes your situation and responses.[9]

Eye Movement Desensitization and Reprocessing (EMDR)

EMDR is used to assist in resolving trauma-related disorders resulting from exposure to a traumatic or distressing event. EMDR may be used for other symptoms, such as anxiety or cravings. In EMDR, you focus on a second stimulus, such as eye movement or rhythmic tapping, while processing traumatic events. The rhythmic nature of EMDR is thought to assist with soothing the limbic system of the brain.

Systematic Desensitization

Systematic desensitization, sometimes called graduated exposure therapy, is a process that begins with learning coping strategies, such as relaxation, breathing, visualization, and meditative skills. Once you have these skills, you are asked to put them to use when faced with stressors. Effective coping through skill use can make it possible to view stressors as less threatening, based on personal successful coping.

Community Support Groups

Peer support, twelve-step, and other recovery groups are effective means to develop supportive connections. Participation in these groups provides opportunities for sharing challenges, experience, strengths, and hope for recovery. They also offer a variety of educational resources and successful methods to use as you continue in recovery. The slogan "I can't, we can" is rooted in the value of being a part of a supportive recovery group.

Medical Interventions

Medical interventions are integrated services focused on providing support in the areas of detoxification, psychiatric stabilization, ongoing medication management, pain management, disease education and management, and general physical health concerns.

Detoxification

Detoxification is the withdrawal of substances from the body. As the body and brain start to learn to function without the substances after long-term use, you may experience uncomfortable or disturbing symptoms both physically and mentally. Some traditional medications, as well as alternative medicines, may be used in the detoxification treatment plan to help reduce these symptoms. Added support through counseling, education, and nutrition can be beneficial as well.[10]

Pain Management

Pain management is a means of improving the quality of life for those living with chronic pain. The typical pain management team includes medical and mental health professionals. It also includes a variety of alternative approaches, such as massage, acupuncture, and biofeedback methods. Pain sometimes resolves promptly once the underlying cause has been addressed. Other times, especially with long-term pain management, you may require an extensive, ongoing treatment plan to manage the symptoms for a successful recovery.[11]

Medication Management

Medication management is a coordinated effort by you and your treatment team. Medication management assures the safe and effective use of medications to support your health. It can include monitoring and adjusting medications to reach stabilization, education on both symptoms and the medications prescribed, and ongoing appointments with the prescriber. Other support people such as your therapist, case manager, nurse, family members, and/or friends may help you be responsible for taking your medications as prescribed and assist in monitoring and reporting symptoms.

Getting the best results from medications can take you and your team working together to prevent drug interactions, assuring you have an understanding of your medication therapy, and helping you stick with the prescribed amounts and dosing schedule for your medications. Understanding the body and mind connection can be invaluable in increasing your ability to avoid relapse. Many times people report that when they stopped taking their medications, the symptoms came back, and they used alcohol or other drugs to self-treat the symptoms.

Care Management

Discharge, Aftercare, and Outpatient Planning

Proactive discharge/aftercare planning is essential in order to meet the needs of your increased independence. Prior to your discharge, or change in the level of care, a plan is developed to assure that your needs are met and that you and your treatment team have a clear understanding of the next steps.

Care Management/Client Care Coordination

The care manager, or client care coordinator, is the person who—working in conjunction with you, your treatment team, and other support figures—attempts to ensure, through assessment and planning, that your needs to achieve and maintain recovery are met. Care management includes support in areas such as accessing ongoing treatment, medication and medical management, housing, transportation, financial resources, employment, social support, community twelve-step resources, and family counseling services.

Alumni Services

Alumni support is a way to maintain connections with people who share in your experience of treatment and have the common desire to lead recovery-oriented and mentally healthy lifestyles. Alumni services offer ongoing events and valuable programs to help you achieve your goals for recovery once you have graduated from your program.

CHAPTER ONE
Body and Brain/Mind and Spirit

The Body, Brain, Mind, and Spirit Connection

The body, brain, mind, and spirit all coexist within you. The balance of each part helps determine your health. Prior to entering recovery, you may have struggled with one or two or all of these parts, which resulted in you experiencing imbalance. In this section, you will have the opportunity to explore the relationship between body, brain, mind, and spirit and learn ways that may assist you with staying in balance.

The Relationship: The Body, the Brain, the Mind, and the Spirit

The body and brain are *things*; they are physical objects you can see and touch. Scientists can observe, dissect, test, and prove much about the body and brain. In contrast, the mind and spirit are processes or *actions* and *things* all at once. They are the unseen processes or actions of humanness that produce the behaviors and expressions of thought, reason, emotion, judgment, perception, sensation, reaction, etc.

Body: The physical structure and material substance of a person.

Brain: The part of the central nervous system enclosed in the cranium of the body, consisting of a soft, convoluted mass of gray and white matter and serving to control and coordinate mental and physical actions.[12]

Mind: 1) The element, part, or process in the human brain that reasons, thinks, feels, longs for, perceives, judges, etc. 2) the totality of conscious and unconscious mental processes and activities.[13]

Spirit: 1) An animating or vital principle believed to give life to physical beings 2) an essence: soul 3) the activating or essential principle influencing a person; e.g., *acted in a spirit of love, recovery, etc.*

How Your Brain Communicates with the Body

The brain is the control center for your body, telling all the other parts what to do and when to do it.[14]

The brain has three main processing centers: the brain stem, the cerebellum, and the cerebral hemispheres (cerebral cortex). Each processing center controls different basic functions. Your brain also has two sections that allow integration of basic functions so that your mind can integrate, build, and share learning, which are the brain functions that make human beings capable of higher thinking.[15]

The brain communicates by sending and receiving electrochemical charges along a network made up of special types of cells called *neurons*, or nerve cells. The network passes chemical signals from nerve cell to nerve cell by electrochemical impulses, or firing in the synapse. The synapse is the space between nerve cells. This network regulates and controls any and all information sent to and from the other areas of the body, and it includes the spinal cord and the central and peripheral nervous systems.

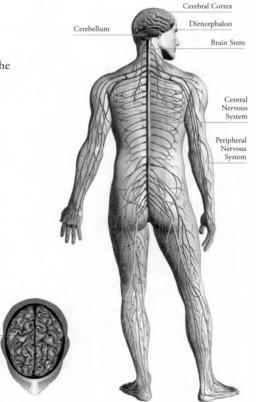

Brain Stem
Central nervous system functions such as heart rate, blood pressure, digestion, basic reflexes.

Diencephalon integrates the brain stem and cerebral cortex, allowing the mind to think and respond about sensory information such as thirst, hunger, and sexual or emotional response.

Cerebellum
Processing of information about balance and movement, extremities, arm and leg coordination.

Cerebral Hemispheres (left and right; together called the cerebral cortex)
Thought, speech, memory.

Left: logic, verbal, detail, science, names, math, strategizing, organizing, thinking, and writing.

Right: pictures, stories, general themes or ideas, observation, patterns, beauty, imagination, and possibilities.

Corpus callosum integrates the two cerebral hemispheres, allowing logic and creativity to interface.

The Message

There are parts of your brain (brain stem) that function on autopilot and control life-sustaining functions of the body, such as breathing and your heartbeat. There are other parts of your brain that function under the direction of the mind (cerebellum and cerebral hemispheres). These functions of the mind are willful, or voluntary choices, and range from choosing to move a finger to running a marathon.

Each neuron or nerve cell has a body, an axon, and dendrites. The cell body holds the specific message of that cell, and the axon and dendrites reach out to connect to or transfer the message to other nerve cells in the form of electrochemical charges, or the firing of the synapse.

The Messengers and What They Signal

The different nerve cells throughout the brain and body hold various types of messengers, or **neurotransmitters**. Think of the nerve cell as the student in class, and the neurotransmitter as the note being passed. The neurotransmitters each have various effects, but only two functions: to slow or inhibit an effect or to speed up or excite an effect. While there are more than fifty identified neurotransmitters, research is still expanding. Considering there are millions of nerve cells in the brain system, there is much more to be learned. Dopamine, serotonin, norepinephrine, gamma-aminobutyric acid (GABA), acetylcholine, and glutamate are the most commonly studied neurotransmitters and the ones most readily affected by addiction and mental health issues.

As neurotransmitters naturally pass between nerve cells, the message is mixed or transformed. These messages prompt the mind toward an infinite number of emotional and physical responses. Each message that the mind interprets, prompts learning—learning based on your individual experience.[16]

External chemicals or an unnatural signal can start or alter a natural signal.[17] Prescribed medication, alcohol and other drugs, or toxins can interject themselves into the loop, starting a signal or altering an original signal begun by the brain, mind, or body. Both natural and unnatural signals are chemical, and they travel on the network. Barring injury or defect, the physical brain has a pathway for all natural signals. If a medication or substance has an effect, it is using this network of pathways to send the signal and cause that effect. The brain does not make "judgment calls" on how to respond to chemical messages. It simply interprets the message and sends the signal on down the line automatically. If an unnatural signal enters the network and the physical brain does not have a pathway for it, nothing happens.

Signals		
Neurotransmitter	**Effect**	**Function**
Dopamine	Fine movement, emotional behavior, reward-based learning	Inhibitory
Serotonin	Sleep, mood, eating, behavior, anxiety	Inhibitory
Norepinephrine	Arousal, wakefulness, learning, anxiety, focus, impulse	Excitatory
GABA	Anxiety states (level of want/anticipation)	Inhibitory
Acetylcholine	Arousal, attention, movement	Excitatory
Glutamate	Learning and memory, balance. Glutamate comes before GABA, another neurotransmitter that helps glutamate work.	Excitatory

For simplicity, only the core categories or primary neurotransmitters are listed to illustrate the process. There are many additional elements to each synaptic reaction.

Learning through Signals

Everyone, obviously, does not respond or adjust to life the same way. We all have had different experiences, different signals, and have stored information in a different way. Each signal teaches the mind something,[18,19] and the mind stores that knowledge for later use. Your mind is as unique as your fingerprints. You have common ground with others, and you may share general ideas, or even reach similar conclusions. Your body and brain function the same way as those of other people, but your mind is yours alone.

Learning happens in the mind, but it begins in the brain. How does that work? When you were born, your brain came with all the neurons it will ever have, but many of them were not connected to each other. When you experience things, the messages in the form of sensory signals (touch, taste, smell, hearing, or sight) travel from one neuron to another, over and over. Eventually, the brain starts to create connections (or pathways) between the neurons, so things become easier, and you can do them better and better with less effort or thought. You experienced it, you stored it, and then you recognized it the next time you experienced it. Over time and with repeated experience, the signal communicates to the brain, and the brain recognizes the signal and responds without the mind ever thinking about it. Once the brain learns the experience, then the pathway is built.

Mental health issues and addiction interfere with brain functioning.[20] They can affect your ability to use portions of your body, senses, or the normal functions of your brain and mind. They can wipe away memory and, thereby, the experience and records that your mind uses to make decisions or judgments. In addition, they can affect your ability to learn and make changes in your life.

Being overwhelmed with constant chemically altered signals can train the brain to use new, maladaptive, autopilot pathways and responses. The mind becomes distracted by the constant barrage of sensory information. Your concentration, focus, or ability to think clearly can be significantly affected.

Mindfulness is key to changing these altered, automatic responses in the brain, giving it new recovery-focused instructions. Simply stated, the brain will continue to respond to the way it is trained unless you consciously and mindfully change it. You can learn to observe and control your mind by developing new skill sets, increasing self-awareness, and taking actions to offer the brain a new way to process.

There is an old recovery slogan that goes, "Nothing changes, if nothing changes."

The Body-Mind Connection: A Balancing Act

The wealth of knowledge and depth of study on the human spirit, brain, body, and mind is vast. Yet, with all that is known, there are many things yet to be discovered. You are learning some core information, which will help you better understand substance use disorders, mental health conditions, and the benefits of integrated treatment focused on the whole self—mind, body, and spirit. This awareness can prepare you to take an active role in your treatment and ongoing recovery.

A good way to better understand and visualize the body-mind connection is to imagine your whole self as a scale. Emotional functioning (mind)[21] is happening on one side of the scale and your physical functioning (body) on the other. Your spirit is represented by the axis of the scale, which has both the ability to keep the scale centered and even and bears the impact of imbalances.

If your physical or mental health is out of balance, your spirit is affected by the stress or strain; if your spirit is injured or weakened, the body and mind are likely to be affected by the instability of the axis.

Physical and Emotional Health

In recovery, the body is often the first place you may notice something is going on with your balance of mind, body, and spirit. In early recovery, many people are distracted by outside circumstances, thus having limited insight into what is going on emotionally or spiritually. Your body often responds to how you think, feel, and act, and when stressed, anxious, or upset, your body may let you know that something isn't quite right.[22] For example, it may do this by causing your heart to race or your blood pressure to go up. Your muscles could get tense, you might experience nausea, perhaps you have trouble sleeping, or you could experience increased levels of pain. There are many ways our bodies provide clues that we need to find some balance in our lives.

As you continue to develop and practice a solid recovery plan, maintain daily self-care, and keep an open mind to new feelings and ideas, things that come your way may be less likely to overwhelm you. By taking care of your body, mind, and spirit needs, your scale, or whole person, will be able to effectively adjust and balance with as little distress as possible.

> **Recovery tip:** "HALT" is a slogan that can remind you in a crisis to ask if you are becoming too Hungry, Angry, Lonely, or Tired, as this affects your overall balance and well-being. The solution to a complex problem can often be as simple as slow it down (HALT), eat some food (H), allow the anger to pass (A), talk to someone (L), and rest or sleep (T).

Here is a simple exercise that may assist you in understanding more about the connection between your body, mind, brain, and spirit.

When I Physically Experience	I Often Emotionally Feel
tiredness	
heart palpitations or high blood pressure	
stiff muscles or neck	
pain	
headaches	
injury or illness that prevents activity	
hunger	

When I Emotionally Feel	I Often Physically Experience
sad	
angry	
happy	
disappointed	
panicked or anxious	
frustrated or stressed	
out of control	

Putting It All Together and to Use

For all the wonder of the body and brain's communication, it is your mind that thinks, judges, engages, seeks, and learns. As you move forward in your recovery, you can begin to utilize the knowledge of how the body and mind work together. This mindfulness can help you develop a greater understanding of your choices. These choices can have the power to either positively or negatively impact your body, mind, and spirit. Developing and understanding the body-mind connection can be a significant advantage in supporting your recovery.

Notes

CHAPTER TWO
Addiction and Dependency

"Chemical dependency is an illness characterized by preoccupation with alcohol or drugs and loss of control of its consumption. It is typically associated with physical disability and impaired emotional, occupational, and / or social adjustments as a direct consequence of excessive use."

American Medical Association[23]

Addiction is defined as a state in which a person engages in a compulsive behavior, even when faced with negative consequences. The behavior is reinforced through the reward system in the brain, and so it continues in spite of the impact on the mental, emotional, family, spiritual, social, economic, physical, and/or legal aspects of your life. Through years of research, scientists have learned a great deal about the biochemical, cellular, and molecular bases of addiction.

Addiction Is an Illness

Research clearly indicates that addiction is a brain disorder that affects the reward pathways and changes brain functions. Addiction targets the underlying neurology (the developed structure and functioning of the brain), not outward actions. It is not a free-will issue, a moral issue, or a lack of willpower.[24]

Numerous factors contribute to addiction, including biological predisposition, psychological state, and social/environmental factors. As such, treatment needs to incorporate all aspects of an individual.

Addiction is defined as a primary disease, meaning that it's not the result of other causes, such as emotional, psychological, or psychiatric problems. You may have, however, already begun the addictive process as a result of some of these other problems. Like cardiovascular disease and diabetes, addiction is recognized as a chronic disease; it must be treated, managed, and monitored over a person's lifetime. Addiction is also considered a progressive and fatal disease if left untreated.[25]

Substance use disorders are varied by substance, intensity, frequency, and duration of use, and they present in differing ways. The use of alcohol and/or other drugs interrupts the normal functioning of the "reward pathway" in the brain.[26] As addiction develops, the problem moves outside the realm of free choice and develops into a long-term mental and physical neurological disorder. The need to seek and continue the use of substances is neurologically driven. The cravings and triggers to use are based in primitive, biological brain signals and structures, and they do not arise by choice. The brain's motivational center becomes structurally reorganized. The priorities are shuffled so that finding and using the substance (or another substance that will produce similar effects) becomes top priority as far as the brain is concerned. In this sense, the drug has essentially taken over the brain, and the individual is no longer in control of his or her behavior.

> "The brain regions and processes that underlie addiction overlap extensively with those that are involved in essential cognitive functions, including learning, memory, attention, reasoning, and impulse control. Drugs alter normal brain structure and function in these regions, producing cognitive shifts that promote continued drug use through maladaptive learning and hinder the acquisition of adaptive behaviors that support abstinence."[27]
>
> —T. J. Gould

In the addicted brain, a network of new, active neurological pathways, which the brain creates through increased neurotransmitter levels, is established to support the continued drive for reward. These neurological pathways are permanently established, and they will not simply disappear. Even after the discontinuation of drug use, you can have long-term, overpowering cravings. These cravings are, in reality, spontaneous nerve impulses and are outside of conscious control. The brain now thinks its survival is dependent upon using these substances.

The brain is affected in numerous other ways as well, complicating the recovery process. Withdrawal,[28] mental health symptoms,[29] the use of medications, and the absence of the "survival" chemicals significantly affect brain functioning. It is for this very reason that health and recovery require a daily and long-term commitment. It takes some time for the brain to reestablish healthy pathways and support the recovery process with ease.

The Reward Pathway

Research has shown considerable evidence that the dopamine reward pathway (mesolimbic dopaminergic pathway) plays a direct part in how you are attracted to and follow through with goal-directed behaviors. The reward pathway has been shown to be key when there is the perception of incentive, or something to be gained.

Substance use increases dopamine concentrations in some areas of your brain; these both intensify the experience of the reward of the substance and also prompt cravings for more when the reward is no longer present. More recently, research suggests that these heightened levels of dopamine are not as much about reward as they are about learned expectation of reward, meaning that the anticipation of the experience of the reward is what is actually increasing the dopamine levels.

Conditioned learning is a cornerstone in both human behavior and motivation. With the dopamine reward pathway intensifying reward and prompting a return to heightened levels by pointing back to the reward to prompt motivation, repeated behavior and conditioned learning is a natural outcome. With continued reinforcement of the neurochemical reward pathway through repetitive use of the substance, the development of "well-worn" structural neuropathways occurs. Just as repetitively traveled paths become larger over time, in the same manner these neuropathways increase and change. This process is referred to as drug-induced change in neural plasticity.[30]

Detox and Withdrawal

It is important to remember that detoxification and withdrawal[31] are not the disease of addiction. They are consequences of active addiction and are present in the early stages of recovery for some people with the disease. As these early stages pass, the disease is not cured. The disease of addiction is a chronic, incurable, progressive, and fatal condition if not treated.

The problem in the brain is not the presence or even the absence of the substance; it is the change in the biological and structural makeup of the brain that causes a primitive response to believe the drug is now an essential part of survival.

Use of Medications for Treatment and Withdrawal

Withdrawal can be life-threatening and must be managed with the support of your medical team and a carefully monitored medication protocol.[32] The National Institute on Drug Abuse and the National Institutes of Health strongly caution against limiting treatment to detox only, stating, "Patients who go through medically assisted withdrawal but do not receive any further treatment show drug abuse patterns similar to those who were never treated." The different approaches to detox focus on medication protocols. Medication protocols used in detox may be referred to as the following:

Taper: The same or similar drug of addiction that is reduced over time for medical safety or comfort.

Comfort: Medications to treat the symptoms that emerge during the detox process.

Assistive: Medically necessary interventions, such as fluids, electrolytes, or medications, to maintain or correct vital signs.

Medications can be used in various ways to assist in correcting brain function that has been improperly wired by substance use. The difficulty is that these drugs work primarily on one category of substance or another, and the majority of individuals with severe addiction problems are users of more than one drug and often present with medical or mental health conditions that may complicate the process.

During the detoxification process, behavioral treatments are introduced to help you engage and take an active role in your treatment process. Change is more likely to occur if you take an active role in the treatment process instead of taking a passive role. As you actively engage in treatment, change your belief about the rewards and consequences related to substance use, and increase your healthy life skills, some medications can be more effective.

In limited circumstances, medications may also be considered in the ongoing treatment of addiction. These medications may be used to block, reduce, or relieve cravings or create negative associations in addictive patterns.

If behavioral treatment to build alternate skills and motivation does not accompany use of this type of medication, the brain may recognize the use of chemicals as a solution that is within reach, and the mind may believe this to be true.

> **Note:** Research shows that overdose risk increases when the return to opioid use occurs following any period of abstinence. When return to use occurs, especially following the use of opioid blockers, the risk for overdose appears to increase substantially for two reasons. First, return to use often follows substantial periods of abstinence. Second, sufficient time has not lapsed between use of the opioid blocker and opioid use. When the drug fails to have the desired effect, more is consumed. When the blocker fully clears the body, an amount that just barely produced an effect one day can be a fatal dose the next.

Post-Acute Withdrawal Syndrome

Post-Acute Withdrawal Syndrome (PAWS) is a set of secondary symptoms that the mind experiences after initial withdrawal is over. The body and brain have detoxified from the substance, which is a step toward recovery. However, the mind is now missing the alcohol or other drugs that acted as messengers (neurotransmitting substances) along its pathways. Remember, the mind has built pathways to handle information with those substances present in the brain. The mind following detox has to take these tasks back from the brain because the pathway it previously provided for use is no longer valid. The mind's workload is significantly increased because, essentially, it has to relearn or establish valid pathways that are sustainable with only naturally occurring neurotransmitters or maintenance medication.

PAWS can last an estimated six to eighteen months after the last use. The trend of PAWS, if you plotted it on a graph, would show continual improvement over time; however, it can have periods where symptoms seem to alternate between improvements and decline. It is important that you be aware of PAWS because its symptoms can decrease your motivation, reduce your rewards of maintaining abstinence, and further complicate addressing mental health symptoms.

PAWS: Four Major Areas of Impact

Cognitive: The way your mind thinks.

- Racing or recycling thoughts
- High distractibility, low focus, concentration, and attention span
- Scattered thoughts, difficulty pulling together cohesive thoughts
- Rigidity in thoughts, black-and-white thinking
- Difficulty with abstract and conceptual thoughts
- Cause-and-effect reasoning becomes more challenging
- Difficulty recognizing themes and ideas; threads connecting disparate events may not be apparent
- Difficulty prioritizing information
- Creates stories to rationalize using as a solution

Physical: The way your body responds.

- Difficulty sleeping (too much/too little)
- Weight gain/loss
- Skin sensitivity to temperature
- Cravings for sugar

- Body aches and pains
- Uncomfortable in your own skin

Emotional: The feelings you experience and the meaning you attach to them.

- Deficiency or excess of emotion
- Tendency, compared to social norms, to experience too much or too little emotion for a given situation
- Tendency to let events, thoughts, and ideas take on exaggerated emotional importance
- Shame
- Repetition of events, thoughts, and ideas in your mind without the ability to solidify associated emotion
- Social awkwardness or social withdrawal
- Anhedonia, or numbing of emotions

Memory: Recall of ideas, events, etc.

- Problems with short-term memory: Recently learned information (thirty minutes to one hour) cannot be recalled without prompting. This can impair implementation of new skills or practice of taught skills.
- Problems with mid-range memory: After a short period, three to twenty-one days, information that was held when used regularly may be difficult or impossible to recall.
- Problems with long-term memory of past events: Events past more than thirty days are no longer contiguous or are absent all together.

Being able to embrace the difficulty that PAWS brings as simply being a part of the recovery process will be an important step in maintaining your motivation and reducing frustration and self-judgment. Friends and family will benefit from understanding what they are seeing. Many people in early recovery have reported that PAWS is exacerbated by stress and improved with consistent sleep, nutrition, and daily routine.

Recovery Is a Process

During the early recovery process, activities may be offered to you beyond your medical care, such as discussion groups, films, or other social activities. Although it may be difficult to simply get out of bed or take a shower, your willingness to attend the activities at any level is an important part of the process. Change, as well as the effectiveness of medications, is more likely to occur with a hopeful attitude and your active participation.

Re-establishing your health and developing a solid recovery plan will require medical and social support. It is a complex process for the brain to heal and reestablish itself and for you to embrace recovery. This may take some time. As the old recovery slogan goes, "Easy does it." This valued suggestion is something to consider as you begin to develop a daily and long-term commitment to a healthier lifestyle.

Recovery is a process of change—a change in thoughts; self concept; perception; behavioral habits; skills; social habits, family roles, rules and rituals; spiritual state; judgment; emotional reactions; sleep patterns; pain tolerance; body awareness; social relations; overall worldview... and absolutely everything else!

Recovery is a developmental process.

Chart of Substance Use at a Glance

Axis	Substance Category	What Do They Do?	Withdrawal Symptoms	Associated Neurotransmitters
I	**Central Nervous System Depressants:** Alcohol Barbiturates (tranquilizers) Benzodiazepines (Valium, Ativan, Librium, Xanax)	**Slow down body functions:** (Heart, respiration/breathing, blood pressure) **Reinforcer/reward:** Calmness, decreased anxiety	**Strong, painful, and potentially lethal acute withdrawal symptoms:** Shakiness, sweats, nausea, headache, anxiety, rapid heart beat, increased blood pressure, cravings, delirium tremens (DTs), seizures, hallucinations **Post-Acute Withdrawal Syndrome (PAWS):** Can cause (and/or prolong existing) depression and anxiety symptoms	Dopamine: Reward Serotonin: Well-being
I	**Central Nervous System Stimulants:** Cocaine Amphetamine Methamphetamine Caffeine Nicotine	**Speed up body functions:** (Heart, respiration/breathing, blood pressure, decrease in appetite) **Reinforcer/reward:** Increased excitement, energy, feeling of strength	**Strong uncomfortable acute withdrawal symptoms:** Depression, guilt feelings, body complaints, irritability, skin-picking, insomnia, anorexia (loss of appetite), anhedonia (loss of pleasure), cravings **PAWS:** Can cause (and/or prolong existing) depression and anxiety symptoms	Dopamine: Reward Serotonin: Well-being
I	**Opiates:** Heroin Morphine Codeine Oxycodone Hydrocodone Methadone Levo-Alpha Acetyl Methadol (LAAM)	**Slows down body functions:** (Heart, respiration/breathing, blood pressure, lowers temperature) **Reinforcer/reward:** Euphoria relaxation, drowsiness, decreased sensory recognition	**Strong painful acute withdrawal symptoms that last ten to fourteen days or longer:** Chills and hot flashes, sweating, cramps, nausea, tremors, loss of appetite, insomnia, dilated pupils, watery eyes, runny nose, yawning fits, diarrhea, panic attacks, bone aches, muscle aches, lethargy **PAWS:** Can cause (and/or prolong existing) restlessness and anxiety symptoms	Dopamine: Reward Serotonin: Well-being
I	**Cannabinols:** Marijuana Hashish	**Speed up body functions:** (Heart, respiration/breathing, blood pressure, increased appetite) **Reinforcer/reward:** Feeling of general well-being and relaxation	**Limited mild acute withdrawal symptoms:** **PAWS:** Can cause (and/or prolong existing) irritability, anxiety, physical tension, decreased appetite, depressed mood	Dopamine: Reward Serotonin: Well-being

Axis	Substance Category	What Do They Do?	Withdrawal Symptoms	Associated Neurotransmitters
I	**Hallucinogens:** LSD (Acid) Mescaline (Cactus) Psilocybin (Mushrooms) MDMA (Ecstasy)	**Speed up body functions:** (Heart, respiration/ breathing, blood pressure, elevated blood sugar) **Reinforcer/reward:** Great sense of pleasure, empathy, emotional insight, increased sociability, anxiety and exhilaration	**No acute withdrawal period established; symptoms vary in intensity and duration:** **PAWS:** Flashbacks, cognitive and perceptual distortion, irritability, anxiety, physical tension, decreased appetite, depressed mood, may cause and contribute to depression and anxiety	Dopamine: Reward Serotonin: Well-being
I	**Solvents:** Aerosol sprays Glue Paint thinner Gasoline	**Speed up body functions:** (Heart, respiration/ breathing, blood pressure) **Reinforcer/reward:** Euphoria, dizziness, lightheadedness, feelings of great power, or exhilaration	**Strong, painful, and potentially lethal acute withdrawal symptoms:** Shakiness, sweats, nausea, headache, anxiety, rapid heart beat, increased blood pressure, cravings, delirium tremens (DTs), seizures, hallucinations **PAWS:** Can cause (and/or prolong existing) depression and anxiety symptoms; strong possibility of brain damage	Dopamine: Reward Serotonin: Well-being
I	**Other Drugs of Abuse:** PCP (Angel Dust) Ketamine	**Speed up body functions:** (Heart, respiration/ breathing, blood pressure) **Reinforcer/reward:** Relaxation, drowsiness, euphoria, sensory distortions; or negative effects such as confusion, disorientation, paranoia, agitation, restlessness	**No acute withdrawal period established; symptoms vary in intensity and duration:** **PAWS:** Flashbacks, cognitive and perceptual distortion, irritability, anxiety, physical tension, decreased appetite, brain damage is possible	Dopamine: Reward Serotonin: Well-being

Notes

CHAPTER THREE
Mental Health

Mental health disorders are varied and can present in a number of ways.[33] When looking at symptoms, experiences, or functioning, you and your team will consider many different areas that will help reveal the whole picture.

The most common areas for assessment of mental health include your physical appearance, attitude or rapport, behavior, mood and affect, speech, thought processes and content, perceptions, cognition, insight, judgment, your history, and socioeconomic stressors.[34] Looking at one area of assessment alone may yield no clues; however, looking at a combination may help to clarify the diagnosis and assist you and your team in understanding the best course of action to support your health and recovery. Here are some areas that may be assessed during an interview or mental health appointment:

- **Physical appearance:** Your age, height, weight, manner of dress, and grooming.
- **Attitude/rapport:** Your approach and interactions during the assessment process. For example, are you perceived as cooperative, uncooperative, angry, guarded, defensive, or hesitant to be honest?
- **Behavior:** Your level of activity and excitement, eye contact, posture, and gait. Abnormal movements, such as tremors, tics, repetitive or fidgety movements, or lack of movement of body, eyes, or other body parts, may indicate a neurological illness or symptoms.
- **Mood:** Your overall feelings and how you perceive them. For example, you might be angry, anxious, sad, depressed, happy, uninterested, overwhelmed, or in control. Or, you may lack the ability to express your mood.
- **Affect:** How you express your mood or what shows on the outside. Differences between mood and affect can be symptoms in themselves. For example, how intense is your mood, and/or does it relate to the situation?

- **Speech:** The loudness, tone, clarity, and flow of your speech, as well as how fast or how slow you speak, word choice, repetitiveness, and intensity all assist in providing further information.

- **Thought process:** The quantity, speed, and logical awareness of thought, largely reported by you, and also observed in your speech patterns. Thought process can also be observed in behavior and within your level of focus or distraction.

- **Thought content:** The value you place on ideas, obsessions, phobias, preoccupations, convictions, control of self and others, and thoughts relative to mood or environment. Are thoughts intrusive or commanding? Do they seem rational? Are they observable beliefs?

- **Perceptions:** Any sensory experience that you perceive as real, whether or not it is. Hallucinations are external sensory experiences of sight, smell, hearing, taste, or touch for which there is no external stimulus. Pseudohallucinations are internal sensory experiences of sight, smell, hearing, taste, or touch for which there are no external stimuli. For example, the perception of voices in your head. An illusion is a distortion of a sensory experience when a real external stimulus is present, such as a garden hose being a snake or a patch of dry skin being poison ivy. Other sensory abnormalities include distortions of sense of self, place, time, or reality.

- **Cognition:** This area of assessment includes alertness, responsiveness, orientation to who, what, and where, and attention spans like immediate, short- and long-term memory. Also, it includes spatial functioning, language, and decision functioning, including abstract thought and the ability to process several things at once.

- **Insight:** How do you understand your own symptoms? Can you tell when something is wrong? If currently in treatment or under a provider's care, are you compliant with that treatment and embracing it as needed? Can you accept or refer to the problems as physical illness, mental illness, or addiction?

- **Judgment:** Judgment is highly correlated to impulsiveness, social appropriateness, self-awareness, and short- and long-term planning while considering the outcomes. This area is assessed to better understand your ability to make responsible decisions.

- **History:** This area includes previous treatment attempts, medications previously prescribed, history of substance use, family history of mental health and substance abuse, history or current suicidal/homicidal ideation or intent. Looking at this history helps paint a more accurate picture as to what may be going on today.

- **Socioeconomic stressors:** Many environmental situations can affect your physical and emotional health and your ability to heal. It's important to identify all these variables in order to develop a comprehensive plan.

You and your team will gather and review all of the information assessed throughout the process and develop a formal diagnosis. This will also help your team evaluate if medication may benefit your symptoms.

Receiving a diagnosis can be difficult for many people. Please take a minute to write a few brief sentences on any positive results you see in receiving a diagnosis, as well as any concerns for negative results.

_____

_____

_____

_____

_____

_____

_____

_____

Medications for Mental Health

Medications can be used in various ways to assist in correcting the brain's functioning due to mental health problems. The challenge is that it can often take several different attempts to find the medication or combination of medications that will be the most useful to you.[35] Why? Most medications used to treat mental health symptoms are not "single application" medications. For example:

- Co-occurring symptoms can overlap in causes and cover up other symptoms that may not surface initially.[36]
- Not all people react the same way to the same medications.[37]
- Not all medications are created equal; they often achieve the same end result in the majority of people, but are sent through different message pathways. Your doctor can be on target with your medication needs, but how to achieve the needed effect in your brain can take trying several different medications individually or even combining medications.

Also, over time you may develop tolerance to some medications. Although they might have been initially effective, they need to be changed or increased as your body becomes adjusted to the medication.

Remember Your Therapy

Behavioral treatments can help you engage and take an active role in the treatment process. Change can often occur with active engagement and participation, rather than with passive treatment or medication only. Your healthier life skills can enhance the effectiveness of medications.

Many in recovery who have co-occurring issues struggle with the fear of being judged for their illness, the need for medications, or the time devoted to appointments, meetings, and social limits that they self-impose to guard their recovery. If you find yourself hiding your recovery as if it were a shameful secret, this fear in action can often be the start of a cycle toward relapse.

Beware of Addictive Thinking and Medication Abuse

People with co-occurring mental health and substance issues report automatic thoughts like, *If one made me feel better then two will fix this; Just take the pill, and it will all be fine; I feel okay, so I don't need to take that today.* Your brain might try a few of these autopilot thoughts, so be mindful of how you approach medications today. Are your decisions supportive of your recovery? Consider asking for support and guidance throughout this process.

Please list a few of your beliefs about medications. Are these beliefs supportive of your day-to-day recovery?

_____

_____

_____

_____

_____

_____

_____

_____

_____

_____

_____

_____

_____

_____

_____

_____

Educate Yourself

Anytime you are prescribed medication (or treatment of any kind), you can increase your confidence and understanding by asking your prescriber/medical provider a few specific questions. You may find it helpful to copy the "Questions to Ask" chart and take it with you to make notes when you see your doctor.

Questions to Ask

Questions	Answers
Medication name (brand and generic)?	
How does it work?	
What symptoms led you to believe this treatment was needed?	
What are you expecting it to do for me?	
Are there other alternative treatments?	
How long before I notice an effect?	
What will I notice to tell me it is working?	
What are the expected side effects?	
Will these side effects lessen over time? Is there anything to help reduce or avoid side effects?	
What side effects are danger signs of an allergic or unwanted response?	
If I experience any of these danger signs, what should I do?	
What are the dosing instructions?	
What do I do if I miss a dose? Should I take it late or wait till the next dose?	
Will this medication affect my other medication(s)?	
When do I return for a follow-up?	

Note: These questions can apply to any treatment—acupuncture, physical therapy, mental health therapies, or treatment programs. Simply replace the word medication with the name of the treatment.

If you actively participate with your providers, you can have a better outcome simply by communicating. Your provider needs your input to best care for you. You are also more likely to stay committed to a treatment plan that you participated in creating, rather than one handed to you without your involvement or understanding.

> It is important to educate yourself, as well as trust your team to guide you with your medication choices. It is your recovery. Learning to follow your medication regimen as prescribed and to report effectiveness and/or symptoms of your medications to your team can be keys to maintaining your health, well-being, recovery, and success.

Cautions and Tips

One of the primary physical, as well as psychiatric, concerns associated with long-term recovery is treatment compliance. Treatment compliance is simply "sticking with the treatment plan" that you and your team have agreed upon. This can include plans such as adherence to any prescribed or recommended interventions, for example, medications, group attendance, holistic services, sleep, nutrition, or physical exercise. Your participation in the treatment plan plays a major part in achieving success. For this reason, learning to identify and overcome the barriers is essential to successful long-term recovery. Specific barriers to medication compliance may include the following:

- Difficulty *remembering* to take medications.
- Difficulty *obtaining* medications (due to financial cost, transportation to appointments and the pharmacy, or missed or canceled appointments).
- Unpleasant *side effects* of medications.

Some solutions might include using a pillbox, storing medication where you can see it, posting notes, keeping lists, and remembering to refill prescriptions.

The Pillbox

A pillbox is a simple method to help you to remember your medication. You put your medicine in each compartment of the container, and that way you know if you have taken your medicine for a particular day or not. The pillbox is also a great way of seeing just how often you take your medicine. The memory takes a while to recover. There is no question if yesterday's pill is still sitting in the box.

Medication Storage

"Out of sight, out of mind" is true when it comes to medication. Place your medication out in the open (away from children) where you can see it. This is especially important in the first week or two of taking a new medication.

The Reminder

Some people find that using an outside reminder helps, such as a note on the bathroom mirror, the door you use to exit your home, or any place that you are likely to notice at the start of your day and medication times. Setting an alarm on your wristwatch or cell phone to remind you of medication times can be useful as well.

Keep a Current Medications List

It can be helpful to keep a current medications list, complete with dosage and any special instructions. A list also gives you a reference when you fill up your pillbox weekly, helping you to make sure you don't forget anything.

Refills

Another reason people miss doses is because they forget to refill their prescriptions. Some pharmacies will call to remind you, but that is not always the case. Instead of counting on someone else to remind you, consider listing your refill dates on your calendar. The pillbox can also help with this. Filling up the box for a week will tell you if you are about to run out.

As you start to feel better, it is not uncommon to believe medication is no longer needed. It is important to remember that consistent use of medication results in stability and positive change and it should be continued unless otherwise recommended by your physician.

Diagnosis: Categorization and Communication

A diagnosis is necessary for your team of providers to communicate. It can also help you in talking with your providers about your symptoms and treatment.

Sorting out your symptoms, developing a plan, and applying skills should generally be your focus and that of your treatment team. Also, the treatment team will be interpreting your symptoms into a diagnosis that can guide the direction of the plan. As the symptoms change, the plan and diagnosis can also change.

Not a Definition

If you receive a mental health diagnosis or substance use diagnosis from your treatment team, it means you have enough related symptoms to place you in the grouping of people with similar symptoms and the related diagnosis.[38] It is important to remember that a diagnosis is not a definition of you as an individual. It is a categorization that allows providers to group effective individualized intervention tools based on the symptoms you present. It also supports a way for you and your team to communicate, especially when discussing medications.

Assessment

Mental health and substance use disorders are diagnosed according to the *DSM*, a manual of the American Psychiatric Association that stands for *Diagnostic and Statistical Manual of Mental Disorders*. A diagnosis is based on a system called multi-axial, which has five parts. Each axis, or part, tells you different information about the diagnosis.

- **Axis I** lists mental health and substance use disorders for which symptoms of mind functioning are clinical and generally improvable through corrective measures.
- **Axis II** lists personality disorders. These symptoms of the mind and brain functioning are generally improvable through learning and developing new skills.
- **Axis III** lists general medical conditions, such as the condition and functioning of the body and brain.
- **Axis IV** lists psychosocial and environmental problems, such as situational or environmental concerns.
- **Axis V** is the Global Assessment of Functioning (GAF), reporting numerically with a score of 0–100 of how you, generally, might be functioning in life.[39]

CHAPTER FOUR

Anxiety Disorders and Addiction

Living with Anxiety Disorders and Addiction

This information is meant to help you consider and better understand anxiety disorders and substance use disorders. It is common for these two diseases to exist simultaneously.

Anxiety disorders include the following:

- Generalized anxiety disorder
- Panic disorder
- Obsessive-compulsive disorder
- Post-traumatic stress disorder
- A variety of phobias

This overview can assist you in recognizing the symptoms of conditions associated with anxiety disorders, effective treatments, how to manage situations that can create anxiety, and how best to live with a disorder along with managing a chemical dependency.

What Is an Anxiety Disorder?

Most people have experienced anxiety, nervousness, fear, or panic caused by a threat of danger—a near-miss car crash, a vicious-looking dog approaching, being followed down a dark pathway or alley, being lost or feeling stranded—at some point in their lives. This is usually accompanied by a rapid heartbeat; quick, shallow breathing; sweating or cold, clammy hands; tightening or tense muscles; difficulty concentrating; catastrophic or negative thoughts; and nausea.

All of the above reactions are normal when they are experienced in a potentially threatening or heightened situation. It is also normal for a person to be anxious over financial troubles, going on a first date, speaking before a group of people, a child's safety, getting older, or being physically attractive. A little bit of anxiety can help people perform better; it can sharpen senses and motivate you to meet certain goals.

When anxiety becomes so severe that it interferes with your ability to be productive, reach goals, and/ or intrude on your quality of life, you may have an anxiety disorder. With an anxiety or phobic disorder, these symptoms are triggered at inappropriate times, are persistent and recurring, or may cause you to dramatically change your lifestyle or behavior in order to avoid situations that cause these symptoms.

Anxiety disorders are brain diseases. They are not caused by a weakness of character or lack of willpower. Anxiety disorders are one of the most common illnesses diagnosed today.

More than nineteen million Americans with anxiety disorders experience overwhelming anxiety or fear that sometimes does not get better without help. Anxiety disorders are illnesses that are chronic, tormenting, and grow progressively worse when left untreated. Symptoms can be extremely disruptive to leading a normal life. The good news is that treatment is very effective in relieving the symptoms of anxiety disorders and co-occurring substance use conditions.

Anxiety Disorders and Addiction

Anxiety disorders frequently coexist with depression and addiction.

Many people think that taking a drink or drug will help them relax or be less nervous. It is all too common for those suffering from an anxiety disorder to rely on alcohol or other drugs to medicate themselves in an effort to cope with their feelings of anxiety, fear, or depression. People with anxiety may find that the only time they can feel "normal" is when they are drinking or using drugs. The catch is that although it may ease the discomfort for a short time, in the long run, it doesn't work. Studies show that alcohol may have the opposite effect—increased tension and nervousness. It is also known that the effects of chronic alcohol and other drug abuse is highly destructive to a person's health and life, which only worsens the symptoms of anxiety, fear, and hopelessness.

Active use of some substances, such as marijuana and stimulants, can also cause symptoms of anxiety or panic, as can prolonged use of alcohol or other drugs. Also, many people develop substance use disorders and mental health conditions independently of each other, with each driven by different genetic, social, and biochemical factors.

If you are in early recovery from addiction, you may be experiencing some intense feelings of anxiety and possibly depression.

Some of these symptoms could be caused by withdrawal, new emotions and feelings, or maybe the anxiety was there before you started drinking or using other drugs and it has resurfaced. Feelings of anxiety or depression that result from withdrawal of addictive substances are not considered a disorder as long as they diminish during recovery. If they remain for a prolonged period then consider reviewing these symptoms with your physician.

Many resources are available when evaluating and treating symptoms of addiction and mental illness simultaneously. Trying to do this alone tends to lead toward increased anxiety, which can often lead to self-medicating by drinking and using other drugs.

The good news is that treating and managing anxiety and recovery, with the assistance of others, is very successful. You will be able to stay clean and sober, feel better about yourself, and lead the life you've always wanted.

A Personal Story of Anxiety

Anxiety is a difficult disease. Many thousands of people who suffer from co-occurring anxiety and substance use disorders every day go undiagnosed, under-treated, or untreated.

Here is Judy's story of how her co-occurring disorders affected her life.

"I remember when I was in grade school and had piano recitals. I knew my pieces perfectly, and I was good! But I dreaded when my name would be called. Of course, the other kids would say the same thing. However, now I know that there were distinct differences. Not only would my heart pound, but I felt as if it would come through my chest. Almost every time I would be playing the piece and then completely, utterly forget what I knew by heart! It was like experiencing a white-out—total blankness followed by feelings of humiliation. These were my first experiences with anxiety.

"After that, I would never raise my hand in class for fear of being wrong, even though I was one of the brightest kids in the class. I took a public speaking course in college. My heart would pound, my voice became extremely high-pitched, and often I would cry. I had total breakdowns. I described the heart pounding to doctors, wondering if the palpitations meant anything. They never linked it with anxiety. I also suffered from depression and was on medication for depression since my late twenties, but none of my doctors ever identified that I had anxiety as well. As I got older, I starting drinking more and more, and I became less and less active. That's when the depression really hit. Who's to say which came first, the depression or alcoholism?

"I had other behaviors that indicated anxiety, like constantly peeling my cuticles, biting the insides of my cheeks, and picking at my face. I realized all of this when finally I was given Paxil,

an antidepressant and antianxiety medication. This was the first time in thirty years I felt at peace. I could identify the behaviors that were anxiety-related only because I no longer did them!

"Shortly after being put on Paxil, I celebrated my anniversary in a Dual Recovery Anonymous meeting in front of over one hundred people and shared my experiences, strengths, and hopes. For the first time in my life, I was composed, coherent, and concise. I cannot describe the feeling when I sat down. For the first time, I knew that I had an anxiety disorder that was being helped."

Types of Anxiety Disorders

Following are descriptions of the major types of anxiety disorders:

Panic Disorder: Symptoms include brief episodes (or "panic attacks") of terror or intense fear that may strike often and without warning, and experiencing symptoms or "signs" that are observable by others, including difficulty breathing, dizziness, sweating, abdominal pains, and/or pain in your chest that affect your behavior.

Obsessive-Compulsive Disorder (OCD): Characterized as having anxious thoughts and performing rituals that you can't seem to stop or control. The thoughts are often repeated, intense, and unwanted (called obsessions) and the behaviors (compulsions) may be washing your hands, counting excessively, or checking things repeatedly.

Post-Traumatic Stress Disorder (PTSD): PTSD symptoms occur after experiencing or witnessing a traumatic or terrifying event. You will experience persistent frightening thoughts, flashbacks, or nightmares of the event, accompanied by feeling emotionally numb or dulled.

Generalized Anxiety Disorder (GAD): Recognized by constant and exaggerated worry, tension, and anxiety about everyday things, such as money, health, family, or work. Physical signs include headaches, fatigue, trembling, muscle tension and aches, and nausea.

Social Phobia (or Social Anxiety Disorder): Symptoms for this disorder include anxiety and a disabling and irrational fear of being humiliated and embarrassed in social situations, such as at work, with friends, at school, etc.

Specific Phobias: A phobia is an extreme and irrational fear of something like flying, fear of heights, elevators, driving on a highway or across a bridge, dogs, or injuries involving blood.

Panic Disorder: Each year, approximately 2.4 million people are diagnosed with panic disorder. Women are twice as likely to be affected as men.

Panic Disorder

The main characteristic of panic disorder is unexpected and recurring panic attacks. These can occur at any time, even when sleeping. Attacks can last from a few minutes to several hours, although most attacks peak within ten minutes, but symptoms can last much longer. Panic attacks are often confused with heart attacks. This is how co-occurring panic and substance use disorders have been described:

"I was in a car accident on a bridge five years ago. Recently, when I was about to drive across a bridge, I froze up in fear. I believed that something terrible would happen to me if I kept going. I could barely pull off the road; I couldn't breathe. I thought I was having a heart attack. I started craving drugs again because I wanted to get rid of that awful feeling."

• • •

"I've never enjoyed it, but I've given a handful of business presentations. In the past, I would drink a couple of shots to loosen up—liquid courage, as they say. But I've been clean and sober for three months now, and on this day, when it was time to stand and walk to the front of the room, out of the blue, it was like terror struck me; my legs wouldn't move. I couldn't remember anything, my hands were shaking, and I broke out into a sweat. I thought I was losing my mind. I was mortified. All I wanted was to crawl into a hole and start drinking again."

• • •

"I had my first panic attack after a bad acid trip. Now I never know when the attacks are going to come, so I dread going out in public. I don't want to be humiliated ever again, and I'll never go back to a place where I've had one. I don't have a life anymore. If I don't get help, I'll just stay home and die."

People with panic disorder may live for years without getting proper diagnosis and treatment. Instead, they may seek help at hospital emergency rooms (thinking they've had a heart attack) or go to various doctors for help.

When you are first experiencing panic disorder, you may not be able to anticipate panic attacks. However, after the illness has progressed, the panic may be associated with certain locations or activities, such as riding in an elevator or being in a crowded place like a shopping mall or being around a certain person with whom you've had a bad experience.

Characteristics of Panic Attacks

Here are some symptoms commonly associated with a panic attack:

- Rapid heartbeat
- Hot or cold flashes
- Sweaty or clammy feeling
- Shortness of breath
- Weakness
- Nausea
- Dizziness
- Chest pain
- Feeling faint
- Fear of impending loss or doom
- Tingling or numbness
- Fear of death or losing control
- Shaking or trembling
- Agoraphobia (fear of not being able to escape a place or situation)

About Agoraphobia

One-third of people with panic disorder also have agoraphobia, which is an intense fear of being in places or situations where escape would be difficult or humiliating. If panic disorder is treated early, agoraphobia can often be prevented. Agoraphobia usually develops because of the fear of having a panic attack in public. Those who suffer from panic disorder with agoraphobia often need another person to travel with them, such as on a bus or in a car, and to be with them when entering crowded places, such as a theater, shopping mall, and offices. If left untreated, panic disorder with agoraphobia can lead to a completely restricted and debilitating life, where the person stays home and only goes out when absolutely necessary.

Effective Treatment for Panic Disorder and Substance Use

Treatment for co-occurring panic and substance use disorders is highly successful through treatments such as psychotherapy, medication, self-help groups, or a combination of each of those. When panic and substance use disorders co-occur, treatment is most successful when integrated. Integrated treatment specifically targets both substance use and anxiety symptoms and addresses the relationship between the disorders.

Panic disorder is often treated with anxiolytic medications. However, if you have co-occurring disorders, avoid all addictive prescription medications such as Xanax or Valium. Talk to your doctor about a medication that is safe for you to use.

Obsessive-Compulsive Disorder

Every year approximately 3.3 million people are diagnosed with obsessive-compulsive disorder (OCD). Some individuals with OCD spend several hours a day performing rituals and end up unable to lead normal lives as a result of the illness. The good news is that treatment is highly effective. Obsessive-compulsive disorder involves anxious thoughts and behaviors that you can't seem to control. You may have persistent and unpleasant thoughts or ideas (called obsessions) that cause you to perform repetitive actions (called compulsions) in order to prevent some threatening event.

Following are some ways OCD has been described:

"I was convinced that I had to wash my hands five times in a row, five times a day, to get through the day without anything bad happening to me. I couldn't stop it, even though it didn't make any sense, and it kept getting worse. I was spending hours in the bathroom every day."

• • •

"After my husband died, I was devastated and turned to drugs. Then, I started collecting things like newspapers and magazines. It got so bad that I saved bags of trash, and I could barely walk around my apartment because of the piles of stuff. Once it started, I didn't know how to stop it. I thought the drugs helped me stop feeling so bad, but after a while, they only made me feel worse."

• • •

"Every time I left the house, I checked the stove, the windows, and the locks on the doors three times before I could get out the door. It was irrational, but the thought of leaving the house without

checking created extreme anxiety, so I couldn't stop. My wife kept telling me I just needed to relax, and she'd hand me a drink. But it didn't help. Over time, my rituals just got worse and worse."

Characteristics of OCD

Some common symptoms of obsessive-compulsive disorder include:

- A fear of contamination by dirt, germs, animals or insects, bodily waste or secretions, disease or illness, or environmental contaminants that trigger you to excessively clean or wash or avoid touching contaminated things
- Hoarding, saving, and collecting items or not being able to throw them away
- Need for order, exactness, or perfection that triggers you to repeat, count, or rearrange things such as books, CDs, dishes, clothes, etc.
- Excessive doubt and need for safety and control that triggers you to check things like doors, windows, the stove, etc.
- Behaviors like counting, repetitive tapping, touching, or rubbing yourself or certain items
- Frequent thoughts or images about violence or harm coming to you or others
- Persistent thoughts or images in your mind about religion, illness, death, or sexual acts
- Performing rituals or needing to do something in a particular way in order to avoid something bad happening

Many people do the things listed above, like alphabetizing books or checking the stove before leaving the house. The difference is that for a person with OCD, these activities take at least an hour a day, create distress, and have a negative impact on his or her life.

Effective Treatment of OCD and Substance Use

If you are struggling from OCD, treatment often includes psychotherapy and medication or both. Treatment for co-occurring obsessive-compulsive disorder and substance use disorders is more successful when integrated. Psychotherapy will typically include specific techniques for reducing obsessions and compulsions such as "exposure and response prevention." There are several nonaddictive medications available to help treat OCD symptoms.

Post-Traumatic Stress Disorder

This disorder affects approximately 5.2 million people every year. Post-traumatic stress disorder (PTSD) is caused by symptoms that develop after experiencing or witnessing an event that threatened your life or that of another.

PTSD is characterized by persistent thoughts or memories (for at least thirty days) and re-experiencing the traumatic event, feeling emotionally numb or unresponsive, and going out of the way to avoid things that may trigger memories of the event.

Many people associate PTSD with war veterans. Other traumatic incidents that are known to have caused PTSD are violent attacks such as rape, robbery, or torture; physical or sexual abuse (including domestic violence); kidnapping; serious vehicle accidents; chronic exposure to extremely difficult circumstances or depravity, such as hunger or homelessness; natural disasters; witnessing a violent crime or death; and/or loss of a loved one under traumatic circumstances (including abortion or still birth), and terrorist attacks, such as the September 11, 2001 attacks in New York. Any experience that you feel was terrifying or overwhelmingly traumatic may lead to post-traumatic symptoms.

Here are some ways that PTSD has been described:

"I was twenty-two and going to college when I was beaten and robbed at gunpoint. I tried to finish out the year, but certain streets reminded me of it, and I started having flashbacks that terrified me. I started drinking, and it helped make me forget, but then I'd wake up and it would all come flooding back, worse than before. Even now, if I hear a voice that reminds me of the attacker, I break out in a cold sweat and can hardly breathe."

• • •

"I was driving when my best friend and I crashed. He was killed instantly, and I only broke my arm. I can talk about it as if it happened to someone else. I don't feel anything, just empty. Every year around the date, I can't get the images out of my mind. It's hard to sleep or do anything. It's like I'm reliving the crash over and over."

People who have PTSD experience three things: re-experiencing, arousal, and avoidance.

Re-experiencing

You re-experience the trauma in ways such as having nightmares or flashbacks, feeling like you are reliving it, or responding to things that remind you of the trauma and cause stress. For example, George was beaten severely by some gang members in his backyard. Now, when he goes to the backyard, he breaks out into a sweat, his heart races, and he's constantly looking around to see if danger is near.

Arousal

PTSD causes symptoms of arousal, meaning that you may be in a constant state of attention, as if you are waiting for something bad to happen again. For George, this means he has difficulty falling asleep, is easily startled and feels jumpy, and gets angry without much provocation.

Avoidance

PTSD also causes you to avoid people, places, or things that remind you of the traumatic event. Using the same example, George is reluctant to and tries to avoid going out into his backyard and stays away from individuals on the street who remind him of the gang members. He also doesn't like to talk about his experience and generally feels "numb."

Here are some other conditions that someone with PTSD may experience:

- A sense of mortality. You may have a sense of dread or believe that you are not going to live past a certain age.
- An extreme reaction to the anniversary of a traumatic event.
- Memory loss. You may have experienced a traumatic event (or recurring traumatic events) so horrifying that you will not remember all or parts of the event.

Substance abuse and PTSD often go hand in hand. An experience of trauma is a major risk factor for substance abuse. Children who have experienced or witnessed a traumatic event and have been diagnosed with PTSD are far more likely to develop an addictive disorder later in life. Often, people with co-occurring substance use disorders and PTSD tend to experience even more severe PTSD symptoms than others with PTSD alone.

You may want to believe that using alcohol or other drugs will reduce your symptoms or that using these substances will help you forget or escape any reminders of the trauma. This doesn't work; your symptoms and trauma will remain until you get help. The numb feeling, which is described as "not feeling anything," "deadened," "sedated," or "emotionally frozen" that people with PTSD often have is heightened by alcohol and/or other drug use. You may feel that you can't cope with your symptoms without using, but covering up the symptoms by taking substances does not make the symptoms go away. Treatment does.

Characteristics of PTSD

Following are some symptoms commonly associated with post-traumatic stress disorder:

- Nightmares and disturbing dreams of the event
- Flashbacks of the event, triggered by ordinary situations or events
- Feeling as if the event were happening over and over again
- Avoiding people, places, or things that remind you of the event
- Difficulty sleeping
- Feeling distressed or panicky when reminded of the event
- Inability to remember parts of the trauma
- Feeling numb or emotionally detached
- Withdrawal from family and friends and activities
- Easily startled or jumpy
- Overly alert or watchful
- Loss of interest in things you once enjoyed
- Trouble being affectionate
- Distrustfulness and paranoia
- Irritability or anger
- Feelings of guilt
- Difficulty concentrating

Effective Treatment for PTSD and Substance Use

People's responses to traumatic events vary greatly. Some people may develop post-traumatic symptoms for a limited period of time or not at all, whereas for others, symptoms may last a lifetime if they are not treated.

Treatment for co-occurring post-traumatic stress disorder and substance use disorder is most successful when integrated. Addressing both, simultaneously, specifically targets both substance use and anxiety symptoms and addresses the relationship between the disorders.

Psychotherapy treatment for PTSD involves therapy aimed at reducing the traumatic nature of the person's memories and response to the trauma. A technique called Eye Movement Desensitization and Reprocessing (EMDR) may be used to help process traumatic memories.

Medication may be used on a short-term basis to reduce acute anxiety, but medication will not resolve PTSD symptoms. However, if you have co-occurring disorders, consider avoiding all addictive prescription medications, such as Xanax or Valium. Talk to your doctor about a medication that is safe for you to take.

Generalized Anxiety Disorder

Generalized anxiety disorder (GAD) affects up to four million people every year. GAD often goes undiagnosed because people do not realize that their anxiety is part of a treatable illness.

The main symptom of GAD is feeling excessive anxiety, worry, or apprehension more days than not for an extended period of time (at least six months). Other symptoms of GAD are similar to those experienced in panic disorder. However, with GAD, the anxiety is not acute, rather it is almost constant.

If you are suffering from this disorder you may not realize that you are experiencing anxiety, instead, you may consider yourself to be a "worry-wart," or overly protective of your children, or justify it by being under a lot of stress. If someone close to you thinks that you worry too much, you may have GAD.

GAD often co-occurs with substance abuse mainly because people attempt to calm their anxiety with alcohol or other drugs. This may offer a short-term solution, because for a short time, all the anxiety is gone. However, in the long run, substance use aggravates and worsens anxiety symptoms.

If you are diagnosed with GAD, you may find yourself anticipating disaster or death, constantly worrying about getting sick, financial problems, family, work, etc.

Here is how GAD has been described:

"If I got a headache, I was sure it was a brain tumor. If I heard a noise, there was an intruder in the house, or if the house was quiet, something terrible was about to happen. I was hooked on meth and I thought that's what was making me jumpy. I couldn't get through a day without dreading that something bad was going to happen."

• • •

"When I sent my son to school in the morning, I couldn't stop worrying about him, so I would take a drink. In the afternoon, I'd be worried, so I'd take another drink before calling his school. I'd drink and call several times a day just to check on him. If he wasn't outside waiting for me, I was sure he'd been kidnapped. I'd be drunk and frozen with fear. It was awful."

• • •

"I thought I was just a perfectionist, and that I was in control of my drug habit. Then I started having trouble sleeping, and started lying to my family about using. I was stressing about every little detail from where I put my car keys, to how I would sort the laundry, to how I could craft the best lies. I felt like I was running a marathon and couldn't breathe, but I couldn't stop. My heart was racing and I was shaky. It was out of control and getting worse."

Characteristics of Generalized Anxiety Disorder

Symptoms for GAD persist over a period of time (at least six months). A person with GAD may or may not also experience panic attacks. Here are some symptoms commonly associated with generalized anxiety disorder:

- Anxiety and worry
- Shaking, trembling, or twitching
- Restlessness
- Fatigue
- Difficulty concentrating
- Irritability
- Muscle tension or aches
- Difficulty sleeping
- Dry mouth
- Easily startled and jumpy
- Unable to relax
- Headaches
- Difficulty swallowing
- Sweating
- Hot or cold flashes
- Out of breath
- Lightheadedness
- Nausea
- Frequent urination
- Diarrhea

Effective Treatment for GAD and Substance Use

Medication or therapy or both are used to treat GAD. Treatment for co-occurring generalized anxiety disorder and substance use disorders is more successful when integrated. Addressing both, simultaneously, specifically targets both substance use and anxiety symptoms and addresses the relationship between the disorders.

Therapy often involves learning new ways of thinking about the things that worry you, learning relaxation strategies, and learning new ways to cope with stress. Antianxiety medications are often used to treat GAD. However, if you have co-occurring disorders, you should avoid all addictive prescription medications such as Xanax or Valium. Talk to your doctor about a medication that is safe for you to use.

Phobia Disorders

Phobia disorders afflict as many as 11.5 million people each year. The two main types of phobias are social phobia, also called social anxiety disorder, and specific phobias, such as fear of heights or confined spaces.

Phobia disorders are characterized by an irrational avoidance of a dreaded event, object, or situation that causes severe anxiety. Sometimes, phobias can bring on panic attacks.

Social phobia involves overwhelming nervousness and self-consciousness in a social situation, such as speaking in front of a group of people, attending class with other students, or participating in a social gathering.

Specific phobias include a fear of animals or insects, a fear of heights, confined spaces, traveling on planes, and crossing bridges, among others.

Phobias are often accompanied by substance use. If you have social phobia, you are likely to drink alcohol in order to help yourself feel more comfortable, or "normal," in social situations.

Phobia disorders have been described like this:

Social phobia: *"I dreaded the party for a month. I knew there'd be drugs and alcohol and I knew I'd make a fool of myself. I didn't know if I could say 'no' to drugs, and I was also terrified that everyone would see me turning red, sweating, and shaking. I got sick to my stomach even thinking about it."*

• • •

Specific phobia: *"As long as I can remember, I've been afraid to fly. I'm not afraid of heights really, just afraid of being trapped in a plane. If I got drunk enough, I could stumble on a plane, but it would scare the hell out of me. Now, I'm sober, and I imagine myself clawing the walls, trying to get out. It scares me to even think about it. I arrange my schedule so I can drive everywhere instead of fly; otherwise, don't go."*

Characteristics of Phobias

The following are some symptoms commonly associated with phobic disorders:

Social Phobia

- Severe anxiety and worry
- Self-consciousness
- Blushing

- Profuse sweating
- Trembling
- Nausea
- Difficulty talking
- Shallow breathing
- Difficulty sleeping

Specific Phobias

- Panic attack or severe anxiety
- Irrational fear
- Difficulty swallowing
- Sweating
- Hot flashes
- Muscle tightness
- Lightheadedness
- Nausea
- Frequent urination

Effective Treatment for Phobias and Substance Use

Treatment for phobias involves psychotherapy or medication or both. Treatment for phobias and substance use disorders is most successful when integrated. Addressing both, simultaneously, specifically targets both substance use and anxiety symptoms and addresses the relationship between the disorders.

An effective method of treating specific phobias is creating a situation where you are safely exposed to the situation you most fear (with the help of a therapist). Group therapy is an effective treatment for social phobia because the group setting allows you to practice skills and reduce your anxiety in a safe setting with people who you know. Antianxiety medications may be effective for phobias, but if you have a co-occurring disorder, you should avoid addictive medications such as Xanax and Valium. Talk to your doctor about a medication that is safe for you to use.

Effective Skills
Relaxation Techniques

There are a variety of relaxation exercises and techniques that you can use to help you better cope with anxiety disorders, panic attacks and agoraphobia, depression, headaches, fatigue, nervousness, and tension related to stress. And you might even enjoy yourself while you are doing them.

Many people pursue activities that are considered relaxing, such as watching a baseball game. However, this could also lead to more nervousness, anxiety, and stress. Any high-stakes activity will eventually have the opposite effect of relaxation.

Some examples of relaxation techniques and exercises are as follows:

- Breathing exercises
- Body awareness
- Meditation
- Yoga
- Visualization

Breathing Exercises

The simple act of taking a deep breath can make a difference between feeling relaxed or feeling anxious and panicked. Each breath delivers oxygen to your body and allows your body to release carbon dioxide, a waste product. As you pay attention to your breathing patterns, you may notice that your breathing becomes more rapid and shallow when you are nervous, anxious, tense, panicked, and fatigued.

Breathing is one of the least conscious activities that we do every day, from moment to moment. Most of the time, we don't even have to think about it. This section will help you learn how to breathe deeply, slowly, and normally so that your body gets the oxygen it so dearly needs. As you become more aware of your breathing, you will be more likely to focus on the present moment, rather than the past or future.

There are two different patterns of breathing:

Chest Breathing: Take a breath. If your chest expands and your shoulders rise when you breathe, then this is your pattern of breathing.

Chest breathing tends to be more shallow and rapid and may occur when you are under emotional or physical stress, are wearing restrictive clothing, or leading an inactive lifestyle.

Abdominal Breathing: Take a breath. If you inhale air deeply into your lungs and your diaphragm (it may feel like your stomach) expands and contracts as you exhale and inhale, then this is your breathing pattern.

Abdominal breathing is your body's natural pattern of breathing and is how you breathe when you are asleep and when you yawn. Abdominal breathing is your body's best and most efficient way to deliver oxygen and remove waste products. What is your breathing pattern?

Practice Abdominal Breathing

Here are two exercises that will help you practice abdominal breathing:

On the floor

- Lie down on your back in a comfortable position. (It is best to lie down on a rug or blanket on the floor. A sofa or bed will be too soft.)
- Focus your attention on your breathing as you inhale and exhale. Now, place your hand on the spot that seems to rise and fall the most as you breathe.
- Place your hand on your abdomen and press down as you exhale. Let your abdomen push your hand back up as you inhale deeply. Practice a few times until you feel comfortable breathing from your abdomen.

Bending over from the waist

- From a comfortable standing position, with your feet shoulder-width apart, slightly bend your knees. Now, slowly roll your body over, as if you are about pick up something off the floor.
- Relax your body into this hanging position, and take some deep breaths. Focus on breathing using your abdomen instead of your chest and shoulders.
- With your knees still slightly bent, slowly roll your body up to a standing position. It is best to try and roll up from your waist, one vertebra at a time.

Count to Ten and Calm Yourself

This breath-counting exercise will help you relax, calm yourself, and release tension. Practice this exercise regularly when you are not anxious so that it becomes second nature. Then, when you experience anxiety, use this technique to reduce your anxiety quickly.

$$\text{``1} - 2 - 3 - 4 - 5 - 6 - 7 - 8 - 9 - 10\text{''}$$

Hint: It may be helpful to have someone close to you remind you to "count to ten" when you are anxious. This is important because it is common to focus on your anxiety and forget to breathe during periods of intense anxiety.

- Sit or lie down in a comfortable position with your arms and legs relaxed and uncrossed and your back straight.

- Begin to slow your breath and breathe into your abdomen (not your shoulders).

- Next, as you inhale, count to four, "one, two, three, four," pause and count "five, six," and as you exhale, count "seven, eight, nine, ten."

- Continue breathing and counting for a few minutes. Notice how you become more relaxed as your breaths become deeper and slower. It's very difficult to feel highly anxious when you are breathing slowly and deeply.

Yoga as a Practice

Yoga is aimed at integrating the mind, body, and spirit through yoga postures, breathing, and body gestures in order to achieve a state of enlightenment or oneness with the universe. Stated simply, body-centered practices are used to purify the body and activate subtle energies of the body.

It is not a religion, but yoga is considered a spiritual practice for some. The philosophies are universal and can be incorporated within any belief system. Yoga has long been used for its powers of increasing relaxation, concentration, physical toning, promoting flexibility, and also is known for its healing and nourishing values. Most community centers and fitness centers offer beginning to advanced yoga classes. You are encouraged to talk with a teacher to decide if this might be beneficial for you.

Visualization

Have you ever imagined yourself in a happy place or situation? Then you practiced visualization. Visualization has been used by professional athletes to prepare for the highly competitive nature of their sports, as well as for helping to heal patients who suffer from chronic and critical diseases. Studies have shown that visualization can be so effective that it has been found to influence our physiology at a cellular level.

There are many commercial relaxation tapes available that guide the listener to imaginary locations, such as swimming in the ocean or flying amongst clouds. You may want to create your own favorite imaginary location. The idea is that if you can create a visual scene of relaxation then your body will adjust accordingly. Try this for yourself by imagining a favorite relaxing place. Real or imagined, try to recreate this magical location with colors, sights, sounds, tastes, smells, and anything else that comes to mind.

CHAPTER FIVE
Mood Disorders and Addiction

Living with Mood Disorders and Addiction

This section offers information about mood disorders (sometimes referred to as affective disorders), including major depression and bipolar disorder (also called manic depression). This section is written for those who are struggling from a dual diagnosis of depression or bipolar disorder and a chemical addiction.

This overview may assist you in recognizing symptoms, how co-occurring depression or mania and substance use disorders may affect you, and treatment options. People with mood disorders are five times more likely to experience substance use disorders than people without mood disorders. Mood disorders also often coexist with other medical and mental health conditions.

What Are Mood Disorders?

A **mood** is a prolonged emotion, such as elation or depression, which can affect your thoughts, feelings, and judgments about yourself, others, and the world around you.

A **mood disorder** can cause you to experience severe changes in your emotions and the way you care for yourself and interact with others and the world around you. Depending on your diagnosis, this could result in a full or partial depressive or manic episode. All aspects of your life can be negatively affected by a mood disorder—family, work, social, sexual, physical, emotional, and spiritual.

There are two major groups of mood disorders:

Depressive Disorders: This group covers all forms of depression, including major depression; dysthymia (also referred to as chronic depression); a combination of the two, where major depression intermittently occurs for a person who struggles with chronic dysthymia (also called double depression); depression caused by medical or substance use disorders; and depression as part of bipolar disorder.

Bipolar Disorder: Bipolar disorder, commonly referred to as manic depression, is characterized by experiencing extreme mood swings that range from the "highs and lows" of mania to depression. This group includes bipolar I, bipolar II, cyclothymic disorders, and mania caused by medical and substance use disorders.

If you think you may have a mood disorder or have been diagnosed as having depression or bipolar disorder, then your moods and the way you view yourself and others are being affected. If you are reading this section because you have dual mood and substance use disorders, it is important to consider that substance use worsens the course of mood disorders and vice versa.

The symptoms of co-occurring mood and substance use disorders respond very well to treatment that addresses both diagnoses together. Treatment might include medication, psychotherapy, or other treatments depending on your needs and symptoms. While treatment needs vary from person to person, research shows that people with dual disorders respond best to a treatment approach that addresses both conditions simultaneously and in one single setting.

Depression and bipolar disorder are treatable illnesses. It is estimated that 80 percent to 90 percent of all people with mood disorders improve once they receive the appropriate treatment.

Depressive Disorders

At one time or another, almost everyone will experience an unexpected or traumatic loss, a romantic breakup, loss of a job or social status, and profound heartache, sadness, grief, or suffering. These experiences are a part of the human condition. In fact, it is normal to feel sad, lonely, irritable, melancholy, nervous, guilty, get the "blues," and/or have trouble sleeping and eating during difficult times in our lives.

Symptoms commonly associated with depression generally occur during times of stress or bereavement. These symptoms might include sad thoughts or feelings, sleep disturbances, concentration difficulties, and other physiological and/or psychological difficulties.

You may be diagnosed as **clinically depressed** if your depressive symptoms last well beyond "normal" sadness and severely interfere with your ability to work, sleep, eat, study, and take pleasure in activities that you once enjoyed. Clinical depression affects thoughts, feelings, judgment, and the ability to perform everyday activities, as well as your recovery from addiction.

A depressive disorder is not a sign of personal weakness or the lack of being able to "pull yourself together." Depression is nothing to be ashamed of and is a serious health disorder that can be treated.

Without treatment, symptoms can last for weeks, months, or years. The good news is that people with dual disorders who suffer from depression, even extremely severe depression, can be helped with the appropriate treatment.

Depression comes in different forms, and not everyone will experience the same symptoms or severity of symptoms. However, there are general guidelines that help to define the different types of depression.

The Different Types of Depressive Disorders

Here are the common depressive disorders:

- Dysthymia (also called *Chronic Depression*)
- Mood Disorder Caused by a General Medical Condition
- Double Depression
- Seasonal Affective Disorder (SAD)
- Mood Disorder and Depressive Disorder Not Otherwise Specified (NOS)

Depression can make you more likely to use alcohol or other drugs in an attempt to feel better or, likewise, if you have used alcohol or other drugs for a long period of time, then you may experience depressive symptoms. People also can develop substance use disorders and mental health conditions, independent of the other, with each driven by different genetic, social, and biochemical factors.

Note: Did you know that about one half of the people with major depression also experience symptoms of anxiety disorder?

Depression is often described as the "common cold of mental illness."

Here are some ways people describe suffering from co-occurring substance use and depressive disorders:

"Being depressed made me want to drink again. Drinking made me depressed. I was in a vicious cycle."

• • •

"I tried to cover up my bad feelings with drugs and alcohol, but things just kept getting worse, until I lost hope that I'd ever be okay again."

• • •

"I couldn't get out of bed for days. I didn't want to do anything or see anyone. I was taking more and more pain medicine to try and block out my physical and mental pain. Not only did it not help, but I pulled further and further away from my friends and family."

• • •

"Everything seemed bleak and dark, like I was being sucked into a black hole. It was painful. I don't want to go through that again."

• • •

"I felt worthless, like the world was against me and nobody cared, not even my husband and family. I thought they all despised me. With treatment, I know depression was the culprit. They love me, and I love them."

Major Depression

Major depression (also called unipolar depression or clinical depression) is one of the most commonly diagnosed mental health disorders. Symptoms that affect most people include a depressed mood or loss of interest in previously enjoyed activities. Other symptoms vary from person to person, including weight loss or gain, changes in sleeping, fatigue and loss of energy, difficulty concentrating, feelings of worthlessness or guilt, being suicidal, and other physiological and/or psychological symptoms. These may occur as a single episode, be ongoing and persistent, or occur in multiple episodes.

Characteristics of Major Depression

The most common characteristics of depression are as follows:

- Loss of interest in most or all activities that you once enjoyed
- Persistent sadness
- Anxiety
- Unpleasant or empty mood

Other symptoms that may accompany the above symptoms are as follows:

- Hopelessness, pessimism, a negative worldview
- Feelings of guilt, worthlessness, helplessness

- Insomnia, either early-morning awakening or oversleeping
- Any change in appetite resulting in severe weight loss or gain of weight
- Less energy, fatigue, slowed movement
- Using alcohol or other drugs excessively
- Thoughts of death or suicide; suicide attempts
- Restlessness, irritability, physical agitation
- Difficulty concentrating or making decisions
- Slowed thinking
- Delusions or hallucinations
- Decreased sex drive
- Crying spells or feeling too sad to cry

Keep in mind that some medications may cause depressive symptoms as side effects, and even a viral infection can cause the same symptoms. Your doctor will want to rule out these causes through an examination, discussion, and lab tests. If you think this could be happening to you, call your doctor right away.

Effective Treatment for Depressive Disorders

A combination of counseling, medication, and support strategies (for example, twelve-step groups, sponsorship, etc.) can be highly successful at treating co-occurring depression and substance use disorders. There are several styles or approaches of counseling that can be helpful: interpersonal, cognitive-behavioral, supportive, and dynamic. You may be encouraged to work on recognizing negative thoughts and patterns and learn how to change them into more positive thoughts and learn problem-solving skills, as well as learning other helpful tools.

There are many medications available to treat depression, and there are also a number that are particularly helpful in reducing cravings or calming feelings of withdrawal. Talk with your doctor to evaluate the ones that would best suit your treatment needs.

Support strategies include developing healthy support networks. This can occur through attendance at recovery meetings (DRA, AA, NA), obtaining a sponsor, and cultivating relationships with people who support your dual recovery.

Dysthymia Disorder

Dysthymia (pronounced dis-thigh-me-a), also called chronic depression, involves long-term, persistent "smoldering" symptoms that are not disabling, but may interfere with feeling good or functioning well. Symptoms include a depressed mood and decreased energy, devalued self-esteem, general negativity, and an overwhelming feeling of hopelessness and dissatisfaction. Dysthymia does not appear as episodes; symptoms are constant from day-to-day. Dysthymia tends to be more persistent and unceasing than major depression, but its symptoms tend to be less intense or severe in nature.

Characteristics of Dysthymia

Dysthymia disorder includes these traits:

- A depressed, sad, anxious, unpleasant, or empty mood for most of the day, most days, for at least a period of two years
- A change in eating patterns, such as a loss of appetite or overeating
- A change in sleeping patterns, such as insomnia or oversleeping regularly
- Low energy or fatigue
- Low self-esteem
- Poor concentration or difficulty making decisions
- Experiencing feelings of hopelessness
- Feeling sad or "blue"
- Loss of interest or pleasure in most or all activities that you once enjoyed

Note: Symptoms of dysthymia can exist with major depression and other depressive or bipolar disorders and can exist due to substance use. Your doctor or counselor will need to ask you some specific questions about your condition before making a diagnosis.

Effective Treatment for Dysthymia

Since dysthymia is a chronic disorder and often goes untreated, many people with this condition find themselves using mental health and chemical dependency inpatient and outpatient treatment services. However, without a proper diagnosis, many of the underlying causes and symptoms can continue.

Treatment includes counseling, medication, and individual recovery strategies, such as self-help groups and support systems. Counseling may include how-to strategies for identifying and solving problems, keeping a journal, and taking an active role in changing negative behaviors. Both cognitive and behavioral counseling approaches have proven successful. Twelve-step programs such as Dual Recovery Anonymous (DRA), Narcotics Anonymous (NA), Alcoholics Anonymous (AA), or other mutual support programs are also recommended for an effective dual recovery plan.

Antidepressant medications are available to treat dysthymia, and there are also a number of medications that are particularly helpful in reducing cravings or calming feelings of withdrawal. Talk with your doctor to develop an integrated treatment plan to best suit your needs.

Mood Disorder Caused by a Medical Condition or Substance Use

Some mood disturbances are the direct result of a specific general medical condition such as stroke, heart condition, multiple sclerosis, hypothyroidism, or other such conditions. In other situations, mood disturbances can be caused by the use or abuse of substances, including prescribed medications or alcohol and/or other drugs.

For those mood disorders caused by a medical condition, there is a direct physiological cause for the disorder and symptoms occur while taking the medication or drug, while intoxicated, or during withdrawal. Mood-related symptoms are the same as for clinical depression or mania, and the symptoms and treatment are generally the same as for clinical depression or mania.

Characteristics of a Mood Disorder Caused by a Medical Condition or Substance Use

Mood disorder caused by a medical condition or substance use includes these traits:

- Many or most of the symptoms associated with major depression
- Many or most of the symptoms associated with mania

Other symptoms that may accompany the above symptoms are (you may only experience one of these):

- A diagnosis of a medical condition such as chronic pain, hypothyroidism, cardiac problems or recent cardiac surgery, multiple sclerosis, recent stroke, or another condition coinciding with the onset of mood-related symptoms.
- Onset of mood-related symptoms during substance use, while intoxicated, or during withdrawal. Substances can include alcohol and other drugs/medications whether legal or illegal.

Effective Treatment for Mood Disorders Caused by Medical Conditions or Substance Use

It is very important that medical professionals, including your doctor and psychiatrist, are involved in your treatment. Depending on various factors, your symptoms and treatment are generally the same as for clinical depression or mania. In cases of mood disorders caused by medical conditions, it is essential that treatment be provided for the medical condition as well. In cases of mood disorders caused by substance use, consideration must be given to the types of substances to determine the course of treatment.

Double Depression

If you are diagnosed with dysthymia and you experience times when the severity of your symptoms of depression worsens, then double depression may be diagnosed. Usually, when the episode of major depression is over, you will return to your dysthymic state.

Double depression occurs when an individual with dysthymia experiences an episode of major depression in addition to symptoms of dysthymia. A person with double depression is more likely to experience relapses and recurrences than an individual with single depression alone, and women are more susceptible to double depression.

Characteristics of Double Depression

Double depression includes these traits:

- Meets criteria for dysthymia with chronic symptoms over the past two years
- Recent onset of symptoms of major depression

Effective Treatment for Double Depression

Treatment for double depression is essentially the same as for clinical depression and dysthymia. The overall goal for treatment is to treat both the depression and the dysthymia, in addition to any other co-occurring conditions. An evaluation by a good psychiatrist is crucial for deciding if medication might be helpful. Also, counseling, as well as attending a support group, is very important. Work with your counselor to map out the treatment plan that works best for you and your lifestyle.

Seasonal Affective Disorder

Seasonal Affective Disorder (SAD) is not a separate mood disorder. Rather, it is diagnosed when you have periods of depression that are influenced by specific seasons of the year.

The more common version of SAD, winter depression, occurs during the fall or early winter and ends during summer months. The less common SAD, summer depression, usually begins during spring or early summer and lasts until winter. Seasonal patterns are more likely to occur for people who have major depression or bipolar II diagnoses and more commonly occur in women than in men.

Characteristics of Seasonal Affective Disorder

Seasonal affective disorder includes these traits:

- Meets symptoms listed for major depression (or depression as part of bipolar II)
- There is a relationship between the depressive episode and a particular time of the year (not associated with an annual stressful event, such as school beginning each fall)

- The depression either ends altogether or changes (to mania or hypomania) at a certain time of the year
- The seasonal depressive pattern has occurred for at least two years with no symptoms of major depression outside of the pattern
- Over your history, there have been more episodes of depression falling within, rather than outside of, the seasonal pattern

Effective Treatment of Seasonal Affective Disorder

There are a number of highly effective treatments for seasonal affective disorder. These treatments depend on your diagnosis and may include medication, psychotherapy, and light therapy (also referred to as phototherapy), among others.

If you also have a co-occurring disorder, increased substance use (or relapse) is strongly associated with changes in mood-related symptoms. Therefore, it is important to recognize your patterns of substance use (and times of increased cravings) and mood-related symptoms. This will help you understand your conditions better and how they impact or influence each other.

Mood Disorder and Depressive Disorder Not Otherwise Specified

This mood disorder and depressive category, referred to as "Not Otherwise Specified," (NOS) is provided for people who have symptoms of a disorder that don't exactly match a specific diagnosis. Mood disorder not otherwise specified (NOS) is diagnosed when you experience mood symptoms that do not meet the criteria for any specific mood disorder and in which it is difficult to choose between depressive disorder NOS and bipolar disorder NOS.

Depressive disorder NOS is chosen when symptoms include depressive traits but do not meet all of the criteria for that diagnosis. Examples might include:

- A person who experiences a minor depressive episode that lasts at least two weeks but with fewer than five items required for major depressive disorder.
- A person whose counselor has concluded that a depressive disorder is present, but the counselor is unable to determine if it is primary, due to a medical condition or substance induced.

Bipolar Disorders

Bipolar disorder ("*bi*" means "*two*" and "*polar*" refers to opposite states of mind) is the medical name for manic depression, and it is characterized as having pronounced mood swings from the "highs and lows" of extremely elevated moods (mania), to extremely low moods (depression) that are out of proportion with what is actually happening in a person's life. Some people experience a "mixed state" of both manic and depressed symptoms.

Manic episodes are characterized by having grandiose thoughts, being overactive, having persistently elevated or irritable moods, a decreased need for sleep, increased talkativeness, racing thoughts or ideas, inappropriate social behavior, impaired judgment, and having an inflated self-esteem. Sometimes mania is accompanied by symptoms of psychosis, such as feeling that others are trying to cause harm (paranoia), overvalued ideas, delusions, or seeing, hearing, or sensing the presence of others not actually there (hallucinations).

Hypomanic episodes are mild forms of mania. Often, but not always, people who experience hypomania say they like the way it "helps" them function, heightening their sense of creativity or productivity. Hypomania occurs without the same level of impairment in judgment or performance seen with mania and does not include psychotic symptoms. Hypomania might include racing thoughts, extreme agitation, overconfidence, reduced sleep or insomnia, and other physiological and/or psychological difficulties.

Depressive episodes are the opposite of manic symptoms and include feeling low/blue, depressed, helpless, or worthless a majority of the time; a loss of interest in most normal activities; significant changes in appetite or weight; a change in sleep patterns; loss of energy level and fatigue; feelings of inappropriate guilt; and recurring thoughts of death and suicide. As with mania, sometimes depression is accompanied by symptoms of psychosis, including paranoia, delusions, or hallucinations.

If you or someone you know has been diagnosed with bipolar disorder, be aware that there is a high risk of relapse for using alcohol and/or other drugs, especially during manic episodes. In fact, substance use disorders are more likely to co-exist with bipolar disorders than with any other mental health condition. Mania can impair judgment, increase urges, and reduce impulse control. Mania can also worsen existing cravings and symptoms related to substance use diagnoses and, alone or in combination with the substance use condition, can increase the risk of suicide.

Use of alcohol and other drugs can be very dangerous when mixed with certain medications and can result in relapse. Keep in mind that there are therapeutic skills and medications that can help and support you in your recovery.

The Different Types of Bipolar Disorders

Here are the common bipolar disorders:

- Bipolar disorder I
- Bipolar disorder II
- Cyclothymia

Following are some of the ways people describe suffering from general bipolar disorder:

"Although I had a good education and could 'hold it together' to get a well-paying job, I never could seem to hold a job for more than two months. Something would tick me off and I'd just quit, positive that I'd find a better one. Many, many times I found I was spending more money on cocaine than I could make in several years, even if I was able to hold a job. I always felt like I was on the edge."

• • •

"My mom would practically skip from bar to bar, drinking with any man she could, and with no worries in the world. She was a manic mess."

• • •

"I have been using crack cocaine since I was twenty years old. There are times when I felt like it inspired my creativity as well as my bravery. I have started several companies, taken a weekend workshop on investing in China, and convinced my family to invest in my businesses. I've declared bankruptcy twice."

• • •

"There were days when I felt like everything was going my way and I could conquer anything. Then one morning I'd wake up feeling like I didn't have a reason to live, like everything was bleak and without purpose. I would use the pills my doctor gave me for back pain to try to mask the pain deep in my soul."

• • •

"I spent a fortune on exercise equipment and clothes and was all excited about working out every day, but then I lost all interest and started binging on food in the middle of the night. I gained forty pounds and was sleeping all the time."

• • •

Bipolar Disorder I

Bipolar disorder I is a serious condition recognized by dramatic swings of feelings, from episodes of severe lows (major depression) to extreme highs (mania). This is most often a chronic condition. The risk of substance use along with bipolar disorder is high, especially during periods of mania.

Characteristics of Bipolar I Disorder

Mania can be considered the opposite of depression. In bipolar disorder, cycles of alternating periods of depression and mania occur. The most common characteristics of mania, as associated with bipolar disorder, are as follows.

Mania includes these traits:

- Abnormally inflated self-esteem or larger than life notions, such as feeling "on top of the world" or extremely powerful
- Inappropriate elevated or irritable mood that lasts for several days
- Overactive and easily distracted
- Over-talkative (talking too much or too fast, changing topics quickly)
- Excessive use of alcohol or other drugs
- Disconnected and racing thoughts
- Decreased need for sleep (feeling rested after only a few hours of sleep or not sleeping for days without tiring)
- Increased sexual desire
- Increase in goal-directed activities (such as starting ambitious projects, starting a business, or excessive cleaning)
- Physical agitation
- Inappropriate social behavior
- Poor judgment and disregard of risk; may become excessively involved in risky behavior or activities (such as gambling, going on a spending spree, engaging in unprotected sex, using street drugs)
- Delusions (believing things that are not true) or hallucinations (seeing or hearing things that are not there)
- Grandiose behavior (doing or saying things because of an inflated sense of one's power, knowledge, worth, or skills; for example, claiming to be a doctor without reason)

Using alcohol or other drugs (especially "street" or illegal drugs) can cause some people to react with the symptoms listed for depression or mania. Therefore, it is sometimes difficult to know whether a person has bipolar disorder or is simply experiencing the effects of drug use. In order to have bipolar disorder, the symptoms of mania must be present even without drug use.

Effective Treatment for Bipolar Disorder I

If you are diagnosed with bipolar disorder, treatment may, at first, seem very dramatic and possibly negative because it may affect your creativity, energy levels, and/or productivity, which are a result of mania. However, remember that you will have control of your life again, and the extreme lows of depression will no longer be a problem. Consider giving yourself time to regain function of your daily life and reap the benefits of no longer cycling through extreme highs and lows.

Taking medication is typically the first line of treatment. As a rule, it takes several weeks before these medications are effective. It also is very important to ask your doctor whether lab work will be beneficial for monitoring the level of medications in your bloodstream.

Counseling is recommended to help you identify stressful events in your life that could trigger a manic or depressive episode, among other things. Treatment should also include a twelve-step program, such as Dual Recovery Anonymous (DRA), Narcotics Anonymous (NA), Alcoholics Anonymous (AA), or other fellowships that may appeal to you in order to abstain from alcohol and other drugs. Also, you may want to consider attending a depression or manic depression support group in your area.

Bipolar Disorder II

Bipolar disorder II also involves swings in feelings, where the milder form of mania (hypomania) alternates with episodes of major depression. Bipolar disorder II may cause depression with alternating phases of bursts of energy or agitation.

Characteristics of Bipolar Disorder II

"Hypo" is Greek for "below," with hypomania referring to "low or mild" forms of mania. Often, but not always, people who experience hypomania associate their symptoms with good functioning and may feel a heightened sense of creativity or productivity. Hypomania occurs without the same level of impairment in judgment or performance seen with mania and does not include psychotic symptoms.

While hypomania is referred to as a "milder" mania in some of the mental health literature, this term can be deceptive. Hypomania can take the form of severe agitation, anxiety, or severe self-criticism, where racing thoughts can be highly negative, and agitation and sleep problems can be severe.

Hypomania includes these traits:

- Periods of elevated mood
- Inflated self-esteem or grandiosity

- "Racing" thoughts
- Increased productivity, activity, or creativity
- Decreased need for sleep or higher energy levels
- More talkative or pressure to keep talking
- Difficulty paying attention
- Loss of judgment, such as participating in pleasurable activities that have a high potential for painful consequences (buying sprees, sexual indiscretion, gambling)

Effective Treatment for Bipolar Disorder II

As with bipolar disorder I, the first line of treatment is evaluation by a doctor to determine whether a mood stabilizer or other medication is right for you (and to rule out the potential for other medical conditions).

Counseling also is very important to help identify stressful events in your life that could trigger hypomanic, depressive, or substance use episodes. A twelve-step program can play an important role in helping you develop a supportive network for continued recovery.

Cyclothymic Disorder

Cyclothymia (pronounced sigh-klo-thigh-me-a) involves less intense symptoms of both depression and mania which, because of their reduced intensity, don't match exactly a diagnosis of major depression or bipolar disorder I. Since symptoms of cyclothymia are less obvious, it can be more difficult to diagnose than bipolar disorder or major depression. A person with cyclothymia typically has recurring and frequent mood swings.

Characteristics of Cyclothymia

Cyclothymia includes these traits:
- Symptoms that last at least a period of two years
- Over the past two years, hasn't been free of symptoms for more than two months
- Chronic mood fluctuations, ranging from euphoria (symptoms of hypomania) to depression, where the symptoms have not been severe enough to be diagnosed with major depression or mania
- Meets many of the symptoms of depression
- Meets many of the symptoms of hypomania

Effective Treatment for Cyclothymia

Treatment for cyclothymia is essentially the same as for bipolar disorders. It is important to rule out other medical conditions, to be evaluated by a specialist to determine whether a mood stabilizer would be beneficial, and, as appropriate, counseling and other support groups.

Substance Use and Mood Disorders

Many people who have a depressive or bipolar disorder are at risk for using alcohol or other drugs, and vice versa, many people who are using a substance are at risk for experiencing symptoms of a mood disorder.

Depression and Substance Use

It is estimated that 25 to 40 percent of people with major depression have a co-occurring substance use disorder. If you are recovering from a chemical addiction, you are at a higher risk of experiencing a depressive episode.

Co-occurrence can develop because of self-medication (using alcohol or other drugs in an attempt to feel better). In other cases, a mood disorder may occur because of damage done to your body by long-term substance use or abuse. Also, there are many cases where both disorders co-exist as a result of different genetic, social, and biochemical factors. Regardless of these factors, your mental health and substance abuse conditions are best treated in a coordinated and integrated manner. Generally, treating only one may result in a relapse and depression. Remember, you are not alone. Through support groups, medications, and/or psychotherapy, the help you need is available so you can start to feel better and lead the life you've always wanted.

Bipolar Disorders and Substance Use

The majority of people with a bipolar disorder may also struggle with a chemical dependency. Sometimes, the use of alcohol or other drugs will hide the symptoms of a bipolar disorder and not appear until you start a detoxification or abstinence program. It is especially important to be aware that the symptoms of mania can put you at high risk for alcohol or drug relapse. With the proper treatment, however, manic episodes can be well controlled. Manic and depressive episodes can become more extreme and potentially more dangerous when caused by or intensified by the use of alcohol or other drugs. Also, as we discuss in depth later in this section, risks for suicide are higher for people with mood disorders.

The Dangers of Self-Medicating with Alcohol and/or Other Drugs

People with a mood disorder are also more likely to self-medicate their symptoms (take their treatment into their own hands) by using alcohol or other drugs. In other words, if you are experiencing depressed or negative feelings or feeling overly excited or "wired," you may try to make yourself feel better by getting drunk or high. Unfortunately, this can actually cause a depressive episode to worsen and potentially endanger your life. In fact, since alcohol is a central nervous system depressant, drinking will usually make symptoms worse.

People may find temporary relief by self-medicating with drugs or alcohol but, after the high is over, they generally feel worse than ever before. In the long run, depression and addiction form a vicious cycle. The more one tries to self-medicate, the worse the addiction becomes. The worse the addiction becomes, the worse the symptoms of mental illness.

> **Note:** If a person is biologically vulnerable to bipolar disorder, using stimulant drugs could trigger the onset of a manic episode. It is important to get the appropriate treatment for bipolar disorder.

How Common Are Mood Disorders?

Depression is the most commonly diagnosed mental illness and can occur at any age. Approximately one out of four women and one out of ten men will experience a depressive episode at some point in their lives.

About 1 to 2 percent of adults suffer from bipolar disorder, and a majority will have a co-occurring substance use disorder.

Here are some facts about mood disorders:

- It is estimated that up to 100 million people worldwide are affected by depression on any given day.
- An estimated twenty million people in the United States suffer from depression each year and even though highly successful treatments are available to relieve symptoms, less than half get the treatment they need.
- Approximately two million Americans suffer from bipolar disorder on any given day.
- Episodes of major depression can be disabling. An estimated 15 percent of Americans will experience a disabling episode at least once in his or her lifetime.
- It is estimated that almost half of those who are diagnosed with major depression also have an anxiety disorder.
- Twenty-five to 40 percent of people with major depression may have a co-occurring substance use disorder.

> **An encouraging note:** Medications and treatments are constantly being improved to reduce symptoms and enhance the lives of those with mood disorders.

Causes of Mood Disorders and Addiction

There is no single cause of co-occurring mood and substance use disorders. It is important to know that because the two conditions occur together, one condition did not necessarily cause the other, even if one occurred first. Also, by having one condition, you are at an increased risk for the other. Keep in mind that substance use and mental health diagnoses may contribute to, cause, or simply co-exist with each other.

Regardless of what causes mood and substance use disorders, both diagnoses share the following similarities.

Here are some facts about mood and substance use disorders:

- They are biologically and genetically based conditions.
- They arise from common causes with common risk factors.
- They include similar stages of recovery and relapse.
- They can result in feelings of guilt or failure.
- They are "no fault" conditions.
- They respond favorably to education, training, and treatment.

Until recent years, both diagnoses were treated separately and apart from each other. We now know that because more than half of those people with psychiatric diagnoses also have substance abuse conditions (and vice versa); co-occurring conditions are the rule, not the exception. As such, it is very important that both conditions are treated together in a single integrated setting.

Women and Depression

Women experience major depression and dysthymia twice as often as men. Men and women are diagnosed at about the same rate for bipolar disorder. Research continues to try to define the reasons why women are more susceptible to depression. Here are some key factors:

- Menstrual cycle changes
- Pregnancy
- Miscarriage
- Postpartum period
- Pre-menopause

- Menopause
- Additional stresses at work and home
- Single parenting
- Abuse and oppression in a relationship
- Pessimistic thinking, low self-esteem, difficulty handling stress, and feeling like one's life is out of control

In recent years, more attention has been given to postpartum depression, which is a depressive episode that occurs after the birth of a baby. Women are particularly vulnerable during this time of hormonal and emotional changes, along with the added responsibility of caring for a new child. It is common for a new mother to have a period of the "blues," but if the new mother experiences severe and incapacitating depression, then the family should offer emotional support and seek treatment with a family physician.

Suicidal Thinking

If depression becomes severe enough, the pain can lead a depressed person to consider ending his or her life. A suicide attempt is when a person tries to harm him or herself with the intent to die. An estimated 15 percent of people with severe depression commit suicide, and the risk increases if a person has a chemical addiction. Eighty percent of those who kill themselves have tried to do so at least once before.

People who are feeling suicidal usually show changes in behavior, such as:
- Stating, "I'm going to kill myself."
- Giving away possessions and saying good-bye.
- Drawing up a will.
- Suddenly withdrawing and becoming isolated.
- Drinking alcohol or using other drugs to work up the nerve to commit suicide.
- Displaying extreme feelings of hopelessness or demoralization.

Thinking about or attempting suicide happens when a person is desperate and he or she is not receiving appropriate treatment. If left untreated, depression can be debilitating. It is essential for the suicidal person to ask for help. Friends or family may need to seek help and take action immediately. Treatment can ease the feelings of suicide and help relieve symptoms caused by depression.

What You Can Do If You Feel Suicidal

If you are feeling suicidal or contemplating injuring yourself in any way, take immediate action. Don't wait; get help by doing one or more of the following:

- Call 911, a crisis center, or suicide hotline.
- Call your therapist, counselor, or doctor right away and tell him or her how you are feeling.
- Go to the emergency room of a hospital or clinic near you.
- Call a friend or family member and ask him or her to take you to get help.

Create a Safety Plan

If you have any feelings whatsoever of hurting yourself, it's important to create a plan for your safety. Here are some guidelines to get you started, but it is crucial that you enlist the help of a professional as soon as possible.

1. Avoid Being Alone

Find someone to be with and/or talk to, whether it's a friend, family member, professional, clergy member, or anyone else who is willing to listen. List the people or places you can call when you need help.

Person 1 _____ Phone #_____

Person 2 _____ Phone #_____

Agency 1_____ Phone #_____

Agency 2_____ Phone #_____

2. Avoid Alcohol and/or Other Drugs

It's more likely that you'll make poor choices when under the influence of alcohol or other drugs, and they will not solve your problems. List the people or agencies you can ask for help to stay in recovery.

Person 1 _____ Phone #_____

Person 2 _____ Phone #_____

Agency 1_____ Phone #_____

Agency 2_____ Phone #_____

3. Remove Any Means of Hurting Yourself

If you have a gun, a stash of pills, or any other means of hurting yourself, get rid of them. Ask someone for help if you need to. If there is anything you need to do, write it down and do it today.

_____

_____

_____

4. Make a Commitment to Not Hurt Yourself

Make a commitment to yourself, or better yet, to someone else that you will not hurt yourself today and that you will ask for help before deciding to act on suicidal feelings. Remember that all bad feelings pass. However bad you are feeling, it cannot continue forever. You can get help to turn your life around.

Seeking Treatment for Mood Disorders

Co-occurring disorders are highly responsive to treatment. Eighty to 90 percent of people suffering from depression can find relief from their symptoms, but sometimes the most difficult step is asking for help. Since depression can make you feel hopeless and worthless, many people never seek the help they deserve.

One stigma common to substance abuse and depression is that you should be able to "pull yourself together" and make yourself feel better, as though your two diagnoses were a choice. This is incorrect; depression and addiction are not caused by weakness of character; rather, they are serious health disorders that respond to treatment. Treatment for co-occurring disorders usually includes:

- Medication
- Talking with a therapist or participating in group therapy
- Participating in a twelve-step program, such as Dual Recovery Anonymous (DRA), Narcotics Anonymous (NA), Alcoholics Anonymous (AA), or others
- Participating in a support group, such as National Depressive and Manic Depressive Association (National DMDA), National Alliance for Mental Illness (NAMI), or a support group near you

Some people may start to feel better with medication or therapy alone, while others may benefit from a combination of all four types of treatment. You may be hesitant or nervous about seeking therapy or attending recovery groups, but you are not alone, lots of people have those same concerns. Taking the first step is usually the hardest.

Taking Medication

Some people may need to take medication for a limited period of time such as six months to a year, while others may need to take medication for the rest of their lives to maintain a healthy chemical balance. Continual advances are being made in medications that treat mood disorders. Even as you read this workbook, new medications are emerging. Whether you are prescribed these or other medications, it is important that you learn as much as you can about your treatment, its effectiveness, and the side effects of the medicines you may be taking.

It is also important to know that some of these medicines take six or as many as eight weeks before their effectiveness can be determined. Also, since there is no way of knowing which medication works best for you, your physician may need to try several different types before finding those that are exactly right for you.

Be open and honest with your doctor regarding your alcohol and/or drug history and any current use so that you will be prescribed medications that minimize risks to your health. Finally, never abruptly discontinue any medications without talking first with your doctor. Some medications must be slowly discontinued in order to avoid serious medical concerns or symptoms of withdrawal.

Mixing Medications with Alcohol and/or Other Drugs

Medications often are an essential part of mood disorder treatment. However, alcohol and other drugs can be especially dangerous or even lethal when mixed with certain medications. Your doctor can prescribe a medication that has less severe reactions if mixed with alcohol or other drugs and may also offer medications to reduce your cravings for alcohol or other drugs. You should be honest with your doctor about your symptoms. He or she is bound by federal confidentiality laws and guidelines to protect your privacy. Remember, your doctor's first priority is to help you get better.

Note: Consider a professional with experience in integrated treatment to help you with your recovery journey. A therapist with experience in addiction treatment or who is also an addictionologist is an excellent resource for managing your medication treatment.

Twelve-Step Programs, Medicine, and Addiction

If twelve-step programs are a part of your recovery, then you know these programs recommend complete abstinence for a successful recovery from addiction. Some twelve-step programs are Dual Recovery Anonymous (DRA), Alcoholics Anonymous (AA), Narcotics Anonymous (NA), and many others.

Here is something important to keep in mind: Do not confuse abstinence from alcohol and other drugs with medication prescribed by your doctor. You should continue taking those medications exactly as recommended by your doctor.

If you have a mood disorder, then prescription medication may be an important part of your treatment. If so, it is vital that you take your medication as prescribed.

Recovery from Mood Disorders and Addiction

Recovering from mood disorders and substance use disorders can be difficult at times, and you may find yourself wanting to be well in the time it takes to snap your fingers, quickly and without too much effort. In other words, "I want what I want, and I want it now!"

People who struggle with addiction often have the mindset that they should get what they want immediately. Recovery from addiction and mood disorders happens every day. Remember that recovery is a process and sometimes an excruciatingly slow process at that. If you have used stimulant drugs that make you feel good in a matter of minutes, it may be difficult to accept that you probably won't start feeling better overnight. There is a wise saying that is worth repeating, "Good things take time."

Hard Truths about Recovery

1. Medication for a mood disorder can take several weeks to start working.

For people in recovery, it may take even longer because the brain structures that have been damaged by alcohol and/or other drug use are the same structures that respond to medicine. Have patience; it's worth the wait.

2. It might take several tries to find a medication that works for you.

Don't be afraid to tell your doctor if your medication isn't working. Everybody has a different chemistry, and sometimes it's like putting a puzzle together as you and your doctor try to find the one that works for you.

3. You will still have bad days.

It is likely you will have bad days when you feel like you haven't made any progress at all. This is not a reason to give up. We all have bad days; it is a part of life. It is important to develop your coping skills so you can tolerate bad days without relapsing.

4. You may continue to struggle with lapses of depression, mania, and/or substance use.

Recovery from a mood disorder and addiction is not "all-or-nothing." Lapses and relapses happen, and learning to deal with them may be a significant part of your recovery. Learn to accept that you might struggle with these issues, and do your best to continue developing your coping skills.

Skill Sets: Coping with a Mood Disorder and Addiction

If you are living with a mood disorder and addiction, you probably have learned to use alcohol and/or other drugs to cope with life's problems. You may have used these substances to cover up or ignore your problems. Or, you might have told yourself that if you could just get high today, you'll deal with your problems tomorrow. Maybe getting high makes your problems seem "far away" or unreal.

Every person encounters day-to-day problems. The trick is to learn how to cope with problems in healthy ways. Here are some healthy strategies that have been used to cope with depression and addiction:

- Concentrate your efforts on coming up with a solution.
- Make a plan to overcome the problem.
- Ask for help.
- Talk to someone about how you feel.
- Use the experience to grow and better yourself.
- Find comfort in your religion or spiritual beliefs.
- Find healthy ways to express your feelings, such as exercise, arts or crafts, journaling, etc.
- Talk to your sponsor or therapist.
- Take a deep breath, slow down, and put the situation in perspective.
- Calm yourself down before trying to solve the problem.
- Tell yourself, "This too shall pass."
- Tell yourself, "I can handle this."
- Think of how you've overcome a similar problem in the past.

Living with Personality Disorders and Addiction

Personality disorders can sometimes have serious and debilitating effects in all areas of a person's life—in relationships with friends and family, in social situations, in regulating moods and emotional states, and in staying in recovery. Often, a personality disorder can stem from an early traumatic experience in which one learns that people and the world are dangerous. That information can affect the way the person develops relationships and learns how to trust.

If you are struggling with severe ongoing problems or troubles in relationships, work, and in your day-to-day life, then you may have a personality disorder.

This section is designed to offer you the information and tools you may need to better understand personality disorders and chemical dependency and steer you toward leading the positive and fulfilling life that you deserve.

What Is a Personality Disorder?

Your **personality** involves the way you think, feel, behave, and how you relate to others. Everyone has personality traits that fall somewhere on a spectrum, such as being shy versus outgoing. With a **personality**

disorder, certain personality traits may seem exaggerated and extreme and result in distress and serious problems in your life. For example, a person with dependent personality disorder is so shy that he or she may have trouble getting along in life because of difficulties when developing relationships with others.

Personality disorders start developing early in life, and symptoms related to these disorders become present in adolescence or early adulthood. Although a personality disorder may be complicated by substance use, the traits of the disorder exist even when substance use does not occur.

Everyone has good and bad personality traits. People with personality disorders have a variety of characteristics that are more extreme than those of most individuals. As a result, a person with a personality disorder may end up having difficulties in relationships and other aspects of his or her life. This person may be less able to recognize and control emotions and reactions and often has difficulty controlling impulses and behaviors. For example, a person with borderline personality disorder may respond with extreme anger to a situation that others would not find upsetting at all.

Personality disorders, like all other mental health disorders, are illnesses that develop for a variety of reasons, including genetic makeup, the environment in which one was raised, and the experiences one has had. Like other illnesses, having a personality disorder is not your fault. It is a serious problem that requires professional treatment and a commitment to change. Treatment can help you change your behaviors and emotional reactions so that you can experience healthy relationships and a productive, rewarding life. It is not a problem that will go away by itself, overnight, or just because you want it to go away. It will take time to change, but change can happen.

People who suffer from a personality disorder may express vague, general, and chronic complaints, such as:

- "I don't like myself."
- "No one understands me; I don't fit in."
- "I know what I should be doing, but I can't make myself do it."
- "I started drinking because I wanted to fit in. But I still feel different."
- "My life is miserable, but I can't seem to turn it around."
- "The only time I feel normal is when I'm drunk or high."
- "I don't get along with people, and nobody likes me anyhow."
- "I can't hold down a job."
- "My relationships always fall apart."

If you feel like your emotions or your life is out of control, like you don't relate to people the way others do, or you just feel different, then you can ask a psychologist or psychiatrist to evaluate your symptoms for a possible personality disorder. **Please do not try to diagnose yourself.**

Common Characteristics of Personality Disorders

There are ten different types of personality disorders, each with specific symptoms, but here are some common characteristics:

- Chronic distress or suffering when in social situations or at work; problems in relationships with family, friends, and intimate partners.
- Severe difficulty with emotions, such as mood swings, difficulty expressing feelings, or expressing inappropriate emotions.
- Behavior that creates conflict, confusion, or anguish instead of the kind that seeks solutions to problems.
- A pattern of inflexible thought or behavior that differs from and often comes into conflict with recognized social expectations.
- Symptoms can be traced to adolescence or early adulthood and are not explained by another mental illness, substance use, or medical condition.

Having a co-occurring problem of substance use and a personality disorder is very common. Between 11 and 23 percent of Americans are affected by personality disorders, and 50 to 60 percent of those with a substance use disorder also have one or more personality disorders. People with addiction experience symptoms of their personality disorder whether they are using their drug of choice or not. *Using alcohol or other drugs will not make your symptoms go away.* In the short term, you may forget about your symptoms or not feel as bad, but in the end, your life and relationships will suffer. Your symptoms and addiction will intensify and your distress will increase.

Although recovery from a personality disorder and a chemical dependency can be complicated, the chance to achieve a better life begins with a desire to change and a commitment to participate fully in effective treatment. You will begin to feel better and, with each new day, you can choose to stay committed to a healthier lifestyle.

Personality Disorders and Addiction

If you have a personality disorder, it is not uncommon to have a substance use disorder and vice versa.

Since personality disorders begin in adolescence or early adulthood, you may have developed a chemical dependency at an early age as a way to make yourself feel better. Sometimes people with a personality disorder use alcohol and/or other drugs to be accepted by others or to feel more comfortable in social situations. Many people say the only time they feel "normal" is when they are drinking or using other drugs. This is an understandable way to try to fix a serious problem, and it may work in the short run. But in the long run, *it only makes your symptoms—and your life—worse.*

If you developed a chemical addiction when you were younger, this could have influenced your thoughts and behaviors by reinforcing any extreme personality traits you might have had. Addiction and personality disorders can feed off each other, with one worsening the other, creating a vicious cycle.

Here's an example: George was rebellious and angry as a teenager as a result of many difficult experiences in his life. He started drinking to cope with anger; however, this just made his anger worse and left him unable to cope with other life stressors. The increase in stress led him to drink even more. George was diagnosed with antisocial personality disorder because his difficult experiences, his tendency toward anger, and his alcohol use were woven into a complex pattern of maladaptive coping strategies.

A personality disorder diagnosis is the first step toward getting help and feeling well. It is not your fault if you developed a personality disorder. In order to heal and change your life for the better, consider your willingness to work hard, understand yourself, stop using, and get into recovery.

Personality Disorders Overview

There are ten types of personality disorders divided into three different groups and based on shared personality traits and behaviors.

Unusual or Eccentric Behavior

These disorders may appear odd or eccentric, and include the trait of distancing oneself from others. *Paranoid Personality Disorder.* A person with this disorder may be suspicious and distrustful of others without reason, believing that others are exploiting, harming, deceiving, or betraying him or her. The individual might think others are trying to hurt him or her by being dishonest, distrustful, or prepared to cause physical harm. These thoughts are usually without a tangible cause, but the person may be absolutely sure the thoughts are real. He or she may feel jealous or have other suspicious emotions and may have difficulty feeling emotions of happiness or being able to relax.

Schizoid Personality Disorder. Appears to be a "loner" and very indifferent to developing a close relationship with others. Doesn't seem to care about what others think and usually is detached from other people or even from activities that other people usually enjoy.

Schizotypal Personality Disorder. Has difficulty developing relationships with others, even family. May experience odd beliefs or magical thinking. Feels very nervous, anxious, or uncomfortable in social situations. Might speak or behave in an unusual manner.

Dramatic, Emotional or Erratic Behavior

These disorders result in highly dramatic, emotional, or erratic behavior.

Antisocial Personality Disorder. May have a history of breaking the law, being dishonest, or "conning" others. Often makes a decision without thinking about it first. May have a history of physical fighting and job losses. Sometimes may be considered charming by people who don't know him or her well, but these behaviors are not especially sincere. May be accused of using others in order to gain something (sex, money, or power) without considering the person being used.

Borderline Personality Disorder. May be unable to feel happy or satisfied with life or with others for very long. Might feel very empty, sad, or abandoned and, because of this, may feel as though he or she doesn't deserve to be happy. May make harmful and self-destructive choices. Often has a history of relationships that haven't worked.

Histrionic Personality Disorder. May be described by other people as being dramatic or even having strong emotional changes. May feel unappreciated unless he or she is the "center" of whatever is happening. May stretch or even change the truth to get other people's attention. May be an "all-or-nothing" thinker, changing from one dramatic thought to another. May have few friends of the same gender because he or she may use sexual behavior or dress in a way to get attention from the opposite sex.

Narcissistic Personality Disorder. Might feel as though things should be done his or her way most or all of the time. May think a lot about being powerful or acting very powerfully; often tries to rule over or direct other people.

Fearful or Anxious Behavior

These disorders produce behavior that is highly fearful or anxious.

Avoidant Personality Disorder. Feels extreme anxiety when around other people or at social events. Often feels very badly about him or herself. Suggestions from people might feel like criticisms.

Dependent Personality Disorder. Has problems making decisions and may have little or low self-confidence. Might feel extremely afraid to live or spend time alone and may be overly sensitive to rejection or being criticized. Might want others to take care of or make decisions for him or her.

Obsessive-Compulsive Personality Disorder. Strives to be "perfect" to the point that the actual task may get lost in the details. Might be labeled inflexible by others; very literal with rules, i.e., no rule bending.

May overwork and over-structure things in his or her life. Often is a pack-rat, keeping things "just in case." Often becomes so wrapped up in his or her own opinions about how things should be done that offers of help or suggestions about how to do things differently are refused.

Antisocial Personality Disorder

Each year, approximately 3 percent of males and 1 percent of females in the general population are diagnosed with antisocial personality disorder (ASPD). Reports indicate that ASPD is most commonly diagnosed in people twenty-four to forty-five years old, although behavior begins in childhood or early adolescence and continues into adulthood.

Among people with dual diagnoses, ASPD is very common. Substance abuse or addiction often worsens symptoms of antisocial personality disorder and increases the chances of having problems with law enforcement, losing important relationships, and having serious legal troubles.

The main characteristics of ASPD are showing a chronic pattern of taking advantage or infringing on the rights of others and having a history of arrests, physical fights, job losses, or problems following social rules or laws. The individual may have a tendency toward lying and dishonesty that seems to occur without remorse, usually starting around the age of fifteen.

In his or her youth, the person with ASPD may have been without support from parents or was raised in an environment with violence or conflict. Criminal behavior may have been common or the person may have been sexually or physically abused.

This person may be considered charming by those who don't know him or her well, but the individual rarely has truly close relationships. Often this person makes a decision without thinking about it first. He or she may be accused of being a "con" or "using" others to gain something (sex, money, or power) without thinking about the impact on the person being used.

Here is an example of how one individual with ASPD described himself.

> "I guess I've been rebellious since I was a teenager. When I was younger I got arrested a lot, usually for drug or alcohol charges. I've settled down a lot, but I still have a temper and I like to get high and have a wild time once in a while. My therapist says I use my anger to get my way by scaring or threatening people. I guess I do sometimes, but hey, you gotta do what you gotta do. I'm usually pretty nice, though. I drink beer and smoke pot to relax, 'cause if I don't, I'm uptight and irritable and can't sit still."

Characteristics of Antisocial Personality Disorder

A person with antisocial personality disorder possesses these behaviors:

- Takes advantage of or infringes on the rights of others in order to satisfy one's own needs.

- Doesn't like to conform to social expectations and laws, prefers to rebel.
- Uses behaviors that may be grounds for arrest, such as theft, forgery, trespassing, reckless or disorderly conduct.
- Has a history of lying and dishonesty, including having aliases or fake identities.
- Fails to plan ahead, impulsive, doesn't learn from mistakes.
- Has excess irritability and may show aggressive behavior, has "temper tantrums."
- Appears charming and has ability to be conning and manipulative.
- Is self-destructive, shows a lack of concern for the safety of self or others.
- Has trouble forming and sustaining meaningful and lasting relationships, suspicious of others who share emotions such as kindness and compassion.
- Is easily bored and restless, often unable to hold a long-term job.
- Views oneself as a loner who looks out for oneself, no matter what the consequences.
- Lacks remorse; rationalizes and justifies hurting or mistreating another person.
- Has a history of behavior such as fighting, stealing, or truancy that started before age fifteen and persists into adult life.
- Has disregard for authority or authority figures.
- Others may think of one as racist, sexist, prejudiced, or having chauvinistic beliefs or behaviors.
- Has beliefs that one is better, smarter, more powerful, etc. than others.

Treatment Options for Antisocial Personality Disorder

It is not uncommon for those with ASPD to have a chemical addiction or be diagnosed with major depression, anxiety disorder, or mood disorders. Other personality disorders may also be diagnosed, such as narcissistic, borderline, or histrionic personality disorders. Treatment should be tailored for all diagnosed illnesses.

Treatment options may include individual and group therapy sessions. Also, self-help groups made up of peers have proven to be successful in some cases.

Medication is most often used to treat associated symptoms, such as anxiety, rage, and depression. However, since substance abuse is often a concern, your doctor will take this into consideration when prescribing appropriate medication.

Avoidant Personality Disorder

This disorder affects a small percentage of the general population, only about 0.5 to 1 percent. However, it may be underdiagnosed because people with this disorder often do not seek help. When someone has avoidant personality disorder (APD), substance use may contribute to his or her avoidance of social contact and worsen already existing problems. Often, individuals with avoidant personality disorder begin using alcohol and/or other drugs to alleviate social discomfort, to try to fit in, or to feel more socially adept. However, although this may alleviate fears and feelings of inadequacy in the short run, substance abuse inevitably makes problems worse in the long run.

Avoidant personality disorder can be recognized by feelings of inadequacy, increased sensitivity to criticism, withdrawing from or avoiding social situations, and low self-esteem. The individual with APD typically will feel that he or she is unappealing, inadequate, self-conscious and unable to fit in; this person may be lonely and view the world as unfriendly and humiliating. These feelings may interfere with developing relationships. Even low-level criticism may cause intense hurt and pain. Often these feelings of inadequacy result from experiences of rejection as a child by a person who was important to him or her.

Here is an example of how one person with APD has described her behavior:

"I've had trouble connecting to people all my life. I'm so jealous of people who can make friends easily; for me it's a huge struggle because I'm really shy. It scares me to have to go somewhere where I don't know people. I usually just hang out by myself and try not to be noticed. I figure people won't like me anyway, so why should I bother trying to be friendly? I started drinking because I thought I'd be able to fit in better. It worked, sort of, for a while. But now, I drink by myself more than anything."

Characteristics of Avoidant Personality Disorder

A person with avoidant personality disorder possesses these traits:

- Is very sensitive to criticism, rejection, disapproval, and conflict
- Has feelings of inadequacy
- Doesn't like getting involved in a relationship unless certain of being liked and accepted
- Avoids activities that involve being with other people because of fear of being evaluated
- Has low self-esteem; is timid and easily embarrassed
- Hides from calling attention to him- or herself
- Withdraws despite wanting affection and acceptance
- Is reluctant to take risks or participate in new activities
- Believes that one is not as good as others, not well-liked, or is socially inept

Treatment Options for Avoidant Personality Disorder

If you are struggling from avoidant personality disorder, it is not uncommon to also be diagnosed with an anxiety or depressive disorder. Therapy is the most important avenue of treatment for you if you have avoidant personality disorder. Therapy can include individual sessions, but group therapy may also be explored, since this may help you understand how your behavior and symptoms affect you and others. Also, assertiveness training is sometimes recommended as a tool for expressing your needs openly and improving self-esteem.

Medications are used to manage any associated disorders, such as anxiety or depression, and also may be prescribed to be used in particularly fear-inducing or stressful situations. Benzodiazepines are addictive. If you are in recovery for a alcohol or other drug problem, these should not be prescribed.

If you are currently taking a benzodiazepine, please talk with your doctor about changing your medication. Since benzodiazepines are highly addictive, consider *not* taking any of the following medications: Klonopin (clonazepam), Xanax (alprazolam), Valium (diazepam), and Ativan (lorazepam).

Borderline Personality Disorder

Borderline personality disorder, also called BPD, affects approximately 2 percent of the general population. Among people with dual diagnoses, borderline personality disorder is a common personality disorder. Addiction can play into BPD in many ways; it can make mood swings more severe, put further strain on relationships, increase self-destructive behaviors, and contribute to impulsive behavior. The main feature of BPD is instability, and substance abuse can easily worsen this problem.

The person with borderline personality disorder is recognized by having a history of intense relationships that don't work; feeling empty and sad inside, and unable to feel happy or satisfied with life or with others for any substantial period of time; difficulty controlling moods and impulses; distancing oneself from others through erratic behavior; and having a deep fear of being abandoned. A person with BPD may seem to have contradictory behaviors. For example, he or she may have an extreme need for love while also having an extreme fear of closeness.

Those diagnosed with BPD sometimes have reported being sexually or physically abused as a child, and some may have been neglected or abandoned by caregivers.

This is how one individual with BPD has described herself:

> *"My life is crazy, there's never any peace. People don't know what to expect from me because one minute I'm happy and the next minute I'm in a rage. The other day, my boyfriend and I were at a party having a great time. Then all of a sudden, I got so mad at him that I lost it. I yelled and screamed and told him off. I do that a lot when I'm drinking or when I'm high on cocaine. Afterward, though, I was hurting badly. I just curled up in a ball and the pain was so intense that all I could think about was cutting myself to make all the bad feelings stop."*

Characteristics of Borderline Personality Disorder

A person with borderline personality disorder possesses these characteristics:

- Has rapid and dramatic changes in moods and unpredictable outbursts that last hours rather than days or weeks; people around this person "walk on eggshells" for fear of his or her moods.

- Has intimate relationships that develop quickly and are tumultuous; falls in and out of love easily; has "love-hate" and often stormy relationships.

- Is terrified of his or her partner leaving, being alone, abandoned, or separated.

- Is impulsive; may physically mistreat others, abuse substances, become sexually promiscuous, drive recklessly, binge eat, or engage in other reckless behavior.

- Has fluctuating or unstable self-image and all-or-nothing thinking; has periods of not knowing who he or she really is.

- Is threatened by intimate relationships, needs others to prove their love over and over; feels that others are not there for him or her enough.

- Tends to view the world and others in the extreme, as totally good or totally bad, with the view changing from one day to the next.

- Has an extreme fear of intimacy.

- Has feelings of overwhelming helplessness.

- Acts suicidal through threats and self-destructive acts such as cutting, burning, or otherwise hurting him- or herself.

- Has trouble sleeping.

- Has frequent displays or explosions of anger, range, or hostility.

- Is likely to have suffered from traumatic loss or physical, sexual, and emotional abuse.

- Has chronic feelings of emptiness.

- May sometimes "dissociate," or have the feeling that one is separating from one's body or is in a dream.

- Fears that others think he or she is bad or unworthy.

- May abruptly end friendships, therapeutic relationships, or love relationships when he or she feels mistreated.

Treatment Options for Borderline Personality Disorder

Borderline personality disorder is a complex disorder that can be difficult to diagnose and treat. If you have been struggling with BPD, you know how devastating it can be, but there is help and you can get better. If you have BPD, it is not uncommon to also be diagnosed with an anxiety, depressive, eating, or sleep disorder. Characteristics of borderline personality disorder may also mimic, or be similar to, other illnesses such as bipolar disorder.

Addiction, whether to alcohol or other drugs, including prescription drugs and/or street drugs, will aggravate the symptoms and interfere with you feeling better. It is extremely important to participate in a rehabilitation program and/or self-help program, such as Dual Recovery Anonymous (DRA), Alcoholics Anonymous (AA), Narcotics Anonymous (NA), or others and stay on your plan for leading a recovery-oriented life.

Therapy is the most important aspect of treatment for this disorder. If you have been suicidal, self-mutilating, or self-destructive, then sometimes a hospital stay is the most effective treatment. This is especially helpful if your home environment is harmful or abusive or attempts to block you from getting help. Behavior therapy and social skills training have been helpful to those suffering from borderline personality disorder. Also, as your treatment progresses, you may want to seek occupational, recreational, and vocational therapy. One type of therapy, called Dialectical Behavior Therapy, has been developed specifically to help individuals with borderline personality disorder and has had much success.

Medications are often used to stabilize moods or control anger, hostility, or brief psychotic episodes. Medications are also used to manage any associated disorders, such as anxiety or depression.

Dependent Personality Disorder

Dependent personality disorder, also called DPD, affects approximately 2.5 percent of the general population and is more commonly diagnosed in women than men. Substance abuse is less common than with some other personality disorders, but it still does co-occur with dependent personality disorder. Addiction can make one feel even less capable of living independently, therefore worsening symptoms.

This disorder can cause low self-esteem, and decision-making can be extremely difficult. The person may feel extremely afraid to live or spend time alone; he or she may be overly sensitive to rejection or being criticized. He or she might want others to take care of or make decisions for him or her.

Sometimes people with DPD have a history of childhood illness, overly protective parents, aggressive siblings, or report feeling a lack of encouragement as a child. Some people had unpleasant experiences when separated from a parent or caregiver during childhood.

Here is how one individual with DPD has described himself:

"I had a hard time leaving home when I was a teenager. I was scared to be on my own, taking care of myself and making my own decisions. I liked the comfort of my parent's house, but being alone made my anxiety skyrocket. Now I'm married, and I worry about what would happen if my wife

wasn't around. She takes care of everything like cooking, cleaning, and paying the bills. I even let her plan our vacations. I doubt I could make it on my own. I take Xanax, and even though I keep getting the dosage increased, it's not helping anymore."

Characteristics of Dependent Personality Disorder

A person with dependent personality disorder possesses these characteristics:

- Ignores his or her needs and puts others' needs first.
- Tends to be submissive or clinging to other people.
- Has an extreme lack of self-confidence, disregarding his or her capabilities and strengths.
- Feels the need to be taken care of by others.
- Has fears of being left alone or being separated from others; has feelings of helplessness.
- Has difficulty making everyday decisions, may seem "wishy-washy," and needs a lot of advice and encouragement.
- Wants others to assume responsibility and make decisions for major areas of his or her life.
- Has extreme difficulty disagreeing with others or standing up for him- or herself for fear of rejection or criticism.
- Is generally fearful.
- Has difficulty starting projects or doing things on his or her own.
- Has a strong need to receive nurturing and support, will volunteer to do unpleasant things or will tolerate physical, sexual, or emotional abuse to get this.
- When a close relationship ends, this individual immediately jumps into another relationship to receive care and support.
- Has fears of being unable to take care of him- or herself without help from others.

Treatment Options for Dependent Personality Disorder

Fortunately, treating dependent personality disorder is often successful. With the help of a therapist, people with DPD often become more independent, self-confident, and self-sufficient. These types of therapies have proven helpful: behavioral therapy, assertiveness training, and individual, family, and group therapy.

Addiction will aggravate the symptoms and interfere with you feeling better. It is extremely important to participate in a rehabilitation program and/or self-help program, such as Dual Recovery Anonymous (DRA), Alcoholics Anonymous (AA), Narcotics Anonymous (NA), or others, and stay on your plan for leading a recovery-oriented life.

Medications are sometimes used to manage associated disorders or symptoms, such as anxiety, depression, panic attacks, or separation anxiety.

Histrionic Personality Disorder

Histrionic personality disorder, also called HPD, affects about 2 to 3 percent of the general population and is more commonly diagnosed in women than men. Alcohol or other drug abuse can easily contribute to symptoms by exaggerating problems that already exist.

This disorder is recognized primarily by these characteristics: showing dramatic displays of emotion in everyday behavior, seeking attention often through physical appearance or seductive behavior, seeking to be the center of attention in a group, changing from one dramatic thought to another in an all-or-nothing manner, and appearing to be self-involved.

Individuals with HPD have not developed a solid sense of their own importance and worth. It is common to report feelings of emptiness, inadequacy, or being unlovable. They turn to others for affirmation and attention but, no matter how much attention is received, it is not fulfilling for long. Their fragile feelings about themselves make them crave attention.

Adults with HPD have described being raised by caregivers who were emotionally distant or who praised them more for the things they did rather than the person they were (such as looking pretty or completing a task). They may describe parents who were irregular about praise, leaving them confused about how to gain approval, which left them feeling the need to "perform" for and please others. Approval comes from others' judgments, not a feeling of self-worth or inner self-esteem.

Here is how one individual with HPD describes herself:

> *"My friends call me a drama queen and a tease. I do like to flirt and be noticed, and if people are going to notice me, I ought to look good, so I never leave the house without looking my best. But I guess what they're really talking about is the way I can cause a scene. My friends and I go clubbing a lot and take Ecstasy, coke, speed, or whatever we can get. I love the rush and the club scene. But sometimes I end up crying all night and getting hysterical and I've even overdosed once."*

Characteristics of Histrionic Personality Disorder

A person with histrionic personality disorder possesses these characteristics:

- Uses highly dramatic, showy, extroverted, or theatrical behavior.
- Is attention-seeking, very comfortable when considered the center of attention, likes to be considered the "life of the party."
- Seeks admiration and approval much of the time.
- Shows sexual seductiveness or provocative behavior to gain attention.

- Makes things sound more important than they really are; may stretch or change the truth to get a response from others.

- Uses physical appearance to draw attention to self.

- Has a need for reassurance, may use behaviors such as crying or suicidal gestures to have one's way or to affect others.

- Is easily influenced by others or circumstances and may seem fickle to others; likes to follow trends or fads.

- Often considers relationships to be more intimate or close than the other person in the relationship does.

- Has difficulty maintaining deep and long-lasting relationships.

- Looks for heightened sensation experiences through "thrill-seeking," which may have led to trouble with the law, addiction, or sexual promiscuity.

- Is more interested in one's own life than the lives of family and friends.

- May use displays of emotion (crying, rage, etc.) to gain attention from others.

Treatment Options for Histrionic Personality Disorder

The symptoms of histrionic personality disorder overlap with those of borderline, antisocial, and narcissistic personality disorder. People with histrionic personality disorder may also be diagnosed with somatization disorder (Briquet's syndrome).

The treatment of choice is therapy in an individual or group setting. Addiction will aggravate the symptoms and interfere with you feeling better. It is extremely important to participate in a rehabilitation program and/or self-help program, such as Dual Recovery Anonymous (DRA), Alcoholics Anonymous (AA), Narcotics Anonymous (NA), or others, and stay on your plan for leading a recovery-oriented life.

Medications are used to manage associated disorders, such as anxiety or depression, and also may be prescribed if you are experiencing psychotic symptoms.

Narcissistic Personality Disorder

Narcissistic personality disorder (NPD) affects a small percentage of the general population, only about one percent, but that number may be increasing. In addition, this disorder may be underdiagnosed because those with narcissistic personality disorder often do not seek help. Substance abuse is common and can exacerbate one's grandiose feelings and need for attention. Often, symptoms of this personality disorder are blamed on the substance use (*"He's just drunk."*), but the truth is, the problems exist with or without the substance use.

A person with narcissistic personality disorder is recognized as feeling that things should be done his or her way most or all of the time, thinking a lot about being powerful or acting powerfully, often trying to rule over or direct other people and being overly sensitive to the opinions of others.

Some people with NPD describe a childhood where the parents were very demanding, perfectionistic, or critical, pushing the child to be talented or special in some way. Often, nothing the child did was ever "good enough." Other people with NPD describe being indulged and praised excessively, perhaps with few rules or inconsistent discipline, while others describe abuse or neglectful histories.

One individual with NPD describes himself this way:

> *"I thought I would love medical school because I've always done well in school and I have a gift for medicine, but my teachers don't recognize my talent. I feel like I'm stuck in a class with inferior students. Why is it me who's getting bad reviews? Just because I'm late for rounds a couple of times a week doesn't mean I'm not going be a great doctor. Besides, I don't need to go on rounds; it's a waste of time. With all this stress, I've been getting high on cocaine more to get away from it all, but I don't think they'll find out. Even if they did, I'm sure I could get away with it."*

Characteristics of Narcissistic Personality Disorder

A person with narcissistic personality disorder possesses these characteristics:

- Has an exaggerated sense of self-importance, uniqueness, achievement, and talent.
- Has grandiose feelings of being special and better than "ordinary" people, believes that one can only be understood by other special or high-status people.
- Is preoccupied with fantasies of unlimited power and money, success, brilliance, beauty, or ideal love.
- Is ambitious, seeking fame and fortune to reinforce one's belief in one's own greatness.
- Has a strong need for attention and admiration; may seek leadership positions to gain admiration.
- Is often charming and well-liked by others.
- Avoids being criticized or having his or her self-esteem threatened; responds to criticism with anger or attacking back.
- Expects to be treated well and for others to automatically comply with his or her needs or expectations.
- May take advantage of others to get what he or she wants.
- Has difficulty sympathizing with others or understanding others' feelings or needs; may fake sympathy as a way of getting what he or she wants.
- Is envious of others while believing that others are envious instead.

- At times has arrogant, self-righteous, selfish, and haughty behaviors and attitudes while also being charming and likable.

- Demands a lot from others; therefore relationships may be strained and difficult to maintain.

- Has a sense of entitlement or privilege or feeling that he or she deserves special treatment.

- Has fragile self-esteem; underneath the bravado, may feel shamed and weak.

- Doesn't show interest in others while expecting that they are interested instead.

Treatment Options for Narcissistic Personality Disorder

It is not uncommon for an individual with narcissistic personality disorder to also be diagnosed with a borderline, histrionic, or antisocial personality disorder or other mental health disorders such as depression. Narcissistic personality disorder is chronic and may be difficult to treat. It has proven important for the patient to fully accept the diagnosis and want to be helped before treatment can be successful. Any chemical addiction, such as to prescription drugs and/or alcohol or other drugs (including street drugs) will aggravate the symptoms and interfere with you feeling better. It is extremely important to participate in a rehabilitation program and/or self-help program, like Dual Recovery Anonymous (DRA), Alcoholics Anonymous (AA), Narcotics Anonymous (NA), or others and stay on your plan for leading a recovery-oriented life. Ongoing therapy is valuable as part of the treatment plan, as is medication if symptoms of mood swings, depression, and panic attacks occur regularly.

Obsessive-Compulsive Personality Disorder

It is estimated that only one percent of the general population is diagnosed with obsessive-compulsive personality disorder (OCPD), and it is diagnosed more commonly in men than women. Behavior usually begins in early adulthood, especially in those whose backgrounds included harsh discipline. The use of alcohol and/or other drugs to attempt to moderate symptoms of OCPD and alleviate distress is common.

Obsessive-compulsive personality disorder is characterized by behavior that is often preoccupied with perfectionism and the need to maintain a sense of control and orderliness; an excessive devotion to work; difficulty expressing warm and tender emotions; being extremely detail-oriented and overly concerned with rules, systems, and schedules; having rigid beliefs and thinking; and often being indecisive.

Obsessive-compulsive personality disorder is very different from obsessive-compulsive disorder, although some of the symptoms might overlap. Despite its similar name, OCPD does not involve obsessions and compulsions.

Here is how one individual with OCPD describes himself:

"I'm one of those people who wants things done 'just right' and my way, which is usually perfect anyhow. People get frustrated with me, but I'm not going to relax my standards for anyone. My wife calls me a workaholic and tells me that I need to get in touch with my emotions, but to me feelings just get in the way of me accomplishing my work. She also thinks I drink too much, but after a tough day, a six-pack helps me relax. She's the one who needs to chill out."

Characteristics of Obsessive-Compulsive Personality Disorder

A person with obsessive-compulsive personality disorder possesses these characteristics:

- Has difficulty expressing warm and tender feelings, may seem cold and unemotional to others, formal and serious, or lacking a sense of humor.
- Is preoccupied with orderliness, attention to details, rules, lists, organization, or schedules.
- Has a tendency toward perfectionism to the point where the task may not get done because it can't be done perfectly.
- Is excessively devoted to work and productivity to the point of excluding friendships and pleasurable and leisure activities; is sometimes referred to as a "workaholic."
- Others may consider this person inflexible and overly conscientious about matters of morality, ethics, or values; feels the need to preach to others about one's opinions.
- Is considered stubborn in attitude and behavior, and compromising is extremely difficult.
- Is unable to throw away worn-out or worthless items or papers, even when they have no sentimental value.
- Insists that others must do things exactly as one requests.
- Has "penny-pinching" attitude toward self and others, hoards money due to having to save for the future and preparing for future catastrophes.

Treatment Options for Obsessive-Compulsive Personality Disorder

Group and individual therapy have proven helpful for individuals with OCPD to learn to be more flexible and adaptable. Medications to help with anxiety can sometimes be helpful.

Any chemical/substance addiction, such as alcohol and/or other drugs (including prescription and/or street drugs) will aggravate the symptoms and interfere with you feeling better. It is extremely important to participate in a rehabilitation program and/or self-help program, like Dual Recovery Anonymous (DRA), Alcoholics Anonymous (AA), Narcotics Anonymous (NA), or others and stay on your plan for leading an abstinence-based and recovery-oriented life.

Paranoid Personality Disorder

Paranoid personality disorder (PPD) affects up to 2.5 percent of the general population and is more commonly diagnosed in men than women. Addiction can be especially destructive to someone with paranoid personality disorder as paranoia is likely to become more severe. Substance abuse may even lead to a psychotic episode.

This disorder is usually recognized by the following characteristics:

- Shows suspicion and distrust without reason
- Believes that others are exploiting, harming, deceiving, or betraying him or her
- Has doubts that others will be loyal
- Experiences feelings of extreme jealousy
- Thinks the worst from other people and is "on guard" against a hostile world
- Expresses a limited range of emotions, such as difficulty showing warmth or tenderness toward others
- Compliments may be viewed as a hidden criticism or coercion
- May have experienced a childhood filled with criticism, blame, and hostility

Here's how one individual with PPD describes himself:

"Ever since I was a teenager I've felt like it was me against the world. Everywhere I go people are always talking about me behind my back. I can tell by the way they look at me that they're making fun of me. Yesterday, I was eating at a fast food place and just as I walked by this table of teenage girls, they all burst out laughing. Why is everyone out to get me?"

Characteristics of Paranoid Personality Disorder

A person with paranoid personality disorder possesses these characteristics:

- Is suspicious of others; thinks people are out to get him or her
- Thinks others' actions or words were meant to hurt or threaten him or her (when the actions or words really were not meant in that way)
- Suspecting, for little or no reason, that others mean to exploit, harm, or deceive him or her
- Has difficulty showing warm or loving emotions; may seem cold toward others
- Is preoccupied with questioning the loyalty or trustworthiness of friends, family, and colleagues
- Has recurring doubts and suspicions about the fidelity of a spouse or partner; is extremely jealous
- Projects one's own unaccepted feelings on other people
- Can quickly become hostile, irritable, and angry; may appear moody
- Is overly sensitive and may seem to take things personally

- Is impressed by power and rank and disrespectful of others who are seen as weak, sickly, or impaired
- Tends to bear grudges or be unforgiving of insults, slights, or injuries
- Is highly critical of others, and has extreme difficulty accepting criticism of themselves

Treatment Options for Personality Disorders and Addiction

Paranoid personality disorder can co-exist with major depression, obsessive-compulsive disorder, agoraphobia, substance use disorders, and other mental health disorders. People with paranoid personality disorder are most often referred to treatment by a spouse or an employer, and rarely seek treatment themselves.

Psychotherapy is the preferred treatment and can be of great help. Individual therapy sessions are the treatment of choice, but group therapy can sometimes be helpful as well.

Any chemical/substance addiction, such as alcohol and/or other drugs (including prescription and/or street drugs) will aggravate the symptoms and interfere with you feeling better. It is extremely important to participate in a rehabilitation program and/or self-help program, like Dual Recovery Anonymous (DRA), Alcoholics Anonymous (AA), Narcotics Anonymous (NA) or others, and stay on your plan for leading an abstinence-based and recovery-oriented life.

If symptoms of anxiety and agitation are present, medication may be prescribed. Medication may also be used to manage any associated disorders, as mentioned above.

Schizoid Personality Disorder

Schizoid personality disorder (SPD) may affect anywhere from 1 to 7 percent of the general population, but the occurrence hasn't been clearly established. Studies show that it is more commonly diagnosed in men than women. Behavior usually begins in early childhood and is easily noticeable. Individuals with schizoid personality disorder who abuse substances are likely to increase their isolation and withdrawal, further separating themselves from society and relationships.

This disorder's main characteristics include the following: difficulty forming or maintaining social relationships; difficulty expressing a range of emotions; being perceived as a "loner" ; and being emotionally withdrawn and detached from people and activities that others usually enjoy.

Individuals with schizoid personality disorder sometimes have family members who have had schizophrenia. Some describe negative childhood experiences with caregiver or parental rage, as well as other influences that promote child insecurities.

Here's how an individual with schizoid personality disorder describes herself:

"I like to be by myself. I can sit for hours—or days!—in front of my computer and not talk to anyone. Even when I'm around other people, I usually keep to myself. I don't see why people need

to get together all the time, and I don't see what the big deal is about dating or getting married either. I'd rather be by myself than have someone bugging me all the time."

Characteristics of Schizoid Personality Disorder

A person with schizoid personality disorder possesses these characteristics:

- Has a lifelong pattern of preferring to be alone rather than being part of a family or being with friends or colleagues
- Is extremely uncomfortable in social situations and with human interactions; may feel socially awkward
- Is introverted and would rather be alone or isolated; sometimes referred to as "hermit-like" or a "loner"
- Has few or no close friends or confidants
- Has little, if any, interest in having a sexual experience with another person, but may have sexual fantasies
- Tends to be emotionally distant or aloof; has difficulty showing warm or tender feelings
- Rarely experiences strong emotions; tends to always be in the same mood
- Lacks interest and involvement in everyday events
- Is indifferent to praise or criticism, as well as the concerns or feelings of others
- Is unable to express anger or aggression, turning instead to daydreams or fantasies; may seem "zombie-like" to others
- Is comfortable with long silences
- May show extreme affection or attention toward nonhuman interests, such as pets, computers, mathematics, or astronomy
- Prefers being independent and doing solitary activities
- May experience a brief psychotic disorder in response to stress

Treatment Options for Schizoid Personality Disorder

Other disorders that may co-exist with schizoid personality disorder include depression, obsessive-compulsive disorder, agoraphobia, and substance use disorders.

Psychotherapy is the treatment of choice, starting with individual therapy sessions and adding in group sessions as needed. Any chemical addiction, such as to prescription drugs, alcohol, or street drugs will aggravate the symptoms and interfere with you feeling better. It is extremely important to participate in a rehabilitation program and/or self-help program, like Dual Recovery Anonymous (DRA), Alcoholics

Anonymous (AA), Narcotics Anonymous (NA), or others and stay on your plan for leading an abstinence-based and recovery-oriented life.

Medications are used to manage any associated disorders, such as depression. Small dosages of antipsychotics, antidepressants, or psychostimulants can be useful for some people.

Schizotypal Personality Disorder

Schizotypal personality disorder affects about 3 percent of the general population. People with this disorder may be diagnosed or misdiagnosed with schizophrenia, a closely related disorder. Substance abuse can contribute to isolation and to odd behavior in people with this disorder.

A person with this disorder experiences severe discomfort in social situations; tends to be withdrawn and isolated; has difficulty developing relationships with others, even family; and experiences odd thoughts, beliefs, or magical thinking.

Schizotypal personality disorder has been described in this way:

"My parents worry about me because they think I should have friends and go to the movies and stuff like that. But I'd rather be by myself. I don't see what the problem is. People think I'm weird, but that's their problem. My parents think my tarot cards are silly and worthless, but it's important to me to be in touch with the spiritual world. I have the gift of telepathy... I've never had a boyfriend, but by using my telepathic powers, I've found my soulmate and we commune as often as possible."

Characteristics of Schizotypal Personality Disorder

A person with schizotypal personality disorder possesses these characteristics:

- Other people think that person's thoughts, speech, and behavior are strange or different; this individual "walks to the beat of a different drummer"
- Has few or no close friends or contacts and prefers to be alone
- Has odd or "magical" beliefs, such as superstitions, belief in clairvoyance, mental telepathy, or bizarre fantasies
- Is emotionally distant or aloof; has difficulty showing warm or tender feelings
- May have inappropriate emotions; for example, being happy when someone gets hurt
- Has unusual perceptions or beliefs, including illusions about one's body
- Has suspicious or paranoid ideas, believing people are out to get him or her
- Says things that don't make sense to others or are considered magical
- May be involved in cults, the occult, and performing odd religious practices
- Has extreme discomfort with social interactions; doesn't feel that he or she fits in

- Is socially awkward; has difficulty conforming to social norms and expectations
- May appear stiff, have unusual mannerisms, or dress very differently
- May experience a brief psychotic disorder in response to stress

Treatment Options for Schizotypal Personality Disorder

Schizotypal personality disorder may be diagnosed along with borderline personality disorder and avoidant personality disorder. Individual therapy sessions are the most important avenue of treatment for a person with schizotypal personality disorder.

Any chemical/substance addiction, such as alcohol and/or other drugs (including prescription drugs and/or street drugs) will aggravate the symptoms and interfere with you feeling better. It is extremely important to participate in a rehabilitation program and/or self-help program, like Dual Recovery Anonymous (DRA), Alcoholics Anonymous (AA), Narcotics Anonymous (NA), or others and stay on your plan for leading an abstinence-based and recovery-oriented life.

Antipsychotic medication may be useful in relieving symptoms of this disorder, and if depression is present, antidepressants may be prescribed.

Personality Disorder Not Otherwise Specified

If you are experiencing significant distress and difficulty getting along in life, but you don't seem to match the description of one of the personality disorders that have been described in this section, then this category may apply to you. Here are examples of disorders that are included in this category:

- Passive-Aggressive Personality Disorder
- Depressive Personality Disorder
- Sadomasochistic Personality Disorder
- Sadistic Personality Disorder

Personality Disorder Not Otherwise Specified is also the diagnosis given if your symptoms are a combination of two or more personality disorders. This is sometimes referred to as a **Mixed Personality Disorder**. For example, a person may have a mixed personality disorder with some borderline and some histrionic traits. Having a combination of symptoms that do not meet the full criteria for any one disorder is relatively common in the general population.

For more information on your specific type of personality disorder, please talk with your doctor or therapist.

CHAPTER SIX

Medication and How It Can Affect Co-occurring Mental Health and Substance Use Disorders

How Medications Can Help You

This is an overview that will familiarize you with medications, how they can help you, questions you can ask your doctor about them, how they affect you, and the role they have in managing your co-occurring disorders. Consistently taking medication prescribed for you can be one of the most important aspects of your recovery and will help you maintain a good quality of life.

Getting Help

As a person with co-occurring mental health and substance use disorders, your treatment plan may involve:

- **Medication:** Your doctor may prescribe one or more medicines to help treat symptoms of mental or emotional illness, such as paranoia, depression, anxiety, nervousness, hearing voices (or having hallucinations), insomnia and others.
- **Counseling:** This involves meeting with a trained professional, such as a therapist or counselor, one-on-one or in a group setting. You will receive emotional support, guidance about dealing

with problems associated with your illness, and information on how to prevent relapse. Counseling can teach you how to cope with co-occurring disorders.

- **Doctor Visits:** It is important to see your doctor regularly to make sure your medication is working properly. If you are experiencing any unwanted reactions, your doctor may change your medication or adjust the dosage.

- **Support Groups:** Support groups, such as Dual Recovery Anonymous (DRA), Alcoholics Anonymous (AA), or Narcotics Anonymous (NA), have regular recovery meetings with others who have similar problems and give you the opportunity to offer and receive support, as well as provide you with a feeling of community.

- **Sponsor Contact:** Your sponsor is an essential part of your recovery plan. Your sponsor will offer active support, guidance, and direction.

- **Case Manager or Social Worker:** This person helps you coordinate the different aspects of your treatment plan and is available if you have a problem. Your case manager can help you find a doctor or therapist, help you join a support group, help you with your prescriptions, and help you find activities that may interest you.

This section teaches about medications, but all of the above treatment options are important and will help you lead a fulfilling life. Ask your doctor, counselor, or case manager for help if you would like to know more about these treatment options.

Do You Need Medicine?

Many mental illnesses result from a chemical imbalance in the brain and central nervous system, and medications help bring this chemistry back into balance. Sometimes people need to take these medications for the rest of their lives to maintain their chemical balance. Other times, a person may experience periodic serious or severe symptoms, such as depression or anxiety, and may require medication for a limited period of time.

Medications that are prescribed to treat symptoms of mental illness, also called psychiatric medications, are usually taken every day for an extended period of time and come in the form of tablets, capsules, or liquid. These medicines work slowly and may take several weeks before you notice your symptoms are getting better or going away. Typically, when you start feeling better that means your medication is working, and you should continue taking it.

You may not like the idea of taking medication, and may think you can take it like cold or flu medicine—start when you are sick and stop when you feel better. Most people are used to getting a quick response when they take medicine, like aspirin, but in order for psychiatric medicines to work, there has to be a certain amount of it in your system before you start to notice a difference. It is important not to change your dosage or stop taking your medicines without first talking with your doctor.

Some reasons to take medication include the following: decreasing symptoms of a mental illness, restoring a chemical balance in the brain, and/or helping to treat a substance use disorder.

When you start to feel better, it is imperative to keep taking your medicine to maintain a balance in your system and experience good mental health. Periodically, your doctor may want to give you a blood test to verify that you have the appropriate levels of medicine in your system.

You are *not alone* in needing to take medication to help you feel better and relieve your symptoms. Here are some quotes from people sharing about taking medication and being in dual recovery.

"Be aware of how you feel. Your whole mind and everything will be clear when your medicine is working. You'll feel uplifted."

"What works for me is being on my meds, not playing doctor, not taking myself off my meds, making sure I have my blood level drawn, and also listening to my doctor's suggestions."

"I know my medicine isn't working when I don't want to be around or talk to other people. When it's not working, I have no feelings for myself or other people."

"Open up and be honest with your psychiatrist. Tell the truth about how you feel. When I first started to see a psychiatrist, I didn't pay attention, but when I understood that he could help, I explained more about how I was feeling."

"If my medicine isn't acting like I feel it should, I go back to my psychiatrist and ask for help. I ask for help in identifying my feelings."

It is not unusual to be concerned about others finding out that you are taking medications. You may think that taking medicine is a sign of weakness, that it carries a stigma, or it may make you feel embarrassed. If this is the case, tell your doctor. You may be able to take fewer doses and take them in the privacy of your home.

Also, keep in mind that millions of people take medications every day to help control illnesses, such as high blood pressure, diabetes, heart disease, asthma, epileptic seizures, and other illnesses and disorders. A recent report states that over thirty-two million Americans take three or more medications daily. There is nothing wrong with taking medications as prescribed by a physician for whatever illness and/or disorder you may have. Taking medication may be part of your treatment, and it's certainly not something to be ashamed or embarrassed about.

Taking your medications, as prescribed by your doctor, is one of the most important things you can do to enjoy a healthy and contented life. Some mental illnesses can be controlled or improved with medications, whereas others cannot be treated with medication. For example, depression and anxiety disorders can be treated with medications, but personality disorders such as borderline personality disorder and antisocial personality disorder can't.

> **Note:** For treating addiction, appropriate medications such as Antabuse, naltrexone, methadone, and Subutex may be used as part of a comprehensive program of recovery for a person with a co-occurring mental health diagnosis. Also, some medications are helpful in coping with addiction or cravings and withdrawal, such as buprenorphine, clonidine, Zyban, and others. A psychiatrist will not only be able to prescribe medications for common uses, but also for less well-known uses.

What Medicine Do You Take?

It is helpful for your mental health and recovery professional(s) to familiarize themselves with your medication treatment.

List three reasons you need to take medication(s).

1. _____
_____
_____
_____

2. _____
_____
_____
_____

3. _____
_____
_____
_____

List All Medicine(s) You Are Currently Taking			
Medicine Name	**Dosage**	**Time Taken**	**Date Started**

Benefits of Medication

Psychiatric medicines have been proven to relieve symptoms of mental illness. Taking medication may help you feel better in a variety of ways. Here are just a few.

You may:

- Feel happier and more energetic.
- Feel more relaxed and at peace with yourself and your surroundings.
- Sleep better and awaken feeling more rested.
- Have better concentration so you can focus on a particular task.
- Feel more independent and capable to fully function on a day-to-day basis.
- Feel more hopeful and even-tempered.
- Have confidence that you are doing your best to stay in recovery and lead a fulfilling life.

These are just a few of the benefits of taking medication. Talk with your doctor about your specific symptoms, diagnosis, and lifestyle. Your doctor will prescribe the best medication(s) to treat and alleviate your symptoms. Taking medicine is only one part of a treatment plan. Give yourself the best chance at staying in recovery and managing the symptoms of mental illness by taking your medicine every day and continuing with the other parts of your treatment, such as meeting with your therapist and attending regular support group meetings, like twelve-step fellowships, and others.

Dealing with Side Effects

All psychiatric medicines have side effects. Side effects are unwanted reactions that result from taking medicine(s). Since everyone is different, no two people will experience the exact same side effects when taking the same medicine. When your doctor prescribes medication to you, he or she will review the possible side effects with you.

Usually, side effects are most obvious when you first start taking your medicine, but they will get better after about seven to ten days when your body has adjusted to the medicine. This is completely normal, so don't discontinue taking your medication after a few days; give it at least two weeks for the side effects to subside.

Examples of side effects range from experiencing dry mouth or slight shaking of your hands to increased blood pressure or constipation. There is a wide range of various side effects that accompany different medications. You should discuss possible side effects with your doctor.

Be sure to tell your doctor about all medicines you are taking, including cold or allergy medicine and birth control pills, since they can interact with your psychiatric medications and cause side effects.

If you are experiencing troubling side effects, talk with your doctor right away. Most serious side effects can be treated with additional medicine, a change in the amount of medication you are currently taking, or by changing your medicine to something else entirely.

You may also have to live with some side effects, especially if they are not serious and if your medication is relieving your symptoms. It is up to you to decide what side effects you can live with. For example, if your medication makes you gain weight, you can adjust your diet and exercise programs to accommodate this side effect.

Guidelines for Taking Medicine

Here are the six basic steps involved when you first start taking psychiatric medication(s):

1. Your doctor prescribes one or more medications for you.

Keep in mind that medicines affect people in different ways. Two people can take the same medicine and experience two completely different reactions. Because of this, you and your doctor must work together to find the right medicine and dosage to best alleviate your symptoms and minimize side effects.

2. Take your medication at the same time every day (or every week).

Some medicines work for twelve hours and need to be taken twice a day, while others work for a few hours and must be taken throughout the day. If your medicine is extended-release or controlled-release, you may only need to take this once a day. Some other medicines are long-acting, such as Prozac Weekly, and only need to be taken once a week.

If your medicine makes you sleepy, your doctor might recommend taking it before going to bed. If your medicine gives you energy, your doctor may suggest it be taken in the morning.

It is important to follow your doctor's instructions and take your medicine at the same time every day. If you are taking several medicines, it can be hard to keep track of multiple doses.

Do not stop taking your medication without first talking to your doctor. Some medications can cause serious problems if you suddenly stop taking them; they need to be "tapered" (the dose needs to be reduced gradually) to avoid dangerous withdrawal symptoms.

3. Keep an extra week's supply of medication so you don't run out.

In order to avoid running out of medicine, you will need to plan ahead and allow time to get a prescription refilled, but it is also a good idea to have a backup "emergency" medicine supply. Make sure to plan ahead and ask your pharmacy for extra medicine if you plan to be out of town for a while.

4. Give the medication time to work.

Psychiatric medications can take effect slowly. You may feel relief from your symptoms right away or it may take up to a month. Also, you may need your doctor to make an adjustment to the amount of medication you are taking. Sometimes your doctor will start you on a low dose and gradually increase it, so it may take even longer to get to the point where your symptoms are optimally managed.

5. If you experience any serious unwanted reactions (side effects), call your doctor immediately.

Be sure to tell your doctor about any and all medicines you take, even over-the-counter cold medicines, sleep-aids, diet-aids, and any allergies that you may have to medications. If you experience a persistent reaction that causes you discomfort, or a health problem that is troubling, you should call your doctor immediately.

All psychiatric medicines have side effects. Usually they are worse when you first start taking your medicine and will get better after about seven to ten days once your body adjusts to the medicine. This is completely normal.

6. Don't drink alcohol or use other drugs, including street drugs, while taking psychiatric medications.

Some medications are deadly if mixed with alcohol or other drugs, especially street drugs. Make sure that the people who make up your support system (friends, family, therapist, etc.) know what medications you are taking so that they can help you stay on track.

> **Helpful Hint:** Your doctor expects you to call if you have any questions or concerns about taking your medicines.

What Your Doctor Needs to Know

Your doctor is there to help you get better. However, before your doctor can help, you will have to be as open and honest as you possibly can about your health and habits. If you and your doctor can develop trust, mutual respect, and good communication, then your recovery path will be easier and your treatment will be more likely to succeed.

It is *very important* for you to tell your doctor the following:

- All of your symptoms. Make a list of your symptoms and bring it with you to your appointment so you don't forget to tell your doctor.
- A complete history of your mental illness. For example, when you first started having symptoms, the pattern of your illness, and what makes it worse or better, etc.
- Your family history of mental illness. For example, if one of your parents or a brother or sister is diagnosed with a mental illness.
- Any concerns you have about taking medication.
- If you are planning a pregnancy or breastfeeding.
- If your medicine's side effects are not acceptable for you. For example, some medicine may have sexual side effects or make you gain weight. Tell your doctor if this is not okay with you.
- If you have a hard time remembering to take your medicine. Some medicines can be prescribed in time-release capsules to make it easier for you to get the medicine you need even if you forget a dose.
- If you are taking other medicines, such as birth control pills, high blood pressure pills, etc., or over-the-counter medications, such as any cough or cold medicine, allergy medicine, or sleep-aids.
- About your substance use disorder, including what substance(s) you have used and where you are in your recovery.

Questions to Ask Your Doctor

It is essential that you take an active role in your own recovery and treatment program. One of the first steps is to gather information about your diagnosis and treatment. This section provides some tried-and-true questions that you should ask your doctor.

Take these questions with you to your next doctor's appointment. If your doctor doesn't have time to answer all of the questions, request that he or she make a photocopy, write the answers, and mail it to you. Consider asking a friend or family member to join you when you visit the doctor. This person can remind you to ask these questions and can take notes for you. If you've already asked your doctor some of these questions, go ahead and try to answer them. If you aren't sure if your answers are correct, then show them to your doctor for feedback.

Questions to Ask When Starting Treatment

What is my diagnosis? _____

What is my treatment plan and why is a particular medication recommended? _____
_____
_____

What symptoms will be helped by this medication? _____
_____

When can I expect relief from my symptoms? _____

What should I do if I miss a dose? _____
_____

What are the side effects that I should be aware of, and how long will they last? _____
_____
_____

What serious reactions are possible, and what should I do if I experience one? _____
_____
_____
_____

What medical tests or lab work will I need? _____
_____
_____

How long will I need to take medication, and will my dosages likely change?_____
_____
_____

Should I change my diet, activities, or lifestyle in any way?_____
_____
_____
_____

Is the medication dangerous if mixed with alcohol or other drugs, including street drugs, or if I accidentally take too much? _____
_____

Is this medication addictive? _____
_____

What follow-up appointments will I need? _____
_____

Are there any other treatments you suggest? _____
_____

Are there any support groups for me, my family, and friends that you suggest? _____
_____
_____

May I call if I need to talk with you?_____

Ask your doctor for any information leaflets about your condition and treatment, if available.

Notes _____
_____
_____
_____

Questions to Ask If You've Been in Treatment

Are there any newer medications to treat my condition with fewer side effects?

_____

_____

_____

I am still experiencing some symptoms and side effects. (Bring a separate list or a daily journal so you can talk about your symptoms specifically.) Is there anything I can do?

_____

_____

_____

_____

_____

How is my overall health? (Please check my blood pressure, weight, etc.) _____

_____

_____

_____

_____

Do you recommend any changes to my treatment or diet, exercise, lifestyle, etc.?

_____

_____

_____

_____

_____

Notes _____

_____

_____

_____

_____

_____

Different Types of Medicines

Psychiatric medications are drugs that have been designed to help manage symptoms of mental and emotional illnesses, such as anxiety, agitation, altered perceptions and sensations, confused thinking, depression, disrupted patterns of attitude and sleep, poor concentration, profound sadness, hearing voices, and discomfort from physical pain.

Occasionally, two or more medications may be needed to relieve multiple symptoms. Sometimes a second medication is prescribed, such as Cogentin, Benadryl, and Artane to help ease the side effects of another medication.

This section provides a list of medications that are commonly prescribed for different treatments and is provided so you can become familiar with the various medications that are being used today. If you have any questions, please discuss them with your doctor, counselor, or pharmacist.

New versus Old Medications

It hasn't been that long since psychiatric medications were developed, and in a relatively short time, hundreds of medications have been developed to treat chemical imbalances and underlying symptoms of mental and emotional illnesses. When your doctor prescribes your medication, you may want to ask if your medicine is a newer or older one. Even though many newer medications are coming on the market every year, older medications are still available, effective, and widely in use.

Example of an *older* medicine—In 1949, Lithium (lithium carbonate) was discovered to be effective for treatment of mania and is still widely used.

Example of a *newer* medicine—In 2002, Lexapro (escitalopram oxalate) was discovered to be effective for treating depression.

Classes of Antidepressants

Here is a list of the groupings, or classes, of antidepressants, shown from newest to oldest, along with a few examples of medications and their side effects.

Antidepressant Class	Example Medications	Typical Side Effects
SNRIs (Selective Norepinephrine Reuptake Inhibitors)	Effexor	Fewer side effects than older medicines. Can cause dizziness, headaches, nervousness, hypertension, agitation, and dry mouth. Certain restrictions.
SSRIs (Selective Serotonin Reuptake Inhibitors)	Prozac Zoloft Paxil	Gastrointestinal problems (nausea, vomiting, constipation), sexual side effects (decreased libido, anorgasmia), some weight gain, fatigue, agitation.
TCAs (Tricyclic Antidepressants)	Elavil Anafranil	More side effects than newer drugs, including significant weight gain, sedation, constipation, urinary hesitancy, sexual side effects.
MAOIs (Monoamine Oxidase Inhibitors)	Parnate Nardil	More severe side effects than newer medicines. Strict dietary restrictions (no food with tyramine, such as cheese, pickles, bacon, yogurt, chocolate, bananas), no alcohol; can cause hypertensive crisis and strokes.

Pros and Cons

Newer medications tend to have fewer side effects and may require fewer doses each day. Also, as more is learned about the chemical reactions in the brain and how the central nervous system is involved with mental illness, new medicines are developed to take advantage of these medical discoveries.

Many of the older medications are still in use today because of their effectiveness; however, they may cause more side effects than newer medications.

For example, Haldol (haloperidol) is an older medicine often prescribed to help with hallucinations, such as hearing voices. If you take Haldol for a long time, you may develop **tardive dyskinesia**, which is a syndrome that results in stiff limbs and muscle tics, among other symptoms. Some side effects can be difficult to live with but might be better than living with hallucinations. Some people find that the newer medications don't work as well to control their symptoms.

Some older medications are also more dangerous. You can become addicted to them and develop tolerance to them, making it difficult to depend on them for long-term symptom management. Also, they can be dangerous if an overdose is taken, whereas the newer medicines tend to be safer.

Currently Prescribed Medications

On the next few pages, you will see a medicine chart that lists medications, their side effects, and illnesses being treated.

If you are taking a medication that is not included in this chart, do not be concerned. This is only a partial listing since the number of medications available today are too numerous to include here. We encourage you to show this medicine chart to your doctor and have him or her add your medication(s) and side effects in the appropriate places.

Treatment	Effects	Commonly Used Drugs Brand Name (Generic Name)
Antiaddiction (for addictions)	Used to reduce cravings, induce illness when alcohol is ingested, or to help one safely taper off heroin, opiates, nicotine, or narcotics.	Antabuse (disulfiram) LAAM (levo-alpha acetyl methadol) Methadone Morphine Naltrexone Subutex (buprenorphine) Suboxone (buprenorphine & naloxone) Zyban (buproprion)
Antidepressants (for depression and anxiety)	Used to elevate or stabilize moods in people with mood disorders and may also be used for anxiety and pain management.	Adapin, Sinequan (doxepin) Anafranil (clomipramine) Asendin (amoxapine) Aventyl, Pamelor (nortriptyline) Celexa (citalopram) Effexor (venlafaxine) Elavil (amitriptyline) Lexapro (escitalopram oxalate) Luvox (fluvoxamine) Nardil (phenelzine) Norpramin (desipramine) Parnate (tranylcypromine) Paxil (paroxetine) Prozac (fluoxetine) Remeron (mirtazapine) Serzone (nefazodone) Tofranil (imipramine) Vivactil (protriptyline) Wellbutrin (buproprion) Zoloft (sertraline)
Anticonvulsants & Antimanic (for bipolar disorder and seizures)	Used to stabilize moods and control episodes of mania and seizures.	Calan (verapamil) Cibalith-S (lithium citrate) Depakene (valproic acid) Depakote (divalproex sodium) Klonopin (clonazepam) Lamictal (lamotrigine) Lithium, Eskalith (lithium) Neurontin (gabapentin) Tegretol (carbamazepine) Topamax (topiramate) Trileptal (oxcarbazepine)

Treatment	Effects	Commonly Used Drugs Brand Name (Generic Name)
Antipsychotics (for schizophrenia, thought disorders, and mood disorders)	Used to reduce hallucinations and delusions; increase calmness; sedate and relieve confusion, disordered thoughts, and mood swings.	Clozaril (clozapine) Daxolin, Loxitane (loxapine) Geodon (zyprazidone) Haldol (haloperidol) Lidone, Moban (molindone) Mellaril (thioridazine) Prolixin, Permitil (fluphenazine) Risperdal (risperidone) Serentil (mesoridazine) Seroquel (quetiapine) Trilafon (perphenazine) Thorazine (chlorpromazine) Zyprexa (olanzapine)
Anxiolytics* (for anxiety)	Used to provide relief of anxiety and for panic disorder, phobias, OCD, alcohol/drug withdrawal, and other medical problems.	Ativan (lorazepam) Azene, Tranxene (clorazepate) BuSpar (buspirone) Centrax (prazepam) Klonopin (clonazepam) Librax, Librium (chlordiazepoxide) Paxipam (halazepam) Serax (oxazepam) Valium (diazepam) Xanax (alprazolam)
Psychostimulants** (for attention deficit disorder, narcolepsy, and hyperactivity)	Used to increase concentration, wakefulness, alertness, and attention span; relieves impulsiveness and restlessness.	Adderall (amphetamine) Cylert (pemoline) Dexedrine (dextroamphetamine) Ritalin (methylphenidate)

*BuSpar is the only nonaddictive medication in this anxiolytics class. All others listed are benzodiazepines and are addictive and should not be prescribed if you have a chemical dependency.

**The psychostimulant medications are all addictive and should not be prescribed if you have a chemical dependency.

Take Medicine to Avoid Relapse

A relapse can happen if you switch medicines, change dosages, start taking an over-the-counter medicine without telling your doctor, miss doses, or stop taking your medicine. Please contact your doctor before making any changes to your medications.

Any change in your medication could change the balance in your brain chemistry, reduce the amount of medicine in your system, and lead to a full return or worsening of your symptoms.

Many people stop taking their medications because of side effects. Instead of stopping your medicine, call your doctor first. Your doctor might adjust your medication dosage or prescribe additional medication to better control the side effects. With certain medicines, such as Xanax, it is *very dangerous* to stop taking it all at once. If you need to stop, it is important to be tapered off the medicine gradually with a doctor's supervision.

Note about Caffeine: It is best to stay away from caffeine (found in coffee, colas, teas, chocolate, and some medicines) and nicotine (found in cigarettes and chewing tobacco) because they could alter the way medicine works in your body.

Don't Mix Alcohol or Other Drugs (Including Street Drugs) with Medication

It is important to avoid drinking alcohol and/or taking other drugs when taking your medicine because they can cause a dangerous reaction that could result in severe illness, hospitalization, or even death. Drinking alcohol or taking other drugs could also reduce the effectiveness of your medicine, or likewise, they could increase your medicine's potency and cause serious damage to your organs and health. For example, drinking alcohol while taking Valium could cause death from a potential overdose.

Mixing alcohol and other drugs with your medicine is dangerous and will disturb the balance of medicine in your system. This could lead to a return of your symptoms and a relapse.

For people with co-occurring disorders, even using a small amount of a drug, such as drinking one beer or smoking one joint, can reduce the effectiveness of medication and cause a psychiatric relapse. Ask your doctor about what would happen to you if you mixed alcohol and/or other drugs while on your medication. In some cases, your doctor may be able to prescribe an antiaddictive medication to help.

Making Medications Part of Your Life

In this section, we will review how to address your concerns about taking medications, what happens if you stop taking medications, possible side effects, and how medications can be effective in treating co-occurring mental illness and substance use disorders. Medications are an important part of an overall treatment plan and should be taken as prescribed by a doctor.

Concerns about Medications

It is not uncommon for you to be concerned about taking medication. You may even think you no longer need to take medication. This section covers some common concerns when one is starting a psychiatric medication routine.

1. "I feel fine. I don't need medication anymore."

If you have been taking medication for a while and are feeling good, this means that your medication is working. Continue taking your medication and you will continue to feel fine. Unlike some medicines that you can stop taking when you feel better (like cough syrup or throat lozenges), you *must* continue taking psychiatric medication to maintain your feeling of health and well-being, even if you have no symptoms.

Remember that one reason you are feeling good is that the appropriate levels of drugs have been built up in your system and are preventing your symptoms from appearing.

Your doctor will consider several factors when deciding whether you should continue or discontinue your medication, including:

- Your symptoms
- The history of your illnesses
- Current life stressors
- The stage of your dual recovery

Sometimes it is necessary to keep taking medication permanently. Other times, medication might be prescribed to help with a temporary problem, such as during a difficult time in your life.

If you've been told that you need to take medication permanently, then there's a good reason for that and you should make it a regular part of your life. If you are taking medication for a more transient problem and think maybe it is time to stop, talk to your doctor about it. Don't make the decision on your own. Your doctor may want you to slowly taper off the medicine or might offer important reasons you weren't aware of to continue the medicine.

If you stop taking your medication prematurely, your symptoms will likely return and you could experience a mental health relapse, substance use relapse, or both. The simple act of taking a daily medication is one of the most important aspects of your recovery process. Never change your dosage or stop taking your medication without first calling your doctor. Your doctor and therapist are available to listen to your concerns.

2. "What if others find out?"

It is not unusual to be concerned about others finding out that you are taking medicine. You may be concerned that taking medicine is a sign of weakness or something embarrassing. You may be concerned that another person will think you have problems. Tell your doctor or therapist about this concern. You may be able to take fewer doses and take them in the privacy of your home.

Also, consider that millions of people take medications every day to help control illnesses, such as high blood pressure, diabetes, heart disease, asthma, allergies, and other illnesses and disorders. Taking medication is nothing to be ashamed of, and if you tell another person you are taking medication, they are likely to say, "So am I!"

We encourage you to tell your family, friends, and colleagues about your co-occurring disorders. You can be proud of yourself for getting help, working every day toward a full recovery, and setting a good example for others who may be struggling with illness. Remember, you are not alone; millions of people are in recovery!

You may want to ask others to help you in your recovery by joining you at a support group meeting, taking a walk, or enjoying a fun social activity together, such as dinner or a movie.

It is important that you do not feel isolated and alone during your recovery. If you experience feelings of shame or embarrassment, talk with your counselor or therapist.

3. "I keep forgetting to take it."

It is easy to forget to take your medicine every now and then. Unexpected things happen and you may lose track of time or forget to bring your medicine with you. If this rarely happens, then there's no need for concern, but if you are forgetting to take your medicine on a regular basis or miss more than one dose at a time, then this could be harmful to your health and increase your chances of relapse.

Keep in mind that in order for psychiatric medicines to work, there has to be a certain amount in your system to work properly. When you miss too many doses, the amount of medicine in your system decreases and your symptoms will very likely return.

You should take your medicine every day to prevent your symptoms from returning.

If you are taking several medicines every day, then it may be difficult to keep track of the medicines you've already taken and the ones you haven't. Here are some suggestions to help you remember to take your medicine:

> **Pair it with a daily activity.** Take your medicine at the same time every day along with a routine activity to help you remember, like every morning before you brush your teeth, after lunch, when you watch the evening news, or at bedtime.

> **Buy a pill container.** Your pharmacy should sell pill containers that help you pre-sort your doses and place them in individual compartments. For example, a weekly pill container may have compartments for Monday, Tuesday, Wednesday, etc. This can help you keep track of doses you've taken, because if one of the compartments is empty, you know you've taken your pills.

Change your dosage schedule. Talk with your doctor about scheduling your dosages to better match your lifestyle needs. Some people wake early and may want to take their medicine at 6:00 a.m., while others wake up later and may want to take their medicine at 9:00 a.m. You may also ask if the number of dosages could be reduced. ***Warning:*** *Do not make any changes to your dosage or schedule without first discussing it with your doctor.*

Display a reminder. You may want to post a medicine schedule in an obvious place, like on your refrigerator or in your car, to remind you to take your medicine.

Set a watch alarm. Some people prefer to set a watch alarm each time they take a dose. For example, if you take a dose in the morning, then after you take it, set your watch alarm for the next time you should take your medication.

If you miss a dose. If you are taking multiple doses of medicine a day and you miss a dose, do *not* make up for it by *doubling the dose*. This can be dangerous and can produce toxic levels of the drug in your system. Instead, the best thing to do is resume taking your standard dose of medicine at the appointed time.

If you have tried these suggestions and are still missing doses, you might want to:
- Ask your doctor if your medication comes in a time-release capsule, which means you wouldn't have to take it as often.
- Ask for help from a trusted family member or friend to help remind you to take your doses.

4. "I don't feel any difference."

If you have recently started taking medication and don't feel any difference in your symptoms, then give the medicine more time to work. Different medicines work at different speeds and may take up to a month before you feel any noticeable change in your symptoms. In addition, if you have abused alcohol or other drugs for years, you may have damaged the structures in your brain that respond to medication. If so, it might take longer for your medicine to start working properly.

If after a month you experience no relief, then call your doctor. You may need an adjustment to your dose or your doctor may want to prescribe a new medicine.

5. "I feel like a zombie."

Sometimes starting a new medication can make you feel like you are having an out-of-body experience, like you are standing outside of yourself looking down. Or, someone may tell you that you look "dazed" or "out of it" and you may feel like you are moving or talking in slow-motion. All of these may be side effects from your medicine.

If you are experiencing a side effect that interferes with your daily activities or endangers you in any way, call your doctor. Your doctor may be able to adjust your dosage or change your medicine. However, if this side effect doesn't bother you too much, wait a while longer until your system has become more accustomed to the medication because the side effect may disappear.

Remember, you and your doctor want the same thing—for you to feel better. If you are experiencing a serious side effect, do not hesitate to contact your doctor, even if it is after-hours or a weekend. If your doctor is not available, then another doctor will be able to assist you.

6. "I'm afraid of side effects."

There is a large variety of psychiatric medicines from which your doctor can choose to treat your symptoms. Different medicines affect people in different ways. Two people taking the exact same medicine may have two different reactions, where one experiences an unwanted effect and the other person doesn't have any reaction at all.

The kind of reaction you will have to a medicine will depend on many things, including your body's metabolism, chemistry, and the amount of medicine you are taking.

Keep in mind that if side effects are bothering you, your doctor needs to know about them. Sometimes, finding the perfect match of a medicine with a patient is "trial and error," and your doctor expects you to call if there are any problems. Your doctor may need to lower your dosage and could even change the medicine you are taking. Changing your medicine or your dosage is a normal part of finding the right medicine to best relieve your symptoms.

Some side effects are not serious and may be temporary. As you keep taking your medicine, these side effects may go away as your body becomes accustomed to the medicine.

Some side effects can be serious. If you are experiencing side effects that impair your functioning, threaten your life, cause discomfort, or feel disabling in any way, call your doctor immediately.

7. "Why does my doctor keep changing my medication?"

You may feel like you are being treated like a "guinea pig" if your doctor keeps changing medications or dosages. When this happens, you may think, "Why doesn't my doctor know what medicine to give me?" Your doctor cannot tell how you will respond to a medication until you try it. It is normal for your doctor to try several medications or different combinations of medications to find what works best for you.

Your doctor may change your medication or the dosage of your medication for a number of reasons. For example, some medications need to be gradually increased until the most effective dose is reached. If you are experiencing a particularly difficult time in your life or are having new symptoms, then your doctor may make changes. Remember, *never change your dose on your own.* Call your doctor and discuss any problems that may arise. Your doctor knows what is best for you and together you both can decide what will be best for your recovery.

8. "They're too expensive."

If you have ever considered missing a dose or not filling a prescription because you were trying to save money, then it is time to talk with your case manager or counselor and ask for help. There may be a special program, fund, or a discount pharmacy service available to assist you. You may also want to ask your doctor if there is a generic version of your medicine that would be less expensive, but just as effective.

Medicines can be expensive and may be a financial burden, but it is extremely important for you to not miss a dose and to continue taking your medication on a daily basis. If you have insurance, contact your insurance company to see if they cover your medicine. Also, ask if they offer a mail order prescription service since this usually offers valuable savings along with the convenience of receiving medicine in the mail.

Remember, in the long run, staying on your medication will save you money by helping you function at your best. Taking your medication regularly can help you be more effective at work, enable you to get a job, or keep you from missing days of work.

If You Stop Taking Your Medications

Even though you know that taking your medication exactly as prescribed by your doctor is one of the best things you can do for yourself, you may encounter some "trouble spots" when you consider stopping your medication. This section will help you understand what happens if you miss a dose or stop taking your medications entirely.

How Medicine Works

Your medicine has been designed to treat imbalances in your brain chemistry and central nervous system. After taking your medicine for a while, an appropriate amount will accumulate in your system. At this time, your symptoms should subside or even disappear, and you should start to feel better. As mentioned previously, you may need to have a blood test so your doctor can make sure you have the right amount of medicine in your system.

If you stop taking your medicine, the level of medicine in your system will decrease and your symptoms will likely return, causing you to feel worse. This could quickly lead to a serious setback in your recovery or a complete mental health relapse, substance use relapse, or both.

Common Reasons for Not Taking Medicine

Here are the five common reasons that people stop taking their medicine.

- You forget to take your medicine.
- You run out of medicine.
- You don't think your medicine is working.
- You feel fine so you don't think you need medicine anymore.
- You don't like the way it makes you feel and your side effects may be bothering you, so you stop taking it.

Each reason is described in more detail on the following page.

You Forget to Take Your Medicine

This will happen every now and then, but if this happens often, it is a problem that requires immediate attention.

You Run Out of Medicine

We recommend that you keep one week's worth of "emergency" medicine as a backup when you are running low or are completely out of your medicine. Ask your doctor to help you with this. Label your emergency supply by writing the name of the medicine on it and the date received. Keep it separate from the rest of your medicine.

Sometimes it may be hard to get a prescription refilled for these possible reasons:

1. You may forget to refill it. Your backup emergency medicine should hold you over until you can refill your medicine. If you don't have any backup medicine, then take your prescription bottle(s) with you, go to your pharmacy, and tell your pharmacist that you've run out. Most pharmacies will provide you with enough medicine until your refill has been filled.

2. The pharmacy takes longer than you expected to refill it. Pharmacies usually take one or two days to refill a prescription, so plan ahead. It is recommended that you refill your medication one week in advance of running out.

3. It is difficult for you to travel to the pharmacy to pick it up. If transportation is a problem, then consider asking a friend or family member to pick up your medicine for you. Many pharmacies offer convenient drive-through windows to make picking up medicine quick and easy. You may also want to ask your pharmacy if they can deliver medicine to your home. If they don't, ask your nurse or case manager to help you find a pharmacy that has a delivery service.

4. You might be sick and don't feel like leaving home. The first thing to do is to ask for help by calling a friend, neighbor, or family member. If you can't reach anyone, then call your sponsor or pharmacist. Accepting that you cannot do this on your own is an important part of your recovery process.

You Feel Fine So You Don't Think You Need Medicine Anymore

After you've been taking medicine for a while, you may start to feel "normal" again because you are no longer experiencing your symptoms. This means that your medicine is working. Do not stop taking your medicine or your symptoms will most likely return. Try to remember what you felt like before you were taking your medicine.

You Don't Think Your Medicine Is Working

This is a common concern, especially if you've recently started taking a new medication. Some medicines start working immediately, while others may take up to a month before relieving your symptoms.

If you are concerned, talk with your doctor. Be open and honest about your symptoms and feelings. Remember, your doctor is there to help you feel better.

You Don't Like the Way Medicine Makes You Feel

Occasionally, when some people start taking psychiatric medicine, they may experience some side effects that make them feel bad, but this is usually temporary and should be reported right away to the doctor.

If this happens to you, do not stop taking your medicine unless instructed by your doctor. Your doctor can adjust your dosage, prescribe a new medication to alleviate a side effect, or change your medication. In rare cases, a side effect may be serious and/or life-threatening. In this case, go to the nearest emergency room, and ask the nurse or doctor to call your doctor on your behalf.

Remember that although there are often some unwanted side effects, they are often better than having a full return of your symptoms.

Side Effects

As previously mentioned, the term "side effects" refers to unwanted reactions that sometimes result from taking medicine. All psychiatric medications have side effects. The goal is to find a medication that has side effects you can tolerate. No drug affects a person in the same way it may affect others; everybody is different. The kind of reaction you may have when starting a medicine will depend on your age, sex, weight, metabolism, hormones, chemistry, and the dose you are taking.

Your doctor will ask about any other medicines you are taking. Be sure to tell your doctor about any and all medicines, such as those for hypertension (high blood pressure), diabetes, insomnia, asthma, birth control, etc., as well as all over-the-counter cold medicines, sleep-aids, diet-aids, diuretics, vitamins or supplements, and any allergies you may have.

Be sure to tell your doctor that you are in recovery. You will need to avoid benzodiazepines (such as Ativan, Xanax, Klonopin, Librium, and others) and any other addictive psychotropic medications.

Your doctor needs to know about all medicines you are taking since they can interact with your psychiatric medications and cause side effects.

Many side effects will get better after a few weeks. Most lasting side effects can be treated with additional medicine, a change in the amount you are taking, or by changing your medicine to something else entirely. Occasionally, two or more medications may be needed to relieve multiple symptoms. Sometimes a second medication is prescribed, such as Cogentin, Benadryl, Artane, and clonidine, to help ease the side effects of another medication.

Keep in mind that there are hundreds of different medications that have been developed to treat different symptoms. Your doctor may have you try more than one medicine before finding the best one for your conditions.

Sexual Side Effects

Some medications may have side effects that impact your sexual life, such as a loss of or reduced sexual desire, impotence, difficulty with orgasms, and irregular menstrual cycles in women. If you are experiencing a sexual side effect that is troubling you, discuss this with your doctor. Some medications have fewer sexual side effects than others.

Sexual side effects are a result of the medicine and are nothing to be embarrassed about discussing. In some cases, you may find the side effect is something you can live with, if your medicine is doing a good job of relieving your symptoms. Once you and your doctor discuss your options, you will be able to make an informed decision.

Weight Gain

Weight gain is a side effect that bothers many people. Before you decide to stop taking a medication that causes weight gain, consider these facts:

- Weight gain generally occurs in the first one to three months of taking medication.
- The average weight gain is five to fifteen pounds. Very few people gain more than twenty pounds.
- Weight gain is often the result of being more hungry than usual. If you can learn to resist this urge or eat healthy snacks, you can minimize weight gain.
- Weight gain is not dose dependent. That is, you won't gain more weight if your doctor increases your dose.
- Most weight gain can be combated by an exercise regime and a healthy diet.
- Although weight gain is undesirable, it is often not as problematic as people expect it to be.

Get to Know Your Medicine

All medicine comes with printed instructions and information. Read this documentation and what it says about common side effects, as well as rare and potentially dangerous side effects. You should also be aware of other issues specific to your medication such as whether it's safe to try to become pregnant or whether you should monitor your blood pressure while taking the medication.

Twelve-Step Programs, Medicine, and Addiction

If twelve-step programs are a part of your recovery, then you know that these programs recommend complete abstinence for a successful recovery from addiction. **However, abstinence from alcohol and/or other drugs (including street drugs) does not mean abstinence from prescription medication.** You should continue taking your prescription medication as recommended by your doctor.

If you have a mental illness such as depression, an anxiety disorder, or schizophrenia, then prescription medication may be an important part of your treatment. If so, it is vital that you take your medication as prescribed. Abstinence applies only to alcohol and other drugs (including street drugs), not medication prescribed by your doctor. When medications for mental illness were new, many of them (mostly a group of drugs called benzodiazepines) were "addictive." That is, people developed tolerance to them and experienced withdrawal effects when they stopped using them. Therefore, taking these medications is risky if you have an addictive disorder. Because of outdated information like this, you may have received faulty advice warning you to stay away from medication for mental health disorders. However, today there are many, many medications that are not addictive. **It is perfectly safe for you to take them, and it will not put your recovery from addiction at risk.**

Keep in mind that prescription medications that are addictive (benzodiazepines) are sometimes still prescribed, especially for anxiety disorders. Tell your doctor about your addiction so he or she won't prescribe that kind of medication for you. If you are uncertain if your medication is addictive, ask your doctor. Antidepressant medications are also effective in treating symptoms of anxiety.

If you are taking prescription pain medication, be aware that some can be addictive, such as Lortab, hydrocodone, morphine, and Dilaudid. Drugs with opioid ingredients should be avoided or used with caution. Talk with your doctor if you are currently taking prescription pain medication.

Medicines to Treat Addiction

Various medications have become available to help treat different types of chemical dependency. Here are the ways these medications can help.

Alcohol

Naltrexone is primarily used to help reduce cravings for alcohol. When used properly and combined with therapy, it can help reduce:

- The number of days spent drinking or using other drugs.
- The amount of alcohol or other drugs consumed.
- The chance of relapse with destructive drinking or other drug use.

Naltrexone is not intended to replace your recovery program and cannot cure your drinking or drug problem, but if used correctly, it can decrease your cravings. Nausea is the most common side effect, with other side effects such as headache, anxiety, dizziness, fatigue, vomiting, and insomnia.

Antabuse (disulfiram) is a medication that helps reduce your drinking by causing unpleasant side effects such as nausea, headache, vomiting, chest pain, and difficulty breathing when even a small amount of alcohol is ingested. The idea is that you will have an extra incentive to not drink if you understand that drinking will make you seriously ill. This medication is not intended to cure addiction to alcohol, but when used correctly, it can be a useful tool in your recovery.

Zofran (ondansetron) has been found to stop cravings and decrease alcohol consumption and increase abstinence in people who developed addiction to alcohol at an early age.

These medications are usually recommended for individuals who are already abstinent and who need help staying abstinent. They are *not* recommended for someone who is still drinking alcohol regularly.

Heroin or Opiates

The following medications are prescribed to those who are addicted to heroin or opiates and are trying to stop using. ***Caution:*** *If you stop using heroin or opiates abruptly, you may experience serious and dangerous withdrawal symptoms.*

These medications are addictive (they are opiate drugs just like heroin and oxycodone), but are safer and more controlled than street drugs that are often mixed with other harmful substances. The idea with these medications is to be weaned off heroin or opiates by taking smaller and smaller doses over time.

Buprenorphine (sold under the brand name Subutex) is the most recently approved treatment for addiction to heroin and other opioids. This is the first narcotic drug approved for addiction that can be prescribed by physicians in their offices. Buprenorphine does not produce a high, dependence, or result in dangerous withdrawal symptoms.

It offers great advantages compared to the existing treatment medications methadone and naltrexone. For example, buprenorphine is more effective at reducing cravings than naltrexone, and only needs to be taken every other day, as compared to methadone, which is taken daily. Naloxone is sometimes administered along with buprenorphine to decrease the likelihood of abuse. This combination drug is sold under the brand name Suboxone. For the above reasons, buprenorphine may be the best choice among these drugs for opioid withdrawal therapy.

Methadone and Levo-alpha-acetylmethadol (LAAM) have been available for years and are used to treat addiction to heroin or opioid painkillers. These drugs will help reduce your dependence on the opioid safely and without dangerous withdrawal symptoms. Methadone is dispensed at approved methadone clinics.

All of these medications are intended to be one aspect of a complete treatment program and should be paired with other forms of treatment like a therapy program.

> **Warning:** A doctor's supervision is required to take these medications because they can be dangerous. For example, drinking large amounts of alcohol while taking Antabuse can be deadly, and taking heroin or controlled pain medications can be deadly if you are taking naltrexone.

There are other considerations as well in determining whether any of these medications might be appropriate for you. Talk with your doctor for more information.

Pregnancy and Medicine

If you are planning a pregnancy or are currently pregnant, you should tell your doctor right away because your medicines may need to be stopped or changed. Anything you eat or drink, including medicines, can affect the health of your baby.

Keep these points in mind:

- If you are considering getting pregnant, talk with your doctor about whether it would be safe for you to stop taking your medication at this time. For example, if you are having suicidal thoughts or are experiencing extreme symptoms of bipolar disorder, it probably would not be the best time to consider a pregnancy.

- You should not take any psychiatric medicines during the first trimester (three months) unless you are at extreme risk for being suicidal.

- As your pregnancy nears the last trimester (six to nine months pregnant), it is safer to take medications.

- You should *never* drink alcohol or take other drugs, including street drugs, while pregnant.

- During the times when you cannot take medicine, it is recommended that you try to reduce your symptoms through meditation exercises, therapy, and other techniques such as breathing exercises or relaxation exercises.

Safety and Medicine

When your doctor prescribes your medication, he or she considers your diagnoses and symptoms; physical health and existing conditions, such as heart disease, diabetes, high blood pressure, etc.; age and weight; lifestyle; your recovery from a specific chemical addiction; potential side effects; and any other concerns you or your doctor may have.

Your medicine and dosage are tailored to you and should never be given to anyone else. Likewise, you should never take medications from anyone else. Sharing medications can be extremely dangerous. Also, if there are children in your household or visiting your home, keep medicine and any dangerous substances out of reach and away from children and the places they can reach.

Taking an Overdose

Taking an **overdose** of medicine is when you take an extremely large amount of medication at one time. This can happen accidentally or purposefully as an attempt at taking your own life. If this happens, call 911 immediately, and if you can, call a loved one. An overdose of medication can lead to unconsciousness and death.

Ask for help when you need it. Don't wait. If you are experiencing suicidal thoughts, call your therapist or counselor right away and let trusted friends or loved ones know. Also, crisis hotlines are available in most areas. Experienced people are available twenty-four hours a day to take your call.

Some psychiatric medicines are more dangerous than others. If you have been suicidal in the past or are currently having thoughts about hurting yourself, talk to your doctor.

Keep Track of How You Are Feeling

When you start taking a medication for your co-occurring disorders, we suggest that you keep a daily journal, or diary, to keep track of how you are feeling and any changes or side effects that may be caused by your medication. We recommend that you keep this for a minimum of ten days while you become adjusted to the medication, but one month or thirty days is ideal.

Include these descriptions in your journal:

Feelings—Some examples of feelings are (add your own if you'd like):

- Angry
- Anxious
- Confident
- Contented
- Distracted
- Elevated
- Empty
- Frustrated
- Giddy
- Happy
- Hyper
- Indecisive
- Irritable
- Larger-than-life
- Lonely
- Melancholy
- Overwhelmed
- Panicked
- Pleased

- Relaxed
- Sad
- Scared
- Terrified
- Vulnerable
- Worried

Physical symptoms—Some examples are headache, nausea, lacking energy, trembling, drowsiness, slurred speech, coughing, blurred vision, dizziness, etc.

You must be able to describe how you are feeling, including any unwanted reactions from the medicine, in order for your doctor to help you.

Here are some examples of journal entries:

"My hands are shaking. I wonder if this is a side effect."

"Feeling tired and lonely. I don't want to see anyone or do anything. I may be depressed."

"Feeling listless and sad. Not hungry, third day in a row."

"A friend said I sounded drunk, like I was slurring my speech."

"Forgot to take my meds twice today. Feeling jittery, shaky, not sure what to do."

"I felt nervous and anxious, like I was waiting for something bad to happen."

How you are feeling emotionally today? _____

_____

_____

_____

How you are feeling physically today? _____

_____

_____

_____

Here is an example of "Sara's" daily journal. She has co-occurring bipolar disorder and addiction. Her doctor has just prescribed some new medications and recommended she keep this daily journal.

Sara's Daily Journal

October 13 to October 19	How I'm Feeling
Monday, October 13	Forgot my morning dose. Feeling depressed, tired, and craving having just one drink to get me through the day.
Tuesday, October 14	Anxious, kind of wound-up. My hands started shaking today.
Wednesday, October 15	Little less nervous feeling, hands still shake.
Thursday, October 16	Stomachache, diarrhea, ask doctor if this is because of meds?
Friday, October 17	Hands still shaking, but not as much. Stomach cramps went away, but still have diarrhea. Feeling more confident today.
Saturday, October 18	Mouth feels dry. Hands not shaking anymore. Stomach okay.
Sunday, October 19	Mouth dry. Feeling a little happier, not as anxious.

In Sara's case, she'll be able to present this journal at her next doctor's visit and her doctor will be able to make adjustments or prescribe additional medicine, if needed. If she didn't have a journal, she'd most likely forget to tell her doctor what kind of reactions she had to the medicines.

A journal not only helps your doctor, but it can help you, too. You can track how your condition changes, as well as your recovery process. Try to get in the habit of writing a line or two in your daily journal at the same time, like at bedtime or at lunch. Keeping a daily journal helps you learn about your symptoms so that you can control them better.

Notes

CHAPTER SEVEN
Stages of Change

Getting Motivated for Change

Living with a co-occurring disorder can be difficult, to say the least. You may have already tried to stop drinking or using other drugs and found it overwhelming or, at least, more difficult than you thought. It may seem impossible to imagine facing life's problems without alcohol or other drugs. Maybe you've been struggling to control your mental health symptoms for many years with little success. Perhaps you may have been successful for a time, but eventually you fell back to where you started.

You may not have decided yet exactly what you need or if you are ready to take action. Pressure to change may be coming from others who have asked you to change your behavior or from an awareness that your life is not working out as you had intended. It is sometimes hard to even consider making changes when chaos and collapse is happening and that change in the face of mental health and addiction issues can be an overwhelming challenge to confront without support.

Exploring Motivation

This section is designed to help you explore how you can adapt your thought patterns, behaviors, and lifestyle so you can begin to make positive changes in your life. Before you begin to look at how change happens, consider taking a moment to "dream a little." Motivation for your life and recovery goals can come from dreams. One way to keep your motivation fresh is to remind yourself what all this work is for. Where are you headed?

Allowing yourself to dream may help you see what it is you want to change.[40] In a later section, you will have the chance to make your dreams more realistic and practical. Dreams are important.

It can be useful to be creative and dream a little, or think "outside the box," when you think about changes you'd like to make in your life. Use your imagination and think about how you'd like to see yourself and the circumstances of your life.

If you hear yourself saying, "I'll never do that," "This is impossible," "It'll never work," or even "I don't have any dreams or hopes," try to ignore this inner critic. Now is the time to create a vision of yourself that you've always wanted.

What do you dream about for yourself in these categories?

Physical and mental health:

_____

_____

_____

Family:

_____

_____

_____

Social life/friends:

_____

_____

_____

Romantic relationship:

_____

_____

_____

Work/career:

_____

_____

_____

Daily routine:

_____

_____

_____

Hobbies/interests:

_____

_____

_____

Motivation is what prompts action to be considered or taken. Sometimes motivation can come from inside you (internal), and sometimes it is prompted by things outside of yourself (external). Motivation usually results in action, and sometimes it also prompts a decision not to take action. Motivation to change is really motivation to take a different action that may potentially result in a more productive outcome. An example:

> Sam is motivated to get in better shape, so he joins a gym. When it is time to go to the gym, a friend invites him to a movie. Sam is motivated to get in shape, so he makes the decision not to go to a movie and another decision to go to the gym.

Motivation: Body, Mind, and Spirit

Taking care of your whole self (mind, body, and spirit) in a balanced way is an important element in developing the motivation for a healthy life. It is important to listen to yourself. Clues that something needs your attention can come in many forms: physical and emotional pain, anxiety, isolation, disruptive behavior, or feelings of emptiness and loneliness. These are called symptoms.

Symptoms are not disorders. A symptom is simply the alarm or clue that tells you something is wrong. If a symptom prompts an action that meets the need in a healthy way, it has served its purpose. Sometimes, if the symptom is misunderstood, it could lead to unhealthy decisions. When emotions are in turmoil or the mind is overwhelmed, you may take actions to help ease the discomfort, perhaps by using alcohol and/or other drugs, which can compromise your body's physical health in ways that can actually cause more harm.

A key component of motivation and an integrated treatment approach is to learn how each symptom and diagnosis may affect another condition. By considering the whole self—mind, body, and spirit—you can look at what is working in some areas of your life, as well as what isn't working. The team of professionals who work cooperatively with you can help you develop a specific treatment, aftercare, and relapse prevention plan that meets your individual needs.

Motivational Strength

Your strengths, as well as defenses, have successfully brought you to this time in your life. For that, there may be some degree of gratitude to consider. Your skills have worked well in many ways, perhaps by simply offering you the opportunity to learn from your own history. Developing motivational strength can offer you a solid foundation when considering the choices and direction you would like to take next.

When you hear the words "change," "treatment," "recovery," "abstinence," "stabilization," what is the first thing that comes to your mind? Depending on your motivation and your experiences with these words, your thoughts might go something like this:

"I'll get through this. I can just count down the days to my discharge."

"Change? I've tried it. If I could do better, I would. Right now, I can't."

"I wish they understood that I will die; I cannot deal with life! I need to stay in bed. I am not strong enough to challenge this. What I am doing works for me."

"Maybe, just maybe . . ."

"They will fix me."

"I am going to do it. I am determined!"

Stages of Change

All of the responses above can be normal reactions, depending on where you find yourself in the **stages of change**.[41] Every person who makes a change—such as losing weight, stopping smoking or drugs, changing jobs, starting a relationship, moving, getting help for an illness, leading a healthier lifestyle—experiences a similar pattern of behavior along the path to change. Change is a process, not an event. Recognizing that change can, and is happening, may also bring about a feeling of hope. Let's explore the six stages of change: precontemplation, contemplation, preparation, action, maintenance, and lapse/relapse.

The first three stages are about readiness for change and increasing motivation.

1. **Precontemplation:** You are not yet considering a change.

2. **Contemplation:** You are considering a change.

3. **Preparation:** You are planning on making a change.

    The remaining three stages are focused on doing the work or taking actions to achieve and maintain your goals.

4. **Action:** You are actively taking steps toward change.

5. **Maintenance:** You have reached your initial goals and are focused on maintaining these goals and growing in recovery.

6. **Lapse/Relapse:** This stage represents a temporary loss of progress.

Please review the six stages of change on the next page. Consider a problem or situation you would like to change, then you can identify what stage of change you are in.

The Six Stages of Change		
#1 Precontemplation	You are not yet considering change or you may be unwilling or feel unable to change.	*"The DUI was just bad luck. I was in the wrong place at the wrong time. I'm here for the DUI classes and to get some help for my nerves. I don't want to hear about anything else."*
#2 Contemplation	You may acknowledge that change would be good or consider making a change, but you may be undecided or uncertain.	*"I'm sick of feeling wired all the time, having no money because I spent it on coke, and making everything in my life about where I'm going to find my next fix. I don't want to see one of those shrink doctors. I just want to stop feeling anxious all the time."*
#3 Preparation	This is when you are committed to and planning on making a change, and you are considering what to do or how to go about making the change.	*"I picked up some information about trauma. Everything I've read tells me that the pain pills are just one way that many people with trauma try to mask their pain. The not-so-funny thing is that I just keep taking more and more and feeling worse and worse. It's time to get off the drugs and deal with my past!"*
#4 Action	This stage is when you are actively taking steps to make a change, but you have not reached a steady or consistent long-term change in behavior.	*"I haven't used any drugs in over three months, and the relapse prevention plan I developed with my counselor really seems to be working. Over the past few weeks, I've realized that ever since I can remember, I've used drugs to mask my feelings. I'm beginning to see that I can cope with my stress in healthier ways."*
#5 Maintenance	You reach this stage when you have reached your initial goals for making the change and are working to maintain the gains you have made.	*"It feels good to trust that I will get up each day and shower. I trust that by taking my medications and actively being mindful of my needs, skills, and goals that I am working to maintain my progress and build on it."*
#6 Lapse/Relapse	More of an event (series of events) than a stage; lapses or relapses may occur at any time. These reflect a temporary loss of progress when personal distress or social pressures are allowed to interrupt your change process.	*"I knew something was wrong when I was tired and irritated. My relapse prevention plan was to address any mood fluctuations with my team, but I convinced myself it would pass. I found myself thinking that if I could just relax with a drink, I could get back on track again. My lapse started with my thinking and ended with a relapse with alcohol."*

Note: It is normal to be in more than one stage at a time or to go back into previous stages along your path to change. It is also important to know that it is rare to move forward in a steady progression of stages. Recovery is about progressing toward ceasing addictive behaviors and/or effectively managing mental health symptoms. As you build on the knowledge of your individual struggles, triggers, and coping skills, you may find you are having smaller and shorter setbacks along the way. When setbacks or relapses occur, you will spend shorter time periods in early stages before catching back up to speed.

Precontemplation

"If you are in the first stage of change, precontemplation, generally you are not yet considering, able, or willing to change."[42]

When asked to make a change in your life by others or by circumstances that leave no other foreseeable choices, you may feel "numb" or indifferent. If friends or loved ones are pressing you to change, you may feel angry, rebellious, and not ready to accept that anything needs changing. Also, if there are numerous things in your life that you'd like to change, facing these can be overwhelming, especially if you've tried before and felt you weren't successful.

You may not be sure whether or not you want to change or if change is even necessary. Change can be scary, sometimes leaving you feeling frightened of the unknown. Or, you may find yourself wanting to change one moment and the next thinking that you're okay and that nothing needs to change after all. It is a normal part of this stage of change for you to feel unsure or ambivalent.

The Four Rs

The Four Rs—reluctance, rebellion, resignation, and rationalization—are barriers to contemplation or considering a change.

You may be reluctant to change or reluctant to admit the need for change. You might think, *My depression keeps me from getting ahead at work, and it would be nice to feel better, but I don't know if I have the energy for anything more than I'm doing right now.* Or, *I don't need to change. It's my body, and it's my life. I'm not hurting anyone.*

You might feel rebellious against others who are telling you that you need to change. You may be thinking, *Don't tell me what to do; I'm not going to change. This is the only way I have to cope, and no one is going to tell me to stop.*

You may be resigned to the fact that your life is fine the way it is, or that it's not worth changing. You think, *Nothing is going to help me; I've tried four different times, and each time I've failed. Why bother?*

Or, you may rationalize the reasons why everything is fine and you don't need to change, and say, "Sometimes it is easier to just stay the way I am. I'm kind of used to it anyway."

Fear of Change

Reluctance, rebellion, rationalization, or resignation may signal that you are experiencing fear of change. The Four Rs are all good ways to avoid addressing a fear of change. No one likes dealing with the unknown. When you consider making a change in your life, you may feel scared or afraid. A few examples may include that you are afraid of being disliked, embarrassing yourself, failing yourself or others, hurting yourself, hurting someone else, relapsing, letting others down, losing your identity with friends and family, facing the future without alcohol and/or other drugs. You are not alone in experiencing doubt and fear.

Like most things, fear is not always bad. Fear can help by signaling you to defend yourself against danger, to leave or to avoid situations. It can also trigger your body to release adrenaline to help you get out of life-threatening situations. Fear can help you survive, avoid danger, and keep you safe.[43]

When you think about making changes in your life, what fears and negative thoughts come up? Please write them here.

_____

_____

_____

_____

_____

_____

_____

Are any of these fears significant enough to keep you from making your changes? Please describe.

_____

_____

_____

_____

_____

_____

Fear may seem like a daunting barrier, but the good news is that once you discover your desire to improve your life, each step toward change gets easier and more rewarding. Progress in change is closer than you think. If you have been able to identify even a small positive value of changing some of the things that aren't working in your life, then you may well be on your way to embracing the contemplation stage of change.

It may not feel comfortable to hear other people's suggestions. It may be that you struggle with feeling as if you are failing when your choices or behaviors are different from others. Maybe others have made suggestions to you or insisted that you change. It can be easy to dismiss these occurrences. However, it might be helpful to privately consider this input. Another way to identify potential areas for change is to look outside of yourself and consider the questions in the following section.

Has anyone told you that you should consider changing? If so, what change(s) did he or she suggest?

_____

_____

_____

_____

_____

_____

_____

Has your opinion about using substances or taking medications ever been different from that of your friends and family? If so, please describe.

_____

_____

_____

_____

_____

What kind of outside factors in your life are pushing you toward change (such as a significant other, an employer, a physician, a family member, a close friend, a counselor, the court system, etc.)? Please describe.

_____

_____

_____

_____

Confidence

As you begin the journey of change, your motivation and confidence may continue to grow as you move in the direction of your goals. It is important to maintain balance and to remind yourself of the strengths you bring to this process.

Consider the following questions and write a few sentences for each.

What have you overcome that you are proud of?

_____

_____

_____

What did you learn by overcoming this?

_____

_____

_____

What significant changes have you made in your life?

_____

_____

_____

_____

_____

What positive or useful traits do you see in yourself that could help you be successful in making changes?

_____

_____

_____

_____

_____

Please list a few important changes that you have already made in your life. For example: moving to a different environment, new friends, exercise, nutrition, talking to friends and family, not drinking alcohol and/or using other drugs.

_____

_____

_____

_____

_____

Recognizing that you currently have multiple strengths and skills that have brought you this far can serve you well in early recovery. What strengths do you bring to support your recovery process? Read through some of these confidence-building characteristics, and mark as many as apply to you.

Character Traits Useful for Change

Accepting	Active	Adaptable	Adventurous
Affectionate	Alert	Ambitious	Assertive
Assured	Attentive	Bold	Brave
Bright	Capable	Careful	Cheerful
Clever	Committed	Confident	Considerate
Courageous	Creative	Decisive	Dedicated
Determined	Eager	Earnest	Energetic
Faithful	Fearless	Flexible	Focused
Forgiving	Free	Happy	Healthy
Hopeful	Imaginative	Intelligent	Loving
Mature	Open	Optimistic	Orderly

Organized	Patient	Perceptive	Persistent
Positive	Powerful	Prayerful	Quick
Receptive	Relaxed	Reliable	Resourceful
Responsible	Skillful	Stable	Steady
Strong	Stubborn	Thankful	Thorough
Thoughtful	Tough	Trusting	Trustworthy
Truthful	Understanding	Unique	Unstoppable
Visionary	Willing	Wise	Worthy
Zealous			

Note: Precontemplation is simply the state of being before thinking about making a change. If you feel ready to think about or consider making a change, most likely you are moving into the contemplation stage.

Contemplation

"In the second stage, contemplation, you may generally acknowledge that change might be good, and you may also be undecided or uncertain."[44]

When you start thinking about making a change, you may acknowledge that you'd like to change even though you may feel undecided, scared, or uncertain. In this stage of change, you may have an idea of how you want to change, but you may not be ready to take the steps toward making it happen. Contemplation is just what it sounds like: You are simply considering if making a change would enhance your life and health and if you believe it is possible to change. Contemplation has no external action required, just honest introspection or consideration. You may still be unsure whether or not you want to change or if change is even necessary.

In the contemplation stage of change, you most likely are moving forward by gathering information about yourself before deciding if you are willing to put that information to use.

Reasons to (and not to) Change

Sometimes thinking about change occurs because of a crisis, or something serious has happened. Perhaps you, or the people around you, are concerned. For example, you may have had a car accident while driving intoxicated, or maybe there are some mental health symptoms that concern others, making you or others around you suddenly more aware of the need for change.

Not wanting to consider change is often based in fear. Sometimes change can mean stepping into the unknown. Even if you make a decision to change, fear can prevent you from actually taking steps toward change. Your conscious brain may make the choice for change, but the unconscious brain quietly and forcefully proclaims, "Stop! There are too many risks ahead!"[45]

Weighing the Pros and Cons

One way that may help you develop confidence in your choice to change is by looking at both sets of comparisons: the benefits of change and the risks of change and the benefits of not changing and the risks of not changing. The next writing activity contains an opportunity to practice this method of contemplation.

It can be helpful to open yourself up to both the positives and the negatives of staying in your current situation. Doing so may help you decide if you are ready to make changes. Many people attempting change lose sight of their goal and return several times to this point to continue to explore and discuss the drawbacks and payoffs of change. If you find that you have made multiple attempts to engage in a changed behavior, but you revert to old prerecovery activities and engage in relapse behavior, you may consider recontemplating your commitment to change.[46]

Pro and con lists are useful in helping you weigh the things you think you might want to change.

List one personal inconsistency in each block down the first column, and then explore the pros and cons of changing that personal inconsistency as you complete the remaining four blocks in the row. Spend some time contemplating the benefits and risks of changing that inconsistency, as well as the benefits and risks of not changing it.

This activity can also be useful in considering changes by asking "or" questions, such as:

- Do I want to stop using or keep using?
- Do I want to get treatment and take medications for my mental health issue or not?
- Do I want to buy or rent a house?

Personal Inconsistency	Benefits of Change	Risks of Change	Benefits of Not Changing	Risks of Not Changing
I say sleep is important, but I sleep less than four hours a night.	If I slept, I would not be so ragged. I could quit using stimulants at work and fearing a drug test. I might be nicer, less manic, and not make as many mistakes.	I would crash and fail at work if I were not always amped. It would be miserable to deal with the down that comes when I am not using.	I know this drill. I know it isn't good, but I know how to pull it off. If I don't change then I keep the sales buzz that makes me a top sales person.	I could get fired any day now.

I think my health is not great, but I don't go to the doctor.

My wife is threatening to leave if I don't calm down and stay around. |
| I say exercise and health care are important, but I don't exercise or see my doctor. | I could get my money's worth at the health club where I work out.

I would know my real health risks.

It would be nice to know I am doing something good for myself. | I could find out that I have really compromised my health.

I don't know if I could focus enough to go work out and not be obsessive about it. | I would have more me time to "come down" before I have to go home and deal with my family's needs.

I don't have to hear one more person tell me I'm doing it wrong. | Less real catch-up time. My mania and lack of focus continues to take up my time playing catch-up.

I know I am a faker, and some day others will, too. |

Then and Now

Additional ways to explore pros and cons is to explore timeframes. Consider a previous time compared to today, such as:

- Before you were using alcohol or other drugs.
- When your life was going particularly well.
- When your medications were stable.

Consider the advantages and disadvantages of making changes. If you were to engage in making the change, how do you see your life improving? What would be the effect of maintaining this change in one year? In five years?

_____

_____

_____

_____

_____

_____

_____

_____

_____

_____

_____

_____

_____

_____

_____

_____

_____

_____

_____

_____

_____

_____

Preparation

"If you are in the third stage of change, preparation, you have made the choice to change and have started to develop a plan. You are considering what to do or how to go about making the change."[47]

Preparation is the decision-making stage. It is a commitment to change and considering different strategies for your behaviors or lifestyle as you begin to decide on the best plan of action. Deciding often includes trying on a few new behaviors to see if they fit before committing to a plan of action.

Your Changes

You may have already had a chance to write about your hopes and dreams concerning recovery. Now is the time to narrow those dreams to basic changes that may be important to your life.[48] It is important to be realistic about the actual changes you are considering. If you set unrealistic goals for change, then you will likely be setting yourself up for frustration and potential failure.

Preparation allows you an opportunity to see what it's like or to try on the change and see how it feels. You can do this by setting a base or preparation plan and trying it for a short amount of time, such as the next three weeks. Keeping a daily journal to record your experiences, thoughts, and feelings, has proven to be helpful. You may decide to discuss these journal entries with your therapist or someone else on your support team.

The Preparation Plan

Your preparation plan is your blueprint for action. Preparation is a necessary step in building a solid foundation to assist you in reaching your goals. At first these goals may seem insurmountable, time consuming, and often tedious. The Four Rs—reluctance, rebellion, resignation, and rationalization—may even attempt to distract you from the plan. The time and effort you put in the preparation stage can assist in establishing the foundation on which everything else will rest; this initial stage lays the groundwork to assist you with your daily maintenance plan and helps you continue to move toward taking action on your desired changes.

Easy Does It

As you move forward in establishing a preparation plan, the urge to take on more than is feasible may likely be strong. Setting goals too large while skipping the learning and practice steps may seem like a quick road to reach your recovery, but it is usually not. Consider what happens when a house is built on a weak foundation.

Sometimes the desire to rush ahead and be "done" or "recovered" may present itself. It can be useful to be aware of the thoughts and feelings that may be triggers for the desire to want to rush ahead. The desire to hurry through the process and reach the end can be a way to avoid (or protect you from) feeling what is happening today in the here and now.

Focusing on the future or the past may prevent you from being available to manage today. It can serve to protect you from experiencing the fullness of your thoughts and feelings today, and it may also protect you from the potential hazards of things that may be distressing. This self-protectiveness is a quality that has been useful to cope with symptoms in the past and can be helpful to you in recovery as long as you remain aware it is simply a distraction tool.

Laying the Foundation and Framework

Everyone, whether they struggle with mental health and/or addiction issues, creates and maintains a foundation upon which to build their lives. The foundation (the ground you build on) and the pillars (the beams that hold up what you build) represent what is important in the daily maintenance of building and supporting the physical and mental necessities of life, including food, clothing, and shelter. Also included are interpersonal connections, relationships, community participation, and spiritual connection.[49]

A Solid Foundation

In building your recovery, there are usually a few base needs that, when met, can assist in supporting the changes you wish to make. Some of these may include food, shelter, and finances. Whatever your individual discoveries are about the recovery you want to build, you can build a strong foundation based on a solid preparation plan.[50]

Initial Preparation Goal Plan				
Foundation	My Goal	Action Steps to My Goal	Goal Date	Who Is Responsible
Physical health (self-care based on need)	Maintain physical health (self-care on a daily basis)			
Mental health (self-care based on need)	Maintain mental health (self-care on a daily basis)			
Food	Eat balanced meals to meet my body's nutritional needs			
Clothing	Wear clothing appropriate to my body's needs for temperature, safety, and social appropriateness			
Shelter	Maintain safe housing			
Interpersonal connection/ community participation	Establish and maintain interpersonal connections Participate actively with my community			
Spiritual connection	Explore, establish, and maintain a spiritual connection actively engaging that connection			
Recovery program	Maintain aftercare and the recovery plan			

Action

What Does the Action Stage Look Like?

In this section we will explore the action stage of change—more specifically, what it looks like in terms of behaviors (actions). You will be introduced to some of the skills and tools that have been shown to be effective in developing a plan of action.[51]

Being in the action stage of change means actively and consistently using the skills and tools you are learning. Along with your support structure, you decide what is important to act on and how to manage everyday life experiences. Sometimes, we may want to change everything at once. This can be a setup for disappointment. It is often wiser to take a more balanced approach in really deciding when to take action.

Remember, the stages of change are fluid.

For example:

- You may be in the action stage of change in practicing your recovery skills for alcohol and/ or other drug abuse, *and* you may still be contemplating if you are willing to address your medication needs in order to stabilize your mental health symptoms.

- You may be in the action stage of change in practicing your learned skills for both substance use and mental health, *and* you may also be resisting or be in a precontemplative stage about addressing your physical or spiritual health.

What Is the Action Stage?

Here is what the action stage may sound like:

"I haven't used any drugs in over three months, and the plan I developed with my counselor really seems to be working. Over the past few weeks, I've realized that ever since I can remember, I've used drugs to mask my feelings. I'm beginning to see that I can cope with my stress in healthier ways."

"I have taken my meds, kept my appointments, and met my basic needs each day. I am starting to see that I can feel better if I meet the tasks in front of me each day and avoid acting on triggers to use old skills. I am starting to believe I am capable of dealing with my life."

The action stage is when you are actively taking steps to make a change, but have not reached a steady or consistent long-term change in behavior.[52]

For example, perhaps you have made a decision to attend twelve-step meetings on a regular basis to support your recovery rather than every now and then. You have been attending almost daily for two weeks.

When you are addressing a problem or a symptom, the action stage of change focuses on what it is you want to change and what it takes to achieve that change.

Recognizing the Positive Effects of Change

Positive reinforcement—or, simply stated, being recognized for your efforts—is an excellent tool in recovery. If you can develop the ability to recognize your successes, then you can begin to see the relationship between your decisions and actions in a positive way. This type of thinking generally encourages and inspires people to consider making further changes. Recognizing the reward and giving yourself credit for the action: These two acts can increase the likelihood that you will reach for the skills and behaviors that produced the positive effect (reward).[53]

For example, let's say you wanted to save money by decreasing the amount of your electric bill. A reward would be opening the envelope and seeing a lower bill. By paying attention to your day-to-day actions (each time you turn off lights, change the thermostat, or run only a full dishwasher) and paying attention to the bill when it comes, you can see your actions causing the reward of the bill going down. Then you continue to be mindful of electricity usage because it has rewards. You monitored it (by being conscious of the actions you were taking); it worked (by having a lower bill); so, you will likely repeat it (after discovering action equals reward). What would happen if you wanted to save electricity, but you didn't pay attention to your actions or never opened the bill to see the results? Do you think you would become a person who was conscious of electricity usage if you were not mindful of your goal or didn't reinforce the action?

Now, say you are used to the feelings of a hangover in the morning or have grown accustomed to symptoms of depression. Try to see the rewards of abstaining from drinking alcohol or the benefits of taking your psychiatric medications for a while. You may be having fewer headaches, have more energy, have clearer thoughts, improved memory, more inspiration to accomplish tasks, or even interest in things that haven't interested you before. Paying attention to the results of your action toward change can help you to reinforce the positive results and rewards of change. If you have difficulty identifying the rewards of the actions you are taking, ask your therapist to help you recognize and acknowledge the positive effects that change is having on you and your life.

Dedication to Change

When making changes, you may find that being dedicated and mindful helps. In order to maintain focused dedication, you might need to periodically remind yourself of the reasons you are making these changes. Perhaps one of the best things you can do to support and reinforce your decision to change is to remember why you did it in the first place. This is where friends and journaling can help sharpen your memory to remember the goals. It may take a while for you to make your desired changes, and you may encounter scary and unknown things about yourself as you sort through the results of each attempt, but keep moving forward and keep practicing the skills you have learned.

Here is an exercise that may assist you.

Can you recall how it was and how it is now? Here are a few ideas to get started.
Sometimes friends and family can see the changes that you cannot see.

Then **What Stood Out the Most about My**	Now **What Stands Out the Most about My**
Attitude	Attitude
Goals	Goals
Confidence	Confidence
Other	Other
As you review these changes, what surprises you the most?	
What surprises you the least?	

Flexible Dreamer

When you started the process of recovery and change, you were likely unaware of some of your abilities. You may also have been unaware of some of your limitations. A twelve-step fellowship member once said in his talk to a regional convention, "If I only went after what I thought I could do, I would have sold myself short." This statement is the perfect example of how perspective affects goal-setting and why effective action goals and plans are always under review.[54]

It can be useful to be creative and dream about the goals you are setting. Using your imagination, try to see yourself and the circumstances of your life at a future time. Try and ignore the inner critic and stretch your imagination as to what you hope for. This is the time to intentionally dream without limitations.

Then, on a piece of paper, write down something you see yourself doing or becoming. This could be going to school to be a doctor, writing a novel, lying in a hammock on the beach, or getting married and having a family.

As your perspective changes, your dreams, goals, and plans are likely to change as well. This in itself is a sign of progress and growth. The idea that the use of alcohol and/or other drugs may have altered your perspective is important information to consider.

Distress, Triggers, and Our Emotions

Distress is sometimes defined as anxiety, sorrow, pain, grief, worry, or sadness. Distress can be different from person to person. It can range from withdrawal, isolation, or avoidance to panic, anger, yelling, or aggression. Also, it can keep you from taking action.[55]

If an old behavior or use of a substance helped to relieve distress before, you're likely to reach for it again in a time of need. We learn most effectively based on the experiences we have had. For instance:

- You may have learned to avoid touching a hot stove by having a negative experience of pain.
- You may have learned to eat when you were hungry by experiencing that eating brought relief of the discomfort of hunger.
- You may have learned that taking a drink or drug resulted in reduced anxiety.

It may seem confusing at times as to why you might respond or react to things the way you do, particularly when the outcome seems negative.

Reacting to a situation generally occurs when there is not a relaxed or mindful space between the trigger (impulse or urge) and the action. Without this space of time to think about things clearly, the response is likely to be based on past experience, habits, or using old gratification behaviors. Developing the recovery skills for mindfulness[56] can assist you in practicing distress tolerance skills.

By beginning to identify people, places, and things that may have previously been associated with an undesirable outcome, you may assist yourself in preparing for the distress likely to be experienced or triggered in response to these situations. Effectively handling distress offers the possibility to experience things in a new way and, by doing so, introduces the brain to new experiences that can become new responses to distress.

Triggers

Your knowledge, based on experience, has helped you gain relief or pleasure and avoid or reduce distressing symptoms in the past. These behaviors may continue to present themselves as viable options or triggers as you walk forward in your recovery. You may consciously say to yourself that you know they are not beneficial to your recovery, but knowing alone may not insulate you from feeling their pull. Once you have discovered that a behavior or solution worked, even if only in the short run, you can be at risk to use it again in times of need. If you reinforced a behavior as a solution by repeating it multiple times, your mind holds that knowledge as a "favorite" response.

The way your brain learns can be a stumbling block; it may be negatively triggering the use of those familiar short-term coping skills. However, your ability to learn new skills, to experience and then reinforce that learning and build on it, can also be a valuable tool in your recovery.

Emotions

The natural life cycle of an emotion is much like a wave; it begins, gathers strength, swells, crests, breaks, and then washes away. Left to its own devices, an emotion will live itself out in twenty to thirty minutes. On paper, that doesn't seem so long to wait out a distressing emotion with the promise that it will pass, and it isn't, until you are swept up in it. Distress tolerance skills can help you develop the ability to avoid getting caught up in or swept away by the emotional wave.

Negative Thoughts

Learning how to cope with negative thoughts[57] and moods that could lead to a relapse is challenging. We all have bad days and experience some negative thoughts and moods. Some of us, however, have them more often and more severely than others. These negative thoughts may sometimes make you feel anxious, depressed, pessimistic, or worthless. These emotions, untreated or unaddressed, can often cause you to doubt yourself, question your decisions, and withdraw from others, sabotaging the action stage. Even though negative thoughts may be a part of your life, you can change the way you think and learn to view the world and yourself more positively.

Have you noticed that when you think good thoughts about yourself, you tend to feel better, and when you think bad thoughts about yourself, you tend to lose motivation and feel down? How you *think* about yourself can directly impact how you *feel* about yourself. You might try changing the way you *think* about the world, so you can start *feeling* better!

You might think, *I can't control my thoughts. They just pop into my head. They're how I feel.* The interesting thing is that you often can control your thoughts. The first step is to be mindful or aware of the thoughts and the second is to challenge them. When you know what to look for, negative thoughts are easy to spot.

Negative thoughts often come from thinking in absolutes, as though everything is one way or another, right or wrong, good or bad, black or white. You will hear yourself using words like "never," "always," "everyone," "no one," or "nothing" if you are thinking in absolutes.

If you are accustomed to negative thinking, listening for these sorts of thoughts may take practice. Your efforts at identifying and reversing these negative thoughts can result in a positive, healthy perspective that can support your recovery and those areas you have selected to change.

Here are a few examples of reframing, or changing negative thinking.

Negative thinking: Ted has a job interview. He thinks, *The manager will never like me. I'm no good. I don't have anything to offer. I should cancel the interview since I'm not going to get the job anyhow.*

Positive reframe: Instead, Ted could look at it this way, *I have tried hard to get this interview, and I deserve a chance. I am a good person, and I want this job. If I get this job, I will work hard to keep it. I will walk in there with confidence; besides, I have nothing to lose and a lot to gain.*

Negative thinking: You wake up feeling sick to your stomach and think, *Oh no, I'm sick again. I'm never going to get better. Maybe it's really serious. I could die. Nothing ever goes right for me.*

Positive reframe: Instead, you could change your thinking. *I'm sick. My stomach hurts, but I don't have a fever. I'll probably feel better in a couple of hours. I'll be okay. If not, I can call my doctor.*

Negative thinking: You have gained some weight and start to think, *I'm fat. I'm never going to lose weight. I look ugly. Everyone's going to notice that I've gained weight. I might as well give up and never go out again.*

Positive reframe: Instead, you could turn your thinking around. *I've gained some weight, but hey, I am taking care of my whole self. I'll be mindful and check out what I eat today and call a friend to join me for a walk. This is no big deal; I will ask my doctor for a perspective check at my next appointment. I can handle this.*

Now, it's your turn to give reframing negative thoughts a try. In each of the four blocks below, reframe a recent negative thought.

Please describe an example of a recent negative thought.	Now change the negative thought into a positive one.
Please describe an example of a recent negative thought.	Now change the negative thought into a positive one.
Please describe an example of a recent negative thought.	Now change the negative thought into a positive one.
Please describe an example of a recent negative thought.	Now change the negative thought into a positive one.

Positive Thinking

A helpful hint: When you think negative thoughts, or start to feel bad or depressed, consider stopping for a moment, then try to determine if you can change the negative thought into a more positive one.[58] The saying "Easy does it" can work well here. It doesn't necessarily need to be a rigid approach of yes or no, I can or I cannot, that is good or that is bad, and so forth. Some people find it helpful to think in terms of a middle ground or taking small steps.

Another hint: Don't sweat the small stuff! This means you do not need to waste much energy or time worrying about little things. In a "tunnel vision" or narrow view of life, a problem can look huge because it is all you can see. If you widen your perspective a bit, you may see that it might be "small stuff."

Fear is another thing to keep your eye on. The recovery slogan FEAR—False Evidence Appearing Real—can remind you to recheck your perspectives. Fear in general is not such a bad thing. It certainly offers us a healthy way to determine if something is safe. On the other hand, fear can be frustrating because it can keep you from taking action. It is often a primary prompter for negative thinking.

The Way We Talk

Did you know that the majority of the messages your mind processes are not from others, but from yourself? These messages often are in the form of your thoughts and voice.[59] Some of these thoughts can be generated by your own value system. For example, your thoughts can be triggered by observations, opinions about people, places, events, or your abilities. Some other thoughts, perhaps also generated by your value system, can be triggered from outside of you by things such as receiving a bill, emails, the newspaper, or simple daily interactions with people.

The messages you process may either reinforce or challenge your automatic thoughts. At times, it may seem that you do not have control of how you think. And for some, this may be true. Often people tend to want to make a change when things in fact no longer seem to be manageable. The skills you are learning in your recovery will assist you in regulating your thoughts, and the way you may interrupt them.

Stumbling Blocks

Stumbling blocks are simply anything that can trip you up or detour you in your recovery journey. A stumbling block can be formed as you perceive other people, places, things, beliefs, values, reactions, thoughts, and so forth.[60] Stumbling blocks can be developed when you use ineffective life skills in managing the situations. In the action stage of change, stumbling blocks provide an opportunity to change behaviors and practice new skills has been shown to be effective. Keeping an open mind to new ideas can help you move forward in your recovery.

This concept of an open mind is best shown in the quote by Herbert Spencer that appears in *Alcoholics Anonymous*, also known as the Big Book, "There is a principle, which is a bar against all information, which is proof against all arguments, and which cannot fail to keep a man in everlasting ignorance—that principle is contempt prior to investigation."

Write about what the principle of "contempt prior to investigation" means to you and your recovery. The concept is that there is a common barrier to learning, keeping you stuck in old ways by your rejection of something before exploring it or considering it fully. Some people call it "getting in your own way" or "blocking your own grace."

_____

_____

_____

_____

_____

_____

Developing the Action Plan

There are several steps to making an action plan:

1. Setting your master goals list.
2. Selecting the goals and determining action steps specific to that goal.
3. Setting review dates for each action step.

Let's look at multiple ways to develop and achieve a goal in a simple way. For example, if you want to stop smoking, your choices could include wearing a nicotine patch, chewing nicotine gum, going "cold-turkey" without help, getting therapeutic help, attending support group meetings, and/or enrolling in a nicotine prevention program. If you are able to come up with multiple realistic options and select the best choice for your lifestyle and context, the better chance you will have of staying committed to your decision to change.

My Action Goals

Remember to dream a little, utilize your journal entries, and consider assistance from other people in deciding what it is you want to change. It is sometimes helpful to be realistic in setting the goals and outcomes. Generally, a six to twelve month plan seems reasonable. You may find that once you start planning your changes step by step, they seem more achievable than you had imagined. It is not unusual for dreams and fears to seem larger, more untouchable, and maybe more threatening than they actually are. Keeping an open mind and drawing from many perspectives during planning can help you succeed in this process.

Creating a Realistic Plan

In this section, you will have the opportunity to create a realistic plan for making the changes you desire, one goal at a time. It is very important that you make a plan that will fit your lifestyle. Be honest with yourself and realistic about what you can achieve in any given step. Some steps may require that you take them slowly and carefully, based on your needs, while other steps can be larger.

In the next pages, you will find the following:

- **A completed example of an action plan.** Use this as a guide if you need help when filling out your own action plan.

- **A blank copy of the "My Action Plan" journal page.** Test your skills here on the journal page. Make copies, then you can complete an action plan for each goal on your master list as you are ready to take action on it. Keep the unmarked copy in your notebook so it is there for you anytime you need a new action plan.

Logan's Action Plan (An Example)

What I want to change/My master goal: *Regain control of my emotional state.*

Description: *I want to stop drinking alcohol and smoking pot, and I want to take my psychiatric medications as directed by my doctor! I want to clean up my life, stay in recovery, and reduce my symptoms. I'm tired of waking up feeling awful with hangovers, letting others down, and feeling like my life is out of control.*

How I will know the change has been made: *If I haven't touched alcohol or pot for one month and have taken my meds every day for one month, I'll know I've made the changes, can stay abstinent, and have my symptoms under control.*

I will achieve my goals by taking these actions:

1. *Throw away all of the alcohol and pot in my possession.*　　Completed by: *February 4*

2. *Make an appointment with my psychiatrist to talk about taking meds again and coping with withdrawal symptoms.*　　Completed by: *February 7*

3. *Take my psychiatric medications at 8:00 a.m. and 8:00 p.m. daily.*　　Completed by: *ongoing*

4. *Stop hanging out with Larry and RJ, who drink and use.*　　Completed by: *February 9*

5. *Won't drive by or go into the Corner Pub.*　　Completed by: *February 9*

Logan's Action Plan (continued)

6. Attend DRA meetings two or three times a week.   Completed by: *ongoing*

7. Call and set up a meeting with my sponsor.   Completed by: *February 15*

8. Start exercising to make myself feel better.   Completed by: *February 15*

9. Tell Susan about stopping drinking and using.   Completed by: *February 21*

10. Call my doctor if I have unwanted side effects.   Completed by: *ongoing*

Possible obstacles I may encounter and how I could handle them:

Obstacle: *Craving alcohol or other drugs*   Solution: *Call sponsor*

Obstacle: *Pressure from friends to drink or use*   Solution: *Tell them I'm sober, call sponsor*

Obstacle: *Get bored; want to drink out of habit*   Solution: *Call a friend, go to a movie*

Obstacle: *Forget to take my meds regularly*   Solution: *Ask for one-a-day/week med.*

Support people and how they can help me with change:

Person 1: *K.P. Smith 555-1212*   Relation/Can help by: *Sponsor, helps me stay in recovery*

Person 2: *Susan 555-3434*   Relation/Can help by: *Girlfriend, offers love and support*

Person 3: *Marty 555-5656*   Relation/Can help by: *Best friend, cheers me up*

Person 4: *Mom 555-6767*   Relation/Can help by: *Believes in me, helps with money*

My possible negative thoughts about this change:

I've tried to stop drinking before, but after three days I started drinking again. I'm scared of others thinking I'm "crazy" because I'm taking psychiatric meds. Sometimes I think of myself as weak, without willpower, as someone who's never going to amount to anything in this world.

My revised positive thoughts about making this change:

This is my third try to get into recovery, and this time I'm going to make it. I've learned from past mistakes that I didn't have the support network I needed to make changes. There's no reason to beat myself up, especially because I'm trying now. This time, I'm doing it right, and I know myself better. I am completely committed to stop drinking and smoking and to treat my symptoms. I am good at my job, so imagine how much better I'll be once my symptoms are under control and I'm staying abstinent. I'll rock! I've been on the streets before and survived that, so I know I'm not weak. My childhood stunk, and now I have to say, I'm a pretty good dad anyway. I have willpower because I'm here today, making this change in my life, and that takes guts. If I can do this, I can do anything! Being in recovery with my symptoms under control will help me feel better, lead a better life, and make me feel proud of me. I have seen other people do this successfully, and just as they tell me, I can do it if they can. I will follow their suggestions.

Review date: *Two weeks*

Review outcome: _____
_____
_____
_____

My Action Plan

What I want to change/My master goal: _____
_____

Description: _____
_____
_____

How I will know the change has been made: _____
_____
_____

I will achieve my goals by taking these actions:

1. _____ Completed by: _____
2. _____ Completed by: _____
3. _____ Completed by: _____
4. _____ Completed by: _____
5. _____ Completed by: _____
6. _____ Completed by: _____
7. _____ Completed by: _____

8. _____ Completed by: _____

9. _____ Completed by: _____

10. _____ Completed by: _____

Possible obstacles I may encounter and how I could handle them:

Obstacle: _____

Solution: _____

Obstacle: _____

Solution: _____

Obstacle: _____

Solution: _____

Obstacle: _____

Solution: _____

Obstacle: _____

Solution: _____

Obstacle: _____

Solution: _____

Support people and how they can help me with change:

Person 1: _____ Relation/Can help by: _____

Person 2: _____ Relation/Can help by: _____

Person 3: _____ Relation/Can help by: _____

Person 4: _____ Relation/Can help by: _____

My possible negative thoughts about this change:_____

_____

_____

_____

My revised positive thoughts about making this change: _____

_____

_____

_____

_____

_____

Review date: _____

Review outcome: _____

_____

_____

_____

_____

_____

_____

Brainstorming

If you aren't sure how to create a plan to achieve your changes and goals, try brainstorming[61] with the help of your peers, sponsor, therapist, or other staff. Come up with as many creative ideas as possible, regardless of how unrealistic they may be. Try not to edit or critique ideas as they are generated. The goal of brainstorming is to open yourself up to creative solutions and possibilities previously unconsidered. You'll be surprised how often thinking "outside the box" will help you find the perfect solution for your life.

Accountability: Telling Others about Your Goals and Plans

You will more likely follow through with making changes when you tell another person about the changes you are planning. If the change will affect others, such as loved ones, a significant other, parents, friends, a sponsor, or your therapist, sharing with them about your commitment to change gives them more opportunities to support you in reaching your goals.

Stick with Your Plan

In the action stage of change, you are taking action every day to maintain your foundation and move toward your goals. Sticking with your plan, no matter what, has proven for many to be most effective. Here are some strategies for staying committed to your new life:

Be Kind to Yourself: The early stages of recovery and change can be the most difficult. Treat yourself as you would a dear friend: with support and consideration. Be understanding. If you feel you need a reward, give yourself a small present. If you need a hug, call a friend or sponsor and ask for one. Ask a counselor for support. Check in with yourself regularly and try to be aware of extreme needs or changes in emotions.

Remember Small Steps: Small steps are better than no steps at all. Usually, the most important and lasting changes take considerable work and time.

Believe in Yourself: As you progress in recovery and your plan to change, you can build self-confidence and increase your belief in yourself. The beginnings are already there; believe in your ability to build on your successes.

Allow Mistakes: You will most likely make mistakes along the way. Imperfect attempts and stumbles are a natural part of change and recovery. Many people find it necessary to return to earlier stages of change several times before the change will "stick." If you make a mistake, acknowledge it without being critical or angry at yourself. Step back and consider reframing your negative thoughts, then get back on your plan. Sharing with your sponsor, a friend, or counselor is helpful. Consider going to a community support group like Dual Recovery Anonymous (DRA), Alcoholics Anonymous (AA), Narcotics Anonymous (NA), or other support meetings. The famous quote, "If at first you don't succeed, then try, try again," is good to remember at this time.

Moving Ahead

Being motivated to action is the natural result of the work you have put into your recovery. You are most likely feeling the rewards of success as well as expanding your perspective of the world. When you feel confident in your commitment to your action plans, consider moving on to the next section to learn about maintenance techniques and the maintenance stage of change.

Maintenance

Strengthening Skills and Enjoying the Benefits of a Healthier Lifestyle

Every day of recovery can build confidence for you to maintain the goals and actions you have established in your foundational plan. Actions that seemed almost impossible to do before now take less effort, energy, and concentration. Practice and consistency have extraordinary results.

You may notice some key indicators, kind of like a checklist, that reinforce that you are actively in the maintenance stage of change.[62]

- Do your activities seem like a routine? Examples: getting up, hygiene, work or school, cleaning, exercise, meetings, and so forth.
- Does your confidence reflect thinking about long-term goals such as education, a career, family, and health?
- Have you found yourself making decisions that support your recovery?
- Do you tend to stay focused, and is recovery your first priority?

The maintenance stage is where you can enjoy your recovery and further develop and explore your life. Keeping life in a mindful balance, along with the application of your skills, can assist you in dealing with normal distress and high-risk situations. Maintaining your recovery on a daily basis can be the best relapse prevention tool.[63]

What Is the Maintenance Stage?

The maintenance stage may sound like: *"It feels good to trust that I will get up each day and shower. I trust that by taking my medications and actively being mindful of my needs, skills, and goals, I am working to maintain my progress and build on it."*

Maintenance is the fifth stage in the six stages of change. It is the time to enjoy the rewards of recovery and to cope with distress as it comes. Continuing to practice and sustain the skills you diligently learned in earlier stages is what maintenance is about. No one knows you and your needs better than you; you can now maintain and have confidence in what you have built. As recovery becomes a lifestyle and not a battle, you can begin to find the joy in daily life.

For example, if your action-plan goals include getting sober and seeing a doctor regarding medications, then in the maintenance stage, you would keep your healthy routine and continue attending support group/twelve-step meetings. If you were tempted to relapse, you might use your support network or your counselor to help you apply your healthy skills as a response to stress or any temptations that in the past may have led to relapse.

The maintenance stage is where you further develop and explore your life and keep your life in balance by learning how to deal with stressful and high-risk situations, and you learn about preventing relapse. If you should find yourself avoiding a problem or situation, consider stepping back and assessing the situation, getting support from others, and then resuming your plan of action.

Here are some things others have said during this stage:

"I didn't think I could feel this good again. I've been clean and sober and taking my meds for six months. I'm kind of proud of myself."

"I've been feeling more depressed lately and feel tempted to drink for the first time in a long time. I'm going to call my sponsor and make an appointment with my doctor."

In each of the statements above, these individuals appear mindful, aware, and ready to take action when indicated. They seem to be managing life daily as it comes along. You may also have similar experiences at this point. Perhaps your belief in your abilities to maintain the changes has significantly increased. Perhaps your confidence to set long-term goals is being considered. The point is this: Your success, your actions, and the results are all yours.

Spotting What Needs Your Attention: Accurate Self-Appraisal

Accurate self-appraisal is a valued tool for maintaining recovery. Using your skills to assess and address daily challenges can help you build the confidence to implement the maintenance stage of your recovery. The stages of change are in themselves tools that you can use again and again. If you are able to honestly assess where you are, you can use the stages and your skills to take action at any given time. This simple process is the basis for building new experiences and dreams that have the positive outcomes you identified in your planning stage.[64]

Maintaining Balance

Maintaining balance begins with the maintenance of a healthy body, mind, and spirit. Balance, in the maintenance stage of change, includes being certain to balance negative or stressful events with positive and good events. If you have not begun to take time to build any enjoyment into your recovery, maintenance is the time to do it. All work and no play can make you not only dull (as the saying goes), but it leaves you more vulnerable when stress or high-risk life events come up.[65]

High-Risk or Stressful Event	Healthy Coping Skill
If you have a craving	Many people use the tool of "thinking it through." What would be the end result if you relapsed?
Struggling with sleep	This is a good discussion to have with your physician. Consider learning about the body and detoxification: music therapy before bed, exercise in the day, and helpful foods.
Feeling overwhelmed	Sometimes anxiety or your emotions can get the best of you. Many people rely on their support team during those times: physician, family, sponsor, friends, or meetings.

Maybe you can think of some high-risk situations you have experienced. How would you handle those today in recovery?

High-Risk or Stressful Event   Healthy Coping Skill

_____   _____

_____   _____

_____   _____

_____   _____

_____   _____

_____   _____

_____   _____

_____   _____

The twelve-step programs have a common prayer that can bring clarity to situations. It's known as the Serenity Prayer.

God, grant me the serenity to accept the things I cannot change, the courage to change the things I can, and the wisdom to know the difference.

Checking Your Wellness Scale

Regularly checking in with yourself can offer a clearer picture of where you are today and what changes you would like to make. The following journal is an insightful and practical way to do this.

Consider using this as a guide for your daily and/or nightly journaling.

Wellness Questions

Have my symptoms changed today or in recent days? _____
_____
_____

Have I experienced any cravings or triggers today or in recent days that I am not applying
recovery skills to? _____
_____
_____
_____

Did anything stressful happen to me today or in recent days? If so, how did I handle it?
_____
_____
_____

How is my physical health? Did I have any appointments?
_____
_____

How is my mental health? Did I have any appointments? _____
_____

Am I socializing and developing friends? _____
_____

Have I been eating well? _____
_____

Have I been sleeping well? _____
_____

How am I doing emotionally? _____

_____

_____

_____

_____

Do I feel my life is changing? How? _____

_____

_____

_____

_____

_____

How do I feel today on a scale of 1–10? _____

List three things I did today that indicate my gratitude, confidence, and growth in my recovery.

_____

_____

_____

Maintaining Recovery
Searching Out Joy

Living with a co-occurring disorder can sometimes create a loss of interest or the inability to feel joy. You may be cautious about venturing out socially in the early stages of recovery. Many people in early recovery are fearful about their ability to interact with others or navigate fun without using alcohol or other drugs. Some are self-conscious about themselves and fear that people will reject them due to their mental health symptoms. These defensive actions may be healthy in some ways by protecting you until you're ready to explore this further. It is important to note here that these feelings and responses are common in recovery and can be resolved with the tools you have learned along the way.

As you continue to progress in your recovery, perhaps you would consider having more joy in your life as an identified goal in your plan.

Dealing with Distress

When people experience pain or distress,[66] it is common for them to attempt to avoid these feelings and to seek relief in any way possible. Some with chronic addiction or mental health issues may think the solution is in chemicals. Others may become guarded or defensive. At first, these solutions may work well. Later, however, addiction and the abuse become out of control, the pain and distress increase, and life feels overwhelming. If this cycle continues, many lose their natural coping skills. During the early stages of recovery, even managing the smallest distress seems daunting. The tools we have been discussing will assist you in redeveloping your skills to deal with everyday life.

Thinking Pitfalls

There is a twelve-step slogan that goes like this: "Think. Think. Think."

Maybe you think too much, or maybe you feel you don't think enough. Either way, how you think affects the way you see things.[67] Perhaps the way you see things is still from the perspective of being under the influence of alcohol and/or other drugs. Perhaps your depression or other mental health symptoms have influenced your decisions in what you will or won't do.

Changing a perspective may involve practicing new skills, taking a few risks, and keeping an open mind to new and enjoyable activities.

Black-and-White Thinking is simply the thought of absolutes (limited options).[68] It can be similar to this: "Either this way or nothing at all; my way or no way; it didn't work then and it won't work now." When you find yourself stuck in this type of thinking, you might want to stop for a moment, step back, and look at the limited options you may be offering yourself.

For example, you might think, *I went to a twelve-step meeting a couple of years ago, and I didn't like it. It didn't feel like I fit there. I am not sure why I would try that again.*

Sometimes we change, and often our perspectives also change. In this situation, trying a few different meetings for a while may have a different result.

Cyclical Thinking[69] is simply thinking that goes in a circle. Each thought connects and leads back to and supports the original thought. It all happens very quickly without much time to consider other ways to think or do something. Often times, these rapid thoughts can lead to repeating negative behaviors or relapse-type actions.

There is a recovery slogan and old saying: "Easy does it." The idea to slow things down a bit is probably a well-balanced one. Taking the time to consider how you think about something can sometimes interrupt the cyclical thinking pattern. This new skill of slowing things down may offer you the opportunity to introduce new ideas and actions, as well as a new perspective.

For example:

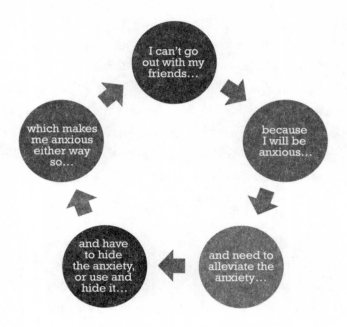

Fighting Boredom

In the early stages of recovery, you may not quite know what to do with your time, which may lead to a sense of boredom and frustration. It will take some practice to develop the skills that allow you to be comfortable exploring new options and having fun in recovery. When you were using alcohol and/or other drugs, you may have spent a lot of time getting high or finding money to buy more. Or, maybe the symptoms of an untreated mental illness contributed to an increase in isolation. Either way, you may be like so many others in recovery when you come to the point of asking yourself, "What do I do with all of this time?"

Perhaps it would be helpful to start identifying the things you like.

Please check the activities that interest you.

☐ Taking a walk   ☐ Going to a movie

☐ Going out to dinner   ☐ Bicycling

☐ Playing golf or tennis   ☐ Playing cards or board games

☐ Bowling   ☐ Taking a class

☐ Going to a park   ☐ Camping

☐ Playing a musical instrument   ☐ Running needed errands, purchasing necessities

- ☐ Spending time on the computer
- ☐ Fishing
- ☐ Playing with a pet
- ☐ Reading a new book
- ☐ Going to a concert
- ☐ Having a picnic
- ☐ Dancing
- ☐ Sitting outside
- ☐ Listening to music
- ☐ Going to the zoo
- ☐ Volunteering to help others
- ☐ Painting or sketching
- ☐ Writing a poem

- ☐ Going to a museum
- ☐ Working on a household project
- ☐ Going to a meeting
- ☐ Going to the gym
- ☐ Going to a ballgame
- ☐ Cooking a special meal
- ☐ Exercising
- ☐ Hiking
- ☐ Gardening
- ☐ Visiting friends or relatives
- ☐ Starting a new hobby
- ☐ Writing a letter to a friend
- ☐ Going to church

If you could do anything with your extra time, what would you do?

_____

_____

_____

_____

Describe a few things you have always wanted to do or achieve.

_____

_____

_____

Note: It may be helpful to review your plans with your support team. Many people have some great ideas and experiences that may assist you.

Trying New Things

Anything new is rarely done perfectly on the first attempt. You've heard the cliché "Nobody's perfect." Well, it's true, and this means you don't have to be perfect either. You have most likely made some important positive changes in your life. Maintaining and developing these changes can be both exciting and challenging at times. As you continue to grow in your recovery, triggers, problems, setbacks, and even relapses may arise along the way. As you apply your new skills to face challenges, consider that you may not always do so perfectly or gracefully. There may be a few bumps in the road, but don't let that stop you.

Avoiding All Mood-Altering Substances

It is old and destructive thinking to believe you can handle getting high just once or getting just one rush of excitement. This has consistently been shown not to work. Some report that it works for a while, then it gets worse later. This is where the problem starts. The brain remembers the positive reward of getting high without a consequence. So, the message is to do it again and again. And soon, of course, the negative consequences come.[70] Another dangerous area is thinking that since you have never used a certain drug, perhaps you would be able to try it a little, such as:

"Beer is okay as long as I don't smoke a joint."

"Alcohol is not my problem; pills are."

Maintaining a Recovery-Centered Life: A Daily Plan

Whenever there is a change, it is extremely helpful to add structure to that change in the form of a plan or roadmap. Call it a treatment plan or a to-do list. People tend to have greater success when they have a plan. In the early stages of recovery, the plan may have to be more detailed. Later in recovery, some people find that once they get the hang of it, they are able to keep up the actions needed without the help of such a detailed plan.

Many recognize a written plan as a *daily* tool to use in recovery. It is strongly encouraged during early recovery and stressful times of change. Consider making time for the following items in your day-to-day planning:

- Taking medications and vitamins (if needed)
- Volunteer work
- Meeting with friends or your sponsor
- Paying bills
- Therapy appointments
- Cleaning up your house or room
- Doctor's appointments
- Dental appointments
- Attending support meetings
- Time for a hobby (art class, music practice, etc.)

- Cooking and mealtimes
- Reading
- Getting a haircut
- Writing in your journal
- Recreation and exercise
- Maintaining your budget

Making a daily plan for recovery serves many different purposes, such as the following:

- Avoiding the trap of too much free time, which can trigger boredom, loneliness, and negative thinking.
- Checking for balance. You can see if you have left out any areas—mind, body, or spirit—or if your day is too heavily focused in one area or another. It is also a good way to check if you have included joy in your day.
- Easing the thinking or decision burden of the day by saving yourself from trying to figure out the next right thing throughout the day, which can be especially helpful in times of stress or upheaval.
- Keeping you focused. If your day gets off track or you get distracted, you have a simple guide to look back to for direction.
- Helping you see your accomplishments as you check off items.
- Building habitual action. The more recovery-driven, self-care activities you do, the more normal they will become.

Maintenance and Self-Help Programs

Self-help programs, such as Dual Recovery Anonymous (DRA), Alcoholics Anonymous (AA), Narcotics Anonymous (NA), Self-Management and Recovery Training (SMART) Recovery, chronic pain groups, etc. are the primary ways to connect to others in recovery outside of the treatment setting. These groups may be twelve-step based or have other sets of guiding principles that support recovery of members through commonly held beliefs and practices. Being connected to a group reminds you that there are others also working toward finding and maintaining their recovery.

Choosing a Home Group

Even though you may attend a number of recovery groups, it is strongly advised that you select a home group. A home group is a group you attend at least weekly that offers a strong support system. By attending your home group consistently, you begin to develop new relationships. These relationships support and encourage the changes you are making in your recovery and help you to be accountable. Most often, your home group is where you might find your sponsor.

Selecting a Sponsor

A sponsor is someone who is willing to assist you through the steps and tools of recovery. Sponsors generally share their own experience and insights. A sponsor is not a therapist or a counselor; however, the relationship is significant, and many with long-term recovery attribute much of their success to their sponsors.

Sponsorship Qualities

While there are no "rules" on how to select a sponsor, it is recommended that you find someone who exhibits the following qualities:

1. Has been abstinent and in recovery for at least one year.
2. Has learned about his or her mental illness and is currently stable. It is recommended that you select someone who understands mental illness and the role of medications in that process.
3. Has worked through the Twelve Steps and will provide a model for you to follow.
4. Is someone who you will not be romantically or sexually attracted to, and vice versa, he or she will not be attracted to you. This means choosing someone who is the same gender as you if you are heterosexual, and/or choosing someone of the opposite gender if you are gay or lesbian.
5. Will challenge you to continue moving forward and who will always hold you accountable to the truth. This may not be someone who makes you feel comfortable and safe; instead, it should be someone whose recovery you admire and whom you think will challenge you to develop a healthy personal program of recovery.
6. Has a similar mental illness and/or similar substance use experience as you, and someone who has a lot in common with your illnesses and recovery. Is someone to whom you relate and find in his or her experiences some similarity to your illness and recovery.
7. Has the time and energy available to be fully committed to you and your recovery.
8. Someone you feel comfortable with, can trust, and with whom you can develop a meaningful relationship.
9. Is "walking the walk" of recovery, not just "talking the talk." In other words, find someone who is actually working the program, not just reciting recovery slogans or recalling phrases verbatim from the Big Book or Basic Text.

When you meet someone with the above qualities, it is a good idea to start developing a relationship with that person before you ask him or her to be your sponsor. This will allow you to be sure that the person really does meet the above requirements.

Asking Someone to Be Your Sponsor

When you are confident that you have selected a person to be your sponsor, after a meeting approach him or her. Then, simply ask, "Will you be my sponsor?"

If the person says "no," don't take it personally. It may be that he or she already sponsors several people and cannot accept another person. Or, he or she may not be at the right place in his or her own recovery to sponsor others.

Recovery means learning to deal with rejection and continuing until you find the help you need. It is common to have to ask several people before you find a sponsor. Don't give up! Remember this is a big commitment on the sponsor's part, and you want someone who is fully willing and committed to take on that responsibility.

It is generally recommended that you have only one sponsor; however, there may be times when a "temporary" or "extra" sponsor might be needed. For example, when you are new to recovery, you should find a "temporary" sponsor immediately. He or she will introduce you to the fellowship, help you find a more permanent sponsor, and, if needed, help you get to meetings. Other times you might need an "extra" sponsor if you are away from home or if your sponsor is temporarily unavailable.

While it may be difficult to think about how to begin the relationship with your sponsor, remember that he or she has been through the same journey and often understands how you may feel. Begin by spending time with your new sponsor during coffee hour and by phone, and your sponsor will take it from there.

If It Doesn't Work Out

There are lots of reasons why the sponsor you choose may not work out. For example, you might find that your sponsor doesn't have enough time or energy for you after all, or he or she may relapse and be unable to continue helping you. Or, maybe you just don't end up feeling as comfortable with him or her as you thought you might. There are even times when you might "outgrow" your sponsor and find him or her leaning on you as much as (or more than) you lean on him or her. These things happen, and they should not prevent you from having the best recovery you can. Sponsorship is not a permanent arrangement. If you can, talk honestly with your sponsor about the issues you're facing, and then find a new sponsor if necessary.

Sponsor Assignments

Typically, a sponsor will give you assignments to help you move forward and grow in your program of recovery. It is a good idea to make notes or keep a journal of your discussions and keep track of your progress with assignments.

You can make copies of this form and use it for your assignments if you think it will be helpful to you.

Sponsor Meeting Place and Date: _____

Discussed: _____

_____

_____

_____

_____

_____

_____

Assignment: _____

_____

_____

_____

_____

_____

_____

_____

Target Date: _____

Outcome: _____

_____

_____

_____

_____

_____

Relapse

The Sixth Stage of Change

In the discussion of the maintenance stage of change, you may have learned that a lack of safeguarding your daily recovery plan might result in relapse for those with co-occurring disorders. The relapse stage emphasizes the importance of developing the skills needed to navigate these dynamics. There are two types of relapses to consider:

A **mental health relapse** is a return of symptoms that interrupt your emotional and physical well-being, possibly resulting in intrusive thoughts, erratic behaviors, and emotional imbalance. It is often characterized by denial of the need for help or assistance and a loss of hope for a solution.

An **addiction relapse** is defined by the use of addictive chemicals after a period of abstinence and recovery. This is usually preceded by thoughts, behaviors, or actions that compromise the decision-making process, supporting and rationalizing the decision to ultimately drink alcohol and/or use other drugs again.

Knowing and understanding your potential for relapse is an important skill of recovery.[71] By learning the seriousness of co-occurring disorders, the importance of a day-to-day recovery plan, and the solutions recovery offers, you are better prepared to achieve a life of abstinence, recovery, and emotional stability.

Oftentimes, we underestimate how powerful the dynamics of addiction and mental health are and, as a result, we minimize the actions we need to take to protect ourselves from relapse. The purpose of this stage is to become intimately aware of your own warning signs and to develop a plan for relapse prevention.

> **Note:** We will explore the various dynamics of relapse and prevention more extensively in Chapter Eleven, "Preventing Relapse."

Notes

CHAPTER EIGHT
Dealing with Trauma

When we typically think of traumatic experiences, thoughts that involve a threat to life or safety come to mind. However, any situation that leaves you feeling overwhelmed, unable to meet your needs, or very alone can be traumatic. It doesn't have to involve physical harm, and it doesn't have to be a single event. Throughout this section we will explore types of trauma, causes, symptoms, treatment, and recovery.

What Is Trauma?

First let's look at how trauma is defined.[72]

1. A serious injury or shock to the body as from violence or an accident.
2. An event or situation that causes great distress and disruption.
3. An emotional wound or shock that creates substantial, lasting damage to the psychological development of a person, often leading to lasting difficulties in resuming or managing daily life events.

In the first two definitions above, trauma is defined as an event. There is also an experience of trauma that accumulates over time—you may not even have recognized the situation(s) as having a traumatic effect.

Note: It can also be helpful to remember that experiencing a traumatic event does not automatically mean that there will be a long-term effect from that event.

Causes of Emotional and Psychological Trauma

Emotional trauma and psychological trauma are often used interchangeably when speaking about trauma. Using the term "emotional and psychological trauma" clearly sets it apart from other traumas, such as physical or body-based trauma.

Emotional and psychological trauma most commonly results from events that happen unexpectedly, repeatedly, and/or in childhood. Or, there may have been an event in which you were unprepared for it, felt powerless to prevent it, and/or suffered intentional cruelty.

As identified previously, emotional and psychological trauma can be caused by one-time events, such as a horrible accident, a natural disaster, or a violent attack. What is a surprising discovery for some is that trauma can also stem from ongoing stress, such as living in a chaotic home, a shameful or bullying environment, a crime-ridden neighborhood, or from struggling with physical or mental illness.[73]

Commonly Overlooked Causes of Emotional and Psychological Trauma

- Injury from a fall or sports
- Surgery (especially in the first three years of life)
- The sudden death of someone close
- A car accident
- Instability (chronic danger due to domestic chaos, poverty, repeated relocation)
- The breakup of a significant relationship
- A humiliating or deeply disappointing experience
- The discovery of a life-threatening illness or disabling condition
- Chronic shame
- Addiction
- Mental illness
- Incarceration

Here is an opportunity to write about your response to the concept of trauma as presented. How does it differ from your belief of what causes trauma and what defines trauma?

_____

_____

_____

_____

_____

Coping and Defense Mechanisms

People may have many conscious and unconscious ways of coping with trauma.[74, 75] While some ways are helpful in dealing with an initial shock, they can often become barriers to a healthy life if used for the long term. For example, withdrawal from the world can initially help support a feeling of safety and, generally, is not a problem unless it prevents you from returning to interacting with others. At the other end of the spectrum, the need to be with people can initially help and is fine unless you become afraid to be alone and cannot enjoy solitude. Denial and dissociation are common ways of coping with the experiences of trauma.

Denial

Denial is often the first and most widely seen response to a shocking or unexpected event. "No," "It didn't happen," and "You have got to be kidding me" are often the first utterances at shocking or unexpected news. Momentary denial is self-protective and can allow you time to process the possibility of a circumstance before accepting it as truth. This type of short-term denial can be useful, but can also become disabling if held onto as a coping skill for too long.

Dissociation

Dissociation is a way to cope with trauma that can occur during or after the event(s) or circumstances have passed. Dissociation happens when awareness separates, and the core (or conscious self) isolates (or encapsulates) itself from the traumatic experience. This is often described as an out-of-body or unconscious experience. This coping mechanism is an attempt to escape the full impact of the trauma. In some instances, the dissociation may be strong enough to replace the traumatic event and may cause amnesia, or a memory gap. Events may also be experienced as though they are only being "watched" or externally observed; you may remain aware of the events, but not connected. This disconnection is often referred to as depersonalization.

Dissociation that brings a "spacey" feeling and distortions of perception, including time, is considered mild; although, the effects can be disturbing. In extreme cases of dissociation, individuals may withdraw into a fantasy world, refusing or being unable to engage in daily happenings without the protection of the fantasy. On rare occasions, adults may develop multiple personality disorder (known as dissociative identity disorder), in which distinct personas separate to deal with compartmentalized needs.

Dissociative symptoms normally dissolve slowly following trauma as you become grounded and your sense of security returns.

During this time, feelings of powerlessness, helplessness, or vulnerability fade. Recovery after a traumatic event may hinge on your ability to ground yourself to the present in a safe environment. However, if the feelings associated with the trauma remain, depersonalization and dissociative symptoms may become stronger and your ongoing outlook may shift to one that keeps you fearful and isolated because you feel vulnerable. If you feel incapable of protecting yourself, long-term dissociation may result. If your environment truly remains dangerous, such as in domestic abuse, wartime, or chronic bullying, then dissociation will likely continue as well.

Psychological defense mechanisms for coping with trauma are endless. Some are conscious, and many are engaged in unknowingly. The use of defense mechanisms is a natural and normal part of dealing with trauma; however, it can cause additional difficulties if used to lock trauma away rather than to ease the process of moving through the experience. Hiding anything takes a lot of energy and can block your ability to engage honestly and mindfully in the present, which can hamper life even after the traumatic event has ceased. Even if a person appears unharmed by a potentially traumatic experience, his or her life can be impaired unless the emotions and energy trapped by these defense mechanisms are processed or let go.

Unconscious Strategies for Coping with Trauma[76]

- **Denial:** Not accepting important aspects of reality.
- **Displacement:** Shifting feelings about one person or situation onto another.
- **Dissociation:** A splitting of awareness; partial or complete separation from the traumatic event.
- **Idealization:** Overvaluing another person, place, family, or activity.
- **Isolation of affect:** Repressing emotions associated with a particular context or ideas associated with particular emotions.
- **Intellectualization:** Thinking about an experience or emotion rather than feeling it directly.
- **Introjection:** An unconscious process by which a person takes into his or her own persona the characteristics of another person or object.
- **Mental illness:** Mental health issues that impede the ability to function, such as depression, addiction, phobia, obsession, or psychosis.

- **Projection:** Attributing unacknowledged feelings to others.
- **Rationalization:** Using reason to justify certain ideas.
- **Reaction formation:** Repressing a conscious impulse and replacing it with its opposite.
- **Regression:** Returning to an earlier developmental phase.
- **Repression:** Keeping unwanted thoughts and feelings out of awareness.
- **Reversal:** Changing feelings or attitudes to the opposite.
- **Somatization:** Converting anxiety into physical symptoms.
- **Sublimation:** Changing a socially unacceptable aim into an acceptable one.
- **Undoing:** Nullifying an unacceptable act.
- **Withdrawal:** Avoiding engaging with others or the world.

Varying Symptoms

Emotional and psychological trauma symptoms can occur when you are unable to relax once a threat or stressful event is over. Hence, two of the primary symptoms of trauma are **hyperarousal**, a heightened sense of awareness, and **hypervigilance**, a constant alertness for danger. Being constantly on guard can rob you of the ability to enjoy the present moment and be mindful, and it can lead to an inability to focus, as well as muscle tension in the head, neck, and eyes.

Hyperarousal is prompted by unresolved physical memories and emotions held in the mind. Hypervigilance results from a felt need to activate a "fight or flight" response for survival. Memories can interrupt your ability to engage in the present and disturb psychological, emotional, and physical well-being and survival instincts by replacing current sensation with a message of potential danger. Let's look at a simple example.

> *Jane works in the city as a photographer and her day is filled with honking horns and people all around her. She has not had any disturbing or traumatic events occur in this environment. She lives in a suburb.*

> *Betty worked with the Peace Corps after college as a photographer. The one time she was in a metropolitan environment, a car bomber hit a library next to the café where she was having lunch. She now lives in the same suburb as Jane.*

> *While at the park, both women hear cars honking, people yelling, and the normal hustle and bustle of an active park. Jane enjoys watching her son play soccer, oblivious to the*

noise. Betty seeks out the source of every horn, squeal, and yelling voice. She is unable to focus on her daughter's game.

This is one way that hyperarousal and hypervigilance can interrupt the ability to engage or enjoy the present moment.

If hyperarousal continues, over time the body-mind connection may adopt the state as standard operation, moving this state from a conscious choice of the mind to an automatic response. Automatic responses can sometimes be difficult to interrupt, manage, or change.

When trauma symptoms are severe, any change or unanticipated experience may be interpreted as a threat, resulting in feelings of overload, confusion, helplessness, anxiety, rage, terror, panic, shame, and/or depression. A simple ringing of the doorbell or horn honking can be overwhelming to process. The constant hypervigilance and physiological stress may also cause psychosomatic illnesses, where the stress presents as physical ailments.

The hyperarousal for danger and fear that accompanies unresolved trauma can prevent exploration and experience, thereby affecting emotional growth. If trauma occurs during childhood, it can affect basic developmental growth, which often goes unrecognized as being a result of trauma, especially if the traumatic event is undisclosed.

Trauma Responses

Symptoms of trauma come from being stuck in abnormal reactions to abnormal events. Recovery from trauma is characterized by a return to normal reactions to normal events and the ability to be mindfully present in order to react to life as it is today, rather than in a hypervigilant stance.

Following a traumatic experience, or repeated trauma, people may experience a wide range of physical and emotional reactions. All are normal attempts to cope with and process shocking and incomprehensible experiences. There is no "right" or "wrong" way to think about, feel toward, or respond to trauma. Judging your reactions or those of other people can worsen the effects of trauma.

There are many symptoms that can result from the initial trauma response as well as from long-term unresolved trauma. Remember, symptoms can be the result of multiple causes. The following categorical lists are some of the specific symptoms associated with experiencing trauma; however, this does not mean that everyone who experiences one or more of these symptoms has been traumatized.

Developmental[77]

- Learning difficulties
- Regression to earlier developmental stages
- Repression of sexuality

Psychological

- Acute sensitivity to light and sound, sudden movements or change
- Amnesia, nightmares, or flashbacks
- Denial of the problem, refusal to address issues or take responsibility for change (blaming of others)
- Low self-esteem and self-confidence
- Psychological defense by limiting emotional engagement or attachment
- Repression or exaggeration of emotional response

Emotional Symptoms[78]

- Shock, denial, or disbelief
- Anger, irritability, and mood swings
- Guilt, shame, and self-blame
- Sadness or hopelessness
- Confusion and difficulty concentrating
- Anxiety and fear
- Depression
- Withdrawing from others
- Feeling disconnected or numb

Physical Symptoms

- Insomnia or nightmares
- Being startled easily
- Racing heartbeat
- Aches and pains
- Fatigue
- Difficulty concentrating
- Edginess and agitation
- Muscle tension

Behavioral Symptoms

- Overeating/undereating
- Poor self-care
- Sexual compulsiveness
- Over-focusing on appearance
- Excessive risk-taking
- Addictive behaviors
- Aggressiveness
- Impulsivity
- Isolation/withdrawal

Feelings of Loss and Sadness

Healthy processing of trauma can take anywhere from a few days to many months. During this time, symptoms gradually fade as the trauma is processed. But, even if trauma is effectively processed, you may be troubled periodically by painful memories or emotions. This may happen in response to triggers, such as an anniversary of the event or an image, sound, or situation that reminds you of the traumatic experience.[79]

Even if a traumatic event does not involve death, grief is a common experience. The loss can simply be the loss of a sense of safety and security, even if only temporarily. The natural reaction to this loss is grief. Those dealing with trauma often go through a grieving process, much like grieving over a death, major change, or loss. This process, while inherently uncomfortable, can be easier if you turn to others for support and talk about how you feel.

Core Emotions

Understanding emotional response is crucial to understanding the effects of trauma. The list of emotions may vary from philosopher to philosopher, but many believe that joy, acceptance, anticipation, surprise, fear, anger, shame, and sadness form the core of each personality. While acceptance, anticipation, and shame are highly affected by thought, they are secondary to the core emotions of anger, sadness, joy, fear, and shame.[80]

Core emotions are the bottom line, and when they are experienced, the body physically responds to these emotions by raising blood pressure, flushing, etc. A range of intensity exists within each core emotion, and emotions can mix to form even more complex emotions.[81]

Healthy

Core emotional responses create a warning system, and these core emotions and the body's response can alarm you to do something. Each core emotion prompts an action urge. Trauma symptoms often result in an overactive, unbalanced, or misguided warning system. It may be that unprocessed trauma has caused the event to remain current in the mind so that the alarm continually sounds. Emotional intensity may be unbalanced, causing you to misinterpret current events. Response to warning signals may become overly impulsive or, on the contrary, you may be numb to the signals.

Trauma Responses versus Healthy Responses

The emotional response pattern begins with an event. An emotion arises, which creates an urge to act, which in turn leads to a behavior. A healthy response to emotion is to acknowledge the alarm or emotion, think (or review the situation or feeling), and choose if and how to respond. Healthy emotional response is deliberate. Core emotions can cause the following action urges:[82]

- Anger can have the action urge to strike out or fight.
- Sadness may have an action urge to deactivate or hide/isolate.
- Joy sometimes has an action urge to get moving.
- Fear can create the action urge of flight or getting away.
- Shame often shows in the action urge to hide, cover up, or keep secret.

Letting the action urge mobilize before attempting to deliberate the action increases the likelihood of impulsivity. Experiencing the emotion before responding to the action urge is the best way to interrupt this pattern.[83]

Emotion Response[84]

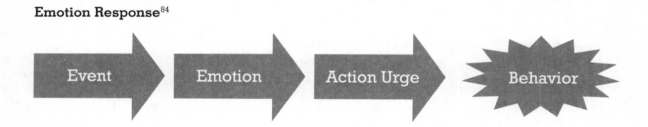

Who Is at Increased Risk for Trauma?

Some experiences that would be considered traumatic events don't necessarily lead to lasting emotional and psychological damage. Some people rebound quickly from even the most tragic and shocking experiences, while others may be shattered by experiences that, on the surface, appear to be less upsetting. Risk factors can make people susceptible to emotional and psychological trauma, just as resiliency factors can make people less likely to be affected by trauma. People are more likely to be traumatized by a stressful experience if they're already under a heavy stress load or have recently suffered a series of losses. People tend to be less likely to suffer lasting effects of trauma if they manage daily stress, have an active support system, and the trauma event is singular rather than compounded stress.

People may also be more likely to be traumatized by a new situation if they've been traumatized before, especially if previous trauma happened in childhood.

Early Life Trauma Affects Risk

Trauma experienced in childhood an have a severe and long-lasting effect, primarily due to the resulting view of the world as a frightening and dangerous place. [85, 86] If early life trauma is not resolved, this fundamental sense of fear and helplessness carries over into adulthood, setting the stage for further trauma.

Early life trauma can result from anything that interferes with a child's sense of safety and security, including:

- An unstable or unsafe environment
- Separation from a parent
- Serious illness
- Intrusive medical procedures
- Sexual, physical, or verbal abuse
- Domestic violence
- Neglect
- Bullying

Post-Traumatic Stress Disorder (PTSD)

PTSD is the most widely talked about diagnosis for trauma. Its primary symptoms include intrusive memories or flashbacks, avoiding things that can remind one of the traumatic event(s), and living in an agitated and nearly constant state of hypervigilance, making it difficult to engage in daily activities and interact with others.[87]

If you've gone through a traumatic experience or suffered repeated trauma, you may be struggling with upsetting emotions, frightening memories, or a sense of constant danger that you just can't change. Or the trauma may have left you feeling numb, disconnected, and unable to trust or engage with other people. When bad things happen, it can take time to move through the pain and feel safe again. With the right treatment, self-help strategies, and support from family and friends, you can begin your recovery from emotional and psychological trauma. Whether the traumatic event happened years ago or yesterday, you *can* heal and move on.

Evidence-Based Treatments

The evidence-based treatments of trauma focus on processing the emotions by alleviating the need for the mind to protect itself through dissociation or other coping skills. Some of these treatments may include Process Therapy, Trauma Grounding Skills and Reprocessing, Somatic Experiencing, Eye-Movement Desensitization and Reprocessing (EMDR), Cognitive Behavioral Therapy (CBT), and Systematic Desensitization.

Process Therapy

Process Therapy is talk therapy in a group, family, or individual setting. It allows for the exploration of an event, topic, or situation with a goal of first identifying an emotional response, effective thoughts and behaviors, as well as providing the opportunity to consider "faulty thinking or behaviors." Process Therapy offers opportunities to replace faulty beliefs with more accurate and beneficial ones.

Trauma Grounding Skills and Reprocessing

This approach is aimed at bringing you to the "here and now" so that symptoms can be processed in an open way, free of protective response (such as dissociation, flashback, protective denial). Grounding can be as simple as allowing you to tell your story in a supportive environment that is actively empathetic, validating, and helpful in normalizing your situation and responses.

Reprocessing of trauma is, very simply, reprocessing the experience of past or unprocessed trauma in a way that allows you to distance yourself from the trauma. When you separate the trauma from you, you may be able to gain the ability to accept the trauma without responding to its triggers.[88]

Somatic Experiencing

With Somatic Experiencing, the body uses its unique ability to heal itself. The focus of therapy is on bodily sensations and learning to self-regulate rather than focus on your thoughts and memories about the traumatic event. By concentrating on what's happening in your body, trauma-related memory, energy, and tension may surface. Somatic therapy encourages releasing pent-up energy through crying and other forms of physical release. You may gradually be able to deactivate the physical and emotional charge related to the traumatic experience.

Eye Movement Desensitization and Reprocessing (EMDR)

EMDR was developed by Francine Shapiro to resolve the development of trauma-related disorders resulting from exposure to a traumatic or distressing event. EMDR may be used for other symptoms; however, its research support is primarily for disorders stemming from distressing life experiences. When a traumatic experience occurs, it may overwhelm the usual ways of coping. The memory of the event may be inadequately processed, and the memory is dysfunctionally stored, prompting a continued reaction to the memory as if it were a current experience.

EMDR uses a structured eight-phase approach and addresses the past, present, and future aspects of the stored memory.

During the phases of EMDR, the client reprocesses the disturbing memory in multiple brief sets of about fifteen to thirty seconds, while simultaneously focusing on an alternate attention stimulus, for example, therapist-directed lateral eye movement, alternate hand tapping, or bilateral auditory tones. EMDR is established as an evidence-based treatment for PTSD.[89]

Cognitive Behavioral Therapy (CBT)

CBT can help you process and evaluate thoughts, feelings, and core beliefs about a trauma. While CBT doesn't treat the physiological effects of trauma, it can be helpful when used in addition to a body-based therapy, such as Somatic Experiencing or EMDR.

Long-Term Chronic Exposure

Chronic exposure or nonevent-based trauma can occur when chronic and unusual stress is present.[90, 91, 92] Like event-based trauma, the mere presence of chronic and unusual stress in and of itself does not mean that trauma will automatically result. Remember, trauma is an emotional wound or shock that creates substantial damage to the psychological development of a person, often leading to lasting difficulties resuming or managing daily life events. It is the result of unresolved response or separation from those stressors.

Looking at some types of nonevent-based traumas may help clarify this.

Long-Term Illness or Adversity May Cause Nonevent-Based Trauma

- Addiction
- Cancer
- Chronic illness
- Chronic pain
- Loss of limb
- Disfigurement
- Significant illness during developmental times of life
- Learning disabilities
- Sociological adversities

- Cultural adversity
- Mental health concerns

Assimilation Issues May Cause Nonevent-Based Trauma

- Cultural-assimilation issues
- Sexual-orientation or sexual-affinity differences
- Religious practices that are different or unaccepted by family
- Financial means that differ from peers or colleagues

It is not uncommon for those who suffer long-term pressure and stress to respond with a variety of emotional symptoms, including shame and fear.

> **Shame:** Some people see themselves as damaged. Sometimes this is the result of a shame-based trauma. This can lead them to isolate, or they may overcompensate to prove they are still capable, able, or worthy, despite not believing it themselves.

> **Fear:** Some people might expect to experience more pain or loss, resulting in a fear-based trauma. This fear, resulting from a need to protect oneself, can often lead to avoidant or aggressive behaviors.

The effect of trauma stemming from long-term chronic exposure is commonly seen in individuals recovering from mental health and substance use disorders. Most often, there is a sense of shame or an ingrained belief that there is a flaw, something to hide or something to compensate for.

Shame is part of our emotions. In normal, healthy development, children seek and need to receive external validation in order to develop the ability to self-validate. When reassured through approval, a developing child gains an internal belief that he or she is acceptable, and the temporary external validation builds the permanent internal self-validation. Before a person can self-validate, they must have received, experienced, and seen approval in action.

It is important to understand that children in and of themselves do not possess the ability for handling emotional cues in a healthy way. They learn from those around them. If a child grows up in an environment where role models react impulsively to emotions, they are likely to do so as well. By the same token, children who observe well-managed or regulated emotions, tend to develop healthier skills.

Seeking approval is the primary defense or reaction against the emotional trigger of shame for children with little emotional skill. If this approval is withheld, then shame is reinforced. The action urge to hide or compensate for this unacceptable part is developed and reinforced in this way. Experiencing chronic shame over time forms automatic thoughts and responses that dictate behaviors and experiences.

Shame through Invalidation

Shame says unworthy. Validation says worthy. Shame through invalidation can occur in many ways, and while the strongest effects seem to be in childhood, chronic invalidation can be traumatizing later in life as well. Some common examples of invalidation that can lead to shame include the following experiences:[93, 94, 95]

- **Being pressured:** Expectations are unachievable here. The bar is set too high and is often perpetrated under the guise of "It's for your own good" or "You need to have goals to reach."
- **Being overlooked:** Primary supports are unavailable, often due to addiction, mental health issues in the home, chronic partner-seeking, and workaholism.
- **Being rejected or blamed:** One child or family member, coworker, or group within a community is the scapegoat for any problems or difficulties of the group.
- **Being sexually shamed:** Gay, lesbian, or heterosexual in a restrictive environment (an environment in which sex is not talked about) are shamed because they are unaccepted and/or no one validates the normalcy of having sexual parts, body responses, thoughts, or feelings.
- **Being religiously shamed:** Exploration of beliefs is restricted, and the forced beliefs appear to reinforce persons as flawed.
- **Being controlled:** Decision-making is not allowed, leaving people incapable of making choices. This can be due to caregivers or spouses having over-controlling tendencies and insisting on conformity. In consistently controlled environments, sometimes there is no room for individual choice because there is no knowledge of anything different, resulting in dependency and a pervasive inability to make decisions.

An invalidating environment is defined as "chronically and persistently rejecting . . . communication of private experiences and self-generated behavior."[96] Childhood invalidation is linked with an inability to regulate emotions in children[97] and psychological distress in adulthood.[98]

While abuse implies intent to hurt the child, invalidation is often unintentional and well meaning. Most invalidating environments reinforce the thought that there may be something wrong with you. Chronic exposure to an invalidating environment can be traumatizing because it may obstruct the ability to self-validate.

If self-validation does not develop, then stability can be lost, creating the following:[99]

- Recurring self doubt
- Low self-esteem/self-worth
- Confusion
- Chronic inability to maintain feelings of satisfaction or contentment

- Wavering, unstable sense of self-purpose and direction
- Difficulty maintaining primary relationships and/or career
- Feeling like an imposter
- Splitting (being different in public or private, or with one person or another)
- Recurring need to escape through addiction

Levels of Validating and Invalidating Environments

Validating Environment	Invalidating Environment
Very high: You are acknowledged in the relationship, and your most treasured dreams are valued. There is a shared moment with mutual experience. You are understood.	**Very high:** Your vulnerabilities and weaknesses are pointed out. Your dreams are ridiculed as foolish. You are threatened physically.
High: You are treated as an equal in the relationship, not inferior or fragile. There are boundaries. For instance, a mom doesn't lean on a child emotionally; she holds the boundary as the mom.	**High:** You are told that your experience isn't normal. You are broken and treated as an incompetent subordinate.
Moderate: You are noticed in the relationship. There is acknowledgment of you, even without approval.	**Moderate:** You are told you don't feel that way, your thoughts are wrong, and your feelings are insignificant or foolish. You are often accused or never given the benefit of the doubt.
Low: You are noticed in the relationship. The other person responds, but is not engaged.	**Low:** Others are too busy or conflicted to notice you.

Note: Validation is the opposite of shame. Recovery from shame-based trauma is moving toward the place where you are able to self-validate and hold the belief that you, your life, and your accomplishments are enough. This can result in self-motivation through your own goals, rather than gaining validation.

Coping Skills that Don't Work

People who suffer from shame-based traumas often respond with maladaptive coping skills. They may overcompensate, judge, fantasize, attack, or adopt others' expectations for themselves.[100, 101, 102]

Here are a few examples:

- **Overcompensation:** With overcompensation, you might have to be the best and hide your vulnerabilities by being the best. Often this is unattainable or not maintainable. When avenues to gain external validation or achieve more are no longer available, then addiction and retreat may seem to be the only ways to avoid having to face the potential experience and feeling of not being acceptable. Core belief: *Life is too painful to be experienced directly, so I will avoid the potential risk of feeling rejected and invalidated by being beyond reproach.*

- **Judgmental:** With this you may degrade others to validate yourself. Or, you might maintain relationships as proof that you are loveable or to validate yourself as loveable. Core belief: *In order to be loved, I must be loveable. Being loved validates lovability.*

- **Fantasy:** You may be searching for the next instant fix. You may not be able to accept life on life's terms, so you idealize that the next thing will fix the shame. When it doesn't work, you then seek to devalue it as "bad" and look for the next thing that might fix it. Core belief: *It is not okay to be normal or average, and when I find the right answer, or fix, I will no longer be ashamed.*

- **Anger:** Here, self-criticism is so constant and overwhelming that if anyone threatens more criticism, it can trigger an anger response. Core belief: *I will show my anger toward someone to avoid being hurt.*

- **Adopting Expectations:** Here you might find you are living the external "should" rather than having internal goals. You may be focused on acting out others' expectations rather than revealing the authentic self. Core belief: *To be acceptable, I must become what they want me to be.*

Overcoming Shame-Based Trauma

Shame-based trauma is an anxiety disorder of shame. Shame is the intrusive emotion. Shame-based trauma interventions treat anxiety and shame, and they build the ability to make a difference in your own life. Resolution of shame-based trauma is achievable through validation and maintainable by establishing the ability to self-validate. The common theme in shame-based trauma is that it results in a failure to develop an intrinsic sense of self.

Getting Treatment for Shame-Based Trauma

Treatment of shame-based trauma is often centered on emotional regulation of anxiety and shame to create a space to contemplate the emotion prior to choosing to respond to the action urge. It generally assists in increasing validation and can provide the opportunity to build internal validation. Internal validation often brings with it the ability to build a higher sense of self-worth and more joy in your life.

Becoming the Master of Your Fate

Choosing to follow your own ideas, passions, and dreams can provide the opportunity for the genuine self to receive external validation and have authentic self-validating experiences and joy.[103]

The art of achieving self-mastery[104, 105] can include the following:

- Learning to recognize and change negative impulses or action-urges triggered by unhealthy shame.

- Expressing your opinion in a thoughtful way, even when you feel it doesn't matter.

- Asking others to treat you respectfully when you feel belittled or disrespected.

- Kindly standing up for your beliefs and values even when you feel that others will judge you harshly. Stand up without invalidating the other person's beliefs or values; no one has to be wrong for you to be right.

- Learning new skills or doing things differently though it will likely be awkward at first.

- Avoiding insincere cheerleading; affirmations can be helpful to self-validate, but if you don't believe them, they don't have much effect and can be invalidating.

- Avoiding seeking validation; it destroys relationships, and you can wear people out.

Regulating Emotion

Dialectical Behavior Therapy (DBT) skills[106] are effective in treating shame-based trauma. Successfully regulating emotion is an authentic experience of self-efficacy. Some skills to consider that are particularly useful are the following:

- Delay, delay, delay. Very few decisions can't wait twenty-four hours. Consider accepting that you can still take action if you think you need to; but, with time, the emotional field opens and allows a perspective that is not narrowed by heightened emotion.

- Use your senses to achieve mindfulness. Focus on a color, a visual cue, or a pleasing sound. Engage with the here and now through your senses.

- Avoid ruminating or repeatedly reviewing the situation that caused the emotion.

- Distract yourself.

- Self-soothe by engaging the senses.

- Apply the "Teflon-mind skill." Decide that what is happening around you will not stick, will not be absorbed, and you not be affected by the situation.

- Use your "one-thing-in-the-moment" skill and look to find the "next right thing."

- Use any of your grounding skills to connect or become grounded in the here and now.

- Use radical acceptance. Some things you can change, some things you can't.

- Ask yourself, "Am I Hungry, Angry, Lonely, or Tired (HALT)?" Look for and address what is making you vulnerable to negative emotion. Self-efficacy (the ability to make a difference in one's life) is influenced negatively by trauma.[107] Many effective treatment methods for trauma are those that are found to increase self-efficacy positively.[108]

Support

Recovering from emotional and psychological trauma may take time and support. Being patient with yourself, while continuing to develop and practice your skill sets, can prove to be beneficial.

It is common to want to withdraw from others; however, being alone can reinforce feelings of vulnerability and lack of support. Connecting to others can help.

Asking for assistance and talking about your feelings can help keep you connected and grounded. You might choose to seek support in a trusted family member, friend, therapist, sponsor, or clergyman.

Finding a Trauma Specialist

Working through trauma can be challenging. Finding the right therapist may take some time. It's very important that the therapist you choose has experience in treating trauma. The quality of the relationship with your therapist is equally important. Trust your instincts; if you don't feel safe, respected, or understood, find another therapist.[109] After you meet a potential trauma therapist, consider the following:

- Did you feel comfortable discussing your problems with the therapist?
- Did you feel like the therapist understood what you were talking about?
- Were your concerns taken seriously, or were they minimized or dismissed?
- Were you treated with compassion and respect?
- Do you believe that you could grow to trust the therapist?

Introduction to Dialectical Behavior Therapy (DBT)

Welcome to DBT

With Dialectical Behavior Therapy, you begin to explore ways to transform your life by changing your behavior, shifting your emotions, and learning concrete skills to decrease emotional pain. Just as you can train your body to lift weights or to run a marathon, you can also train your mind to lessen your emotional suffering. The process of training your mind works just like exercise. It does not happen overnight. However, with consistent practice in thinking about your emotions and struggles differently and coping more effectively, change can occur.

DBT was originally developed by Dr. Marsha Linehan, a psychologist at the University of Washington, as a treatment for Borderline Personality Disorder, and this therapy has since been adapted to many different client populations.[110]

What Is DBT?

DBT integrates elements from two different and highly effective practices: behavior therapy and ancient Zen philosophy.[111] In DBT, you learn how to create the life you want. You strive to let go of focusing on "right" or "wrong," "good" or "bad," and rather on what works and what brings you the results you are looking for. You work on letting go of "judgment" in order to move out of your own way.

DBT is an evidenced-based therapeutic practice. Numerous scientific studies have found DBT to be effective in helping people manage their emotions and, thereby, decrease problematic behaviors, such as substance abuse, suicide attempts, self-harm/cutting, eating disorders, etc.

The Four Areas of DBT

There are four areas of study/practice in DBT: mindfulness, interpersonal effectiveness, emotional regulation, and distress tolerance. Each module has a specific purpose, and you will study and practice skills from each of these four modules.

Mindfulness

The purpose of mindfulness is to get to know yourself better (your thoughts, feelings, and behaviors). Developing the skill of mindfulness allows you to increase your experiences of joy and to "turn your mind" when you are overwhelmed by painful emotions.

Interpersonal Effectiveness

The purpose of interpersonal effectiveness is to learn effective communication skills. In this module, we'll focus on how you can ask to get your needs met in an assertive/non-aggressive fashion, how to say "no" to others in a firm but respectful fashion, how to maintain relationships that you want to maintain, and how to keep your self-respect, even when you are faced with challenging people.

Emotional Regulation

The purpose of emotional regulation is to learn how to decrease emotions that are painful and difficult. You can learn new skills that give you increased freedom with your emotions. You can work to increase your experiences of joy and peace. You cannot eliminate pain or uncomfortable emotions from your life completely, but in this module, you can learn skills for decreasing the frequency and intensity of distressing emotions. You can also explore ways to cope with and prepare for painful emotions.

Distress Tolerance

The last section of study is distress tolerance. This section focuses on surviving an emotional crisis. During this section, you will learn effective coping skills that can replace destructive coping techniques and help you allow your high emotional level to subside.

DBT Groups

DBT-informed skills groups can be more meaningful to you if you first identify the patterns you want to change, the importance of changing these patterns, and what you want most in your life (goals, values, dreams, etc.). Some examples of patterns that you could choose to focus on in this group are repressing emotions, attempting suicide, neglecting others, neglecting yourself, raging at others, physical violence, or using alcohol and/or other drugs.

(Based on what we've found most helpful, Foundations Recovery Network has made a few modifications to the standard DBT model to adapt it to a short-term residential setting.)

DBT: Ten Core Skills

The following are ten core skills of Dialectical Behavior Therapy (DBT).[112, 113, 114]

Dialectical Thinking: This is the concept that two seemingly opposing ideas (for example, "I want to be in recovery" and "I want to use") can coexist, at the same time, without eliminating one another. Considerations include learning how to authentically embrace dialectics with the goal of being able to experience joy and peace even in the midst of profound suffering.

Non-judgment: This is the concept of learning how to turn your mind away from the judgment of self and others. Considerations include learning how to move toward creating the life you want to live, and learning how judgment is counterproductive to making positive life changes.

Wise Mind: This is the concept that we each may have three different states of mind: emotional mind, rational mind, and "wise mind." Considerations include learning how to identify the states of mind, recognize their uses and limitations, and work toward "wise mind" choices and actions.

Turning the Mind: This is the concept of mindfully shifting your focus when you are obsessing on negative thoughts, feelings, or images. Considerations include learning to understand the relationship between what your mind focuses on and the emotions you experience.

Mindfulness: This is the concept of learning how to focus your attention on the present moment for increased self-awareness, joy, and peace. Considerations include learning mindfulness practices to reduce distraction during times of emotional pain.

Interpersonal Effectiveness: This is the concept of learning techniques utilized for clear, confident, and effective communication for maintaining and repairing important relationships. Considerations include learning how to respect yourself more by communicating differently with others.

Ride the Wave of Your Emotions: This is the concept of learning how to practice acceptance of painful emotions. Considerations include "surfing" the emotions until the feelings lessen in intensity, as opposed to pushing them away or obsessing on them.

Cultivating Happiness: This is the concept of learning concrete techniques to increase our experiences of peace, joy, and gratitude. Considerations include five steps to live a happier life.

Radical Acceptance: This is the concept of learning how to embrace the world as it is and still move forward in your life. Considerations include how to embrace the "willingness" to participate in life and work with your current circumstances.

Distract and Self-Soothe: This is the concept of learning how to identify being overwhelmed by emotion. Considerations include how to use new tools to distract yourself from overwhelming emotions until they decrease, and learning techniques to support yourself during intense pain.

These core DBT skills can offer newfound hope, freedom, and practical self-care skills for managing many of the thoughts, feelings, and responses that arise in early recovery.

CHAPTER NINE
Spirituality and Recovery

Spiritual relationships can sometimes change as you develop in your recovery. Some people might begin the journey with a belief in God, or some might be atheists or agnostics. Still others may be undecided, believing in the force of the universe or in nature as a higher power. The list can be endless according to each person's experiences, beliefs, and perspectives.

Your openness to and cultivation of any relationship, including a spiritual relationship, can take many forms, be it through prayer and meditation, reconnecting with nature, formal religion, expressing gratitude, or a simple consideration that there is a power greater than you.

Spirit[115]

1. The principle of conscious life; the vital principle in humans, animating the body or mediating between body and soul.

Spirituality[116]

1. The quality or fact of being spiritual.
2. The unseen or immaterial nature.
3. Spiritual character as shown in thought, actions, life, etc.; spiritual tendency or tone.

Religion[117]

1. A set of beliefs concerning the cause, nature, and purpose of the universe, usually involving devotional and ritual observances, and often containing a moral code governing the conduct of human affairs.

2. A specific fundamental set of beliefs and practices generally agreed upon by a number of persons or sects. (Examples: Christianity, Buddhism)

3. The body of persons adhering to a particular set of beliefs and practices. (Example: a world council of religions)

4. The practice of religious beliefs; ritual observance of faith.

Spirituality and the Twelve Steps

In twelve-step programs, it is not uncommon to hear phrases such as "the spiritual part of the program" or "this is a spiritual program." All twelve-step programs clearly separate themselves from religion, while being equally clear that spirituality plays an important role in recovery and a healthy life.[118]

Spirituality through the Twelve Steps and Twelve Traditions uses four simple yet distinct concepts.[119] These concepts are presented as changes that occur along the road to what is referred to as a spiritual awakening. The result of this spiritual experience is described as the result of working the Twelve Steps.

These four concepts leading to a spiritual experience can be simply defined as shifts from relating to life in a negative way to a positive way:

Fear	Trust
Self-pity	Gratitude
Resentment	Acceptance
Dishonesty	Honesty

Please take a few moments to consider where you see yourself on the continuum of these spiritual concepts. You can use any situation to ask yourself, "In this situation, am I fearful? Do I trust? Or perhaps, am I somewhere in the middle?"

Fear	Trust
Self-pity	Gratitude
Resentment	Acceptance
Dishonesty	Honesty

Write about the idea of spirituality as a part of recovery.

_____

_____

_____

Spirituality through Mindful Activity

Surroundings Awareness[120]

Here is a small exercise. Take a look around you. Don't look for something or in a direction because you need to go there. Just look to see what is. Let your thoughts slow down as you name to yourself what you see.

Start with the big picture: computer, desk, walls, bookshelf, and curtains. Then begin to take in smaller details: your own hands, your fingers, what they're touching. Take in the differing shades of color and light. Use your other senses, too. Do the lights make a buzzing sound? Do you hear a bird outside?

Sometimes the stress of life is such that our thoughts won't let us slow down no matter what. Many have found that there are countless spiritually based practices that tend to support easing the distress of their minds.

Yoga

Yoga is a physical, mental, and spiritual discipline, originating in ancient India. Its goal is the attainment of a state of perfect spiritual insight and tranquility. The word is associated with meditative practices in Hinduism and Buddhism.

The Sanskrit word *yoga* has the literal meaning of "yoke," from the root word *yuj*, meaning to join, to unite, or to attach, and it is a term for a system of abstract meditation or mental focus through positions of the body commonly referred to as poses.

The goals of yoga are varied and range from improving health to achieving mindfulness or calming energy. The ultimate goal of the yoga process is to enjoy an internal relationship with yourself as a complete person: mind, body, and spirit.[121, 122]

Mindful Walking

In this mindfulness activity, you bring your full attention to the simple act of walking as you become consciously aware of and absorbed in the movement of your body as you walk. The great thing about this activity is that you can practice it any time you walk, at a moment's notice.

Any Mindful Activity

Any activity you can think of can be used as a focal point for mindfulness training. Even the most mundane, everyday habit can be transformed into a mindful activity that comes alive with newness, presence, and power when you practice mindfulness. The secret is to place all of your attention on what it is you are doing. Be completely in the now.[123]

Any activity of daily life can become a support for mindfulness when it is undertaken with the intention of developing concentration, clarity, compassion, or insight. A few tips may include the following:

1. Choose an activity you enjoy.

2. Determine to bring your full attention to it.

3. Slowly, carefully, and mindfully begin. Stay relaxed and give your wholehearted attention to what you are doing.

4. Whenever your attention wanders or fades, gently return to being fully aware of what you are doing. If tension arises, relax and smile playfully to yourself.

5. When the activity or designated time period is over, pause for a few moments to reflect on the new richness you have discovered in this familiar activity.

Everything we do throughout the day, even the tasks that we do not like, can become a tool for developing our minds and deepening our concentration. Mindful eating and mindful listening are common mindful activities taught and used.[124]

Spirituality of Personal Values

A personal value is a belief, a mission, or a philosophy that is meaningful or motivating to you. Whether you are consciously aware of them or not, every individual has a core set of personal values.[125] Values can range from common things such as placing importance in family, friendships, honesty, hard work, timeliness, marriage, trust, and so forth.

Personal values can be the foundation and guide to peace, confidence, and contentment when your behavior, thoughts, and actions are consistent with your values. Personal values can also be a source of confusion, shame, and regret when your actions, situations, thoughts, and behaviors are outside of your personal value system.

Please take a minute to list a few of your own personal values. You may want to consider how the use of alcohol and/or other drugs may have affected these.

_____

_____

_____

_____

Personal Standards of Conduct

Personal standards of conduct are the self-imposed standards you set for the way you conduct yourself. There are also external standards of conduct you may be obligated to maintain for your school, friendships, workplace, religious practice, and certainly from the legal system in the form of laws.

Not everyone will hold the same standards. Each person will have standards concerning manners, clothing, hygiene, sex, work, and so forth.

Personal standards of conduct, much like personal values, can either bring confidence, peace, and contentment if kept, or prompt anxiety, shame, and health consequences if your conduct is inconsistent with your personal standards.[126]

Please take a minute to list a few standards of conduct that guide your day-to-day activities.

_____

_____

_____

_____

_____

_____

Reflect on Your Beliefs

What beliefs do you hold about religion, spirituality, or a higher power? Answer the following questions in order to reflect on your beliefs.

- Do you believe in God or a higher power? _____

- Do you believe that spiritual growth is important for you? _____

- Do you believe there is an afterlife? _____

- Do you belong to any religious or spiritual organization?_____

- Do your spiritual beliefs affect the way you live your life? _____

- How frequently do you attend religious services? _____

- Do you pray? How often? _____

- When you have emotional problems, do you turn to your spiritual or religious community for help? _____

- How would you define religion?_____
  _____
  _____

- How would you define spirituality? _____
  _____
  _____

- Do you see any benefits to a relationship with a higher power? If so, what would those benefits be? _____
  _____

- Do you see yourself as a religious or spiritual person? If so, in what way? _____
  _____
  _____

- Are you affiliated with a religious or spiritual denomination or community? If so, which one?
  _____

- Has living with co-occurring disorders affected you religiously or spiritually? If so, in what way?
  _____
  _____

- Has your religion or spirituality been involved in the way you have coped with your co-occurring disorders? If so, in what way?_____
  _____
  _____

Religion and Spirituality Are Not the Same

Spirituality refers to a search for meaning, purpose, or direction of life. It can be in relation to a higher power, universal spirit, or God. Spirituality reflects a search for the sacred, whereas religion refers to participation in a social institution with its accompanying beliefs, practices, symbols, and rituals.

Religion and spirituality can play a significant role in helping people to cope with and protect against stress. Individuals who use religious and spiritual coping efforts demonstrate a greater physical and emotional well-being.

Exploring Sources of Inner Strength

Sometimes exploring your views about courage, peace, or purpose in life can start you on the path to exploring faith and spirituality.[127] For instance, consider the following questions:

- When you are afraid or in pain, how do you find comfort and solace?
- What sustains you in the midst of your troubles?
- From what sources do you draw the strength and courage to go on? What are the deepest questions your situation has raised for you?
- How has this situation shaken your faith in yourself?
- When in your life have you experienced forgiveness?

The topic of spirituality and religion is enormously diverse. There are different views and practices across a broad spectrum. Most people report that these concepts, beliefs, and experiences play a large part in helping them maintain their recovery. It's good to keep an open mind when investigating spirituality and religion.[128]

Notes

CHAPTER TEN

Relationships: Building a Support Network that Heals and Nourishes

Relationships and Recovery

Living with a co-occurring disorder and active symptoms of addiction can frequently place barriers between you and your ability to connect with other people in an authentic and meaningful way. Depression, anxiety, and behaviors associated with addiction can distance you from others and from yourself, and they can leave you feeling isolated and emotionally bankrupt. Like for so many people, learning to live in healthy authentic relationships may not be something you have ever done. Developing a willingness to be open to this aspect of recovery can offer support, hope, integrity, and a sense of well-being.

In many ways, recovery may even be said to be all about relationships. Think about it. What would recovery be like in isolation? And, even in isolation, you would benefit from developing a healthy relationship with yourself in order to manage day-to-day life and understand your needs. It seems that no matter how you slice it, recovery is all about living in healthy relationships.

Think back to when you started the journey of your recovery; how much of your motivation to make changes was about your connections to other people? Perhaps your relationship with your family was strained or your friends had become distant or concerned. As you begin to move forward in recovery, you may find that for as many times as relationships and connections have been positive, they also may have been frustrating or disappointing. Learning effective relational skills can be a key to recovery and healthy relationships.

Developing Your Relationship Skills: Clarifying Feelings

In early recovery, it can be challenging to begin to identify your emotions,[129] let alone communicate them. Many new to recovery have felt numb to their emotions for years, and allowing themselves to feel again might seem like a new experience. It is often helpful to be patient with yourself as you begin to feel your emotions and learn to name the sensations or body cues that entail what you are feeling.

While it is possible to experience a full range of emotions or feelings, the range is a mixture, or varying intensity, of the five core emotions: anger, sadness, joy, fear, and shame.

Communicating effectively in recovery is about sharing your feelings. As simple as that sounds, it can be difficult to do. It can be hard to open yourself up to trusting others to be respectful of your feelings. This trust and the vulnerability it brings are often the very things that create authentic relationships. We encourage you to start simply: You don't have to dress it up or talk around it or play games; just state your real feelings (mad, sad, glad, scared, or ashamed).

For example, when you are communicating with your spouse about him or her coming home late, you could say, "I feel scared when you come home late. I also feel hurt that you don't think to call and let me know you're running late."

Those are feeling statements. They are difficult to argue with because they are "I" statements, and you are the only one who can relate what you feel. The focus is your personal feelings.

If you communicated the same statement as an opinion about the other person's behavior, the focus shifts from the facts of how you feel to an arguable opinion: "It's irresponsible and inconsiderate of you to come home late like that and not call me."

You might believe you are communicating feelings in this example; however, what is conveyed is opinion. You may hope that the implied feelings of fear and hurt are recognizable to the other person, but those feelings may not have been communicated.

> **Tip:** It is helpful to use an "I" statement rather than a "You" statement. For example: "I feel sad," rather than "You made me feel sad."

With practice, you may come to realize that you don't have to defend your feelings, say why you have a feeling, or explain them at all. Feelings just "are." You can state them, and the other person can choose to respond by asking for more information, or respond however they wish.

By learning healthy ways to share your feelings and avoid hurtful opinions, judgments, or accusations, you can learn to communicate with the intention of removing any barriers that might make it difficult for others to hear what you are communicating.

Consider a recent interaction you may have had. What were the core emotions (anger, sadness, joy, fear, or shame)? Did you use "I" statements?

_____

_____

_____

_____

Developing Your Relationship Skills: Being "in Relationship"

Before attempting to apply what you are learning to the various categories of relationships, such as the relationship with yourself (body, mind, spirit), your sexual partner, your family, alcohol and/or other drugs, gambling, food, success, etc., it may be important to have a clear definition of what it means to have a relationship.

It is more accurate to ask, "What does it mean to be 'in relationship' to a person, place, or thing?" Relationships require your participation, whether that participation is in entering into a new relationship, being in an existing one, or a refusal to engage in a relationship. It is the participation that places you there. Learning to identify healthy, reciprocal, and supportive relationships is a skill unto itself. The acronym SHARE is a way to recall the description of what we might strive for in a healthy relationship. SHARE stands for safety, honesty, acceptance, respect, and enjoyment.

- **Safety:** In a healthy relationship, you feel safe. You don't worry that you will be harmed physically or emotionally, and you don't feel inclined to use or be fearful of physical or emotional violence against yourself or others. You can comfortably express opinions, be authentic, try new experiences, and change your mind about something without fear.

- **Honesty:** You don't feel inclined to hide or keep secrets. You can express your thoughts without fear of censure or ridicule. You can admit to being wrong. You have the skills to resolve disagreements by talking and behaving honestly.

- **Acceptance:** You accept the situation as it is. The relationship is not about "fixing" the person, place, or thing to be more than it is. Others in the relationship share this acceptance. You receive and give acceptance. You are mindful of and appreciate unique qualities. If you are not accepted by, or do not accept the qualities of the people, place, or thing you are engaged in relationship with, you may want to examine your motivations for participating.

- **Respect:** There is mutual high regard. You do not feel superior or inferior in important ways. There is mutual respect; you and others have the right to have separate opinions and ideas. This doesn't mean you tolerate everything. Setting limits is a sign of self-respect.
- **Enjoyment:** A healthy relationship isn't just about how you treat others, or how they treat you; it also has to be enjoyable. You feel energized and alive in the relationship. You can play and laugh. You have fun.

Regardless of whether the relationship is with yourself, a romantic partner, friend, or family member, the SHARE acronym can be a helpful tool to measure if the relationship is healthy.

Relationships Come in All Shapes and Sizes

Your Relationship with Yourself

What does it mean to have a relationship with yourself? It simply means treating yourself with the care you would give to a loved one. Taking care of yourself means caring for your body, your mind, and your spirit.

When you have co-occurring disorders, it can become easy to let yourself feel defined by your symptoms and struggles. In recovery, it can be difficult to know or remember who you are. Sometimes, the difficulty can be letting go of the way you viewed yourself in active illness. Other times, it can be about dealing with the new feelings when symptoms are lessened and old skills (unhealthy coping mechanisms) are no longer used.

Whatever you find yourself to be in recovery, developing a relationship with yourself can become natural. Mindfully caring for your whole self is the first essential relationship you may build in recovery.

Developing a Spiritual Relationship

Discussing the spiritual aspect of yourself can be a touchy subject for some. If this is a difficult topic for you, please allow yourself the time to explore the spiritual aspects of recovery at your own pace.

Spiritual relationships come in many different shapes and sizes. They are as varied as the people in them. Spiritual relationships often change with your ability to engage and participate. You may begin your journey in recovery at a place where you are unable to engage and participate fully in a spiritual relationship due to symptoms of mental health concerns or addiction. You might begin your journey with a belief in God or as a hard-line atheist or agnostic. Or, you may be undecided, believing only in the force of the universe or in nature as a higher power.

The openness to and cultivation of any relationship, including a spiritual relationship, can take many forms, be it through prayer and meditation, active mindfulness, reconnecting with nature, formal religion, expressing gratitude, or a simple acceptance that there is a power greater than yourself.

Romantic and Sexual Relationships

Romantic and sexual relationships can sometimes be a small part of life, and they sure can generate some powerful emotions. Romantic and sexual relationships can be challenging in early recovery simply because they involve so many aspects of what makes us human: emotional, mental, physical, and spiritual.

When it comes to entering into a new romantic or sexual relationship, it is often recommended to avoid these new encounters in early recovery, or at the very least be cautious and mindful regarding them. This recommendation is based on the experience of many who have relapsed after entering or exiting a new relationship. Many reported that their focus on romantic and/or sexual relations occupied their time, and they lost interest in establishing their recovery.

Tip: If you are seeking to enter or exit a romantic relationship so that it will "fix your problems," "fill the void," or "make you whole," then you might want to consider focusing on first establishing a relationship with yourself and your recovery for a while.

Relationships with Friends

Friends can play an important role in our lives in a positive way, and sometimes in a negative way. The term "peer pressure" is sometimes associated with youth; however, the concept can exist in all relationships. In recovery, you will often hear it said that you should stick with the "winners." By considering this suggestion, peer influence can then be extremely supportive to your recovery. Developing these positive relationships can result in positive outcomes.

By the same token, developing or staying in relationships with people who are drinking alcohol and/or using other drugs can result in the same behaviors and results, including relapse. It is often difficult, especially for young people, to let go of old friends with whom they drank or used drugs. And some of these friends may be supportive in other ways. Labeling all old friends as "using buddies" is not always the answer. It is important to determine if friends are capable of supporting you and your recovery. It is also important to be sure that you are comfortable navigating through negative peer influence.

Family Relationships

Family relationships in recovery can be stressful. Families living with the presence of co-occurring disorders often have high levels of stress and confusion. Families may be dealing with many emotional, psychological, and behavioral issues, as well as a long history of family dynamics. Such issues are all too often characteristic of the family system—first from the member with the co-occurring disorder and often from others within the family as they struggle to communicate. Living with these experiences over time can put the entire family in unusual circumstances.

Normal routines are difficult to maintain when they are continually interrupted by unexpected or even frightening experiences that are part of living with unmanaged co-occurring symptoms. Inconsistencies between the perceptions and spoken words or behaviors of the struggling family member, and those of the remaining family, can be confusing. Such situations can lead to mistrust, blame, and resentment.

The lack of consistency and safety in the family may lead otherwise healthy family members to become traumatized to varying degrees by the experience. Members of the family may seek to maintain a balance by avoiding, manipulating, or even denying the reality of the addiction or illness in their family. This continual response can leave the family minimizing the situation. The entire family system may become absorbed in managing the addiction and illness and the daily strain it takes.

Further compromising the system is that both mental health and addiction issues are more likely if your parents or grandparents struggled with them; they can be hereditary disorders. The genetic link may mean that there are multiple family members struggling with either mental health and/or addiction issues. Research has long supported the higher incidence of mental health disorders among those with affected family members.[130]

It can be difficult for some family members to accept that all of the answers are not known about these disorders. Why some people from the same families have similar experiences within that family and are without addiction or mental health concerns remains a question.

Write about your current relationships and the effects of your co-occurring disorders on those relationships.

Do you think there is an effect? How? _____

_____

_____

_____

_____

Do you think the relationship would change if you were in full recovery with your co-occurring symptoms? How? _____

_____

_____

Understanding the Effects of Co-occurring Disorders and Relationships

Co-occurring disorders can affect not only your life, but the lives of those around you.[131] They can affect your ability to work, go to school, and interact with others, and they can impair your most basic functions. Relationships with others can be harmed and destroyed due to untreated mental health symptoms, behaviors, and addiction. It can be easy to become focused on avoiding symptoms, hiding symptoms, and/or seeking out substances. Mental health issues and active addiction can become so much the norm that you may be unaware of the effect on others and are honestly confused by others around you having an issue with your behaviors. Co-occurring symptoms can even become so powerful that you seemingly disregard everything else.

The disruption and distraction of day-to-day priorities for you and those around you can damage your relationships and delay or irrevocably damage your hope for future plans. While no one intends to end up with no options and no support, what starts as a simple escape can develop into an addiction, leaving you with more problems on top of the ones you were attempting to escape. Whether you are the product of a family riddled with addiction or have no genetic history of substance use, the potential damage to relationships is a matter to consider.

Identifying Abusive Relationships

Signs of an abusive relationship include blaming, belittling, controlling freedom, excessive guilt, intentionally shaming, intimidation, name-calling, jealousy, and violence.[132] An abusive relationship is in direct contrast to a healthy relationship. Such relationships depend on fear, control, and lack of respect. Often, an abusive relationship may be less threatening at times or may be interspersed with periods of remorse, repair, or even intimacy. Typically, one partner does most of the abusing while the other lives in resentment or fear; however, mutually abusive relationships do exist.

Signs of an Abusive Relationship

There is a good chance you are in an abusive or unhealthy relationship if you find yourself contemplating the possibility based on these descriptions.

Do you:

- Feel afraid of your partner much of the time?
- Avoid certain topics out of fear of angering your partner?
- Feel that you can't do anything right for your partner?
- Believe that you deserve to be hurt or mistreated?
- Wonder if you're the one who is crazy?
- Feel emotionally numb or helpless?

Does your partner:

- Humiliate or yell at you?
- Criticize you and put you down?
- Treat you so badly that you're embarrassed for your friends or family to see?
- Ignore or put down your opinions or accomplishments?
- Blame you for his or her abusive behavior?
- See you as property or a sex object, rather than as a person?

Does your partner:

- Have a bad and unpredictable temper?
- Hurt you or threaten to hurt or kill you?
- Threaten to take your children away or harm them?
- Threaten to commit suicide if you leave?
- Force you to have sex?
- Destroy your belongings?

Does your partner:

- Act excessively jealous and possessive?
- Control where you go or what you do?
- Keep you from seeing your friends or family?
- Limit your access to money, the phone, or the car?
- Constantly check up on you?

Often people in abusive relationships may be aware that the relationship is not in their best interest, but they are afraid to leave it for many reasons. Some reasons are practical, like finances, shared parenting, or extended family supports, while others may be a product of the relationship itself, like wondering if being alone would be worse, or if anyone else would want to be in a relationship with her or him. Some people in abusive relationships have grown up in a home with unhealthy relationships, causing the current abuse to feel normal or familiar. While it may be difficult to leave an abusive relationship and heal the damage, doing so offers opportunities to gain emotional distance and perspective, as well as the potential to make a different life choice.

If you are in an abusive situation, seek assistance as soon as possible.

Addiction and Family Roles

Family roles are simply the way the family views and interacts with specific family members. If a family were a Broadway play, then the family role would be the character each individual plays on stage. True to any theatrical production, family members can share parts, or play more than one. Basic family roles can be broken down into six distinct "characters" that family members unconsciously act out and with whom many people identify:[133]

- **The Hero:** The perfectionist who needs to make everyone and everything look good, refuses to acknowledge problems, and pretends problems don't exist. Despite the exterior display of cheer, the hero is plagued by feelings of guilt, shame, and fear.

- **The Mascot:** The comedian in the family who often uses silliness and off-color humor about people or situations to distract others and him- or herself from feelings of shame, embarrassment, and anger.

- **The Lost Child:** The quiet one who doesn't like to make waves and avoids confrontation to the point of giving up his or her needs. This family member often hides within the family chaos, voices no need or distress, and secretly feels lonely, neglected, angry, and guilty.

- **The Scapegoat:** The troublemaker, the one who acts out in order to divert attention away from the real problem. He or she is often the recipient of the family blame and may be seen as the reason for the family's struggles. He or she rebels against true feelings of shame, guilt, and emptiness through attention-seeking.

- **The Caretaker/Enabler:** The family member who tries to keep everybody happy by meeting everyone's needs. He or she often makes excuses for others' behavior, puts on airs of a problem-free family for outside people, and denies underlying fears of inadequacy and helplessness by fixing others and making themselves needed by others.

- **The Addict:** The elephant in the living room. The family tiptoes around him or her, unsure of what to expect. Family members may gauge the mood or sobriety of the addict before making plans. He or she avoids emotional connections through alcohol and/or other drugs. Although labeled as the family addict, he or she is often not the only person in this type of family unit who needs treatment for addictive behaviors.

Family roles may be useful in helping to identify traits among family members, to normalize the happenings within families that may have previously been unmentionable family secrets, and to open conversations about personal interactions that might otherwise be difficult to initiate. A family system such as this may be seen in other close-knit social situations, such as among friends at work and school.

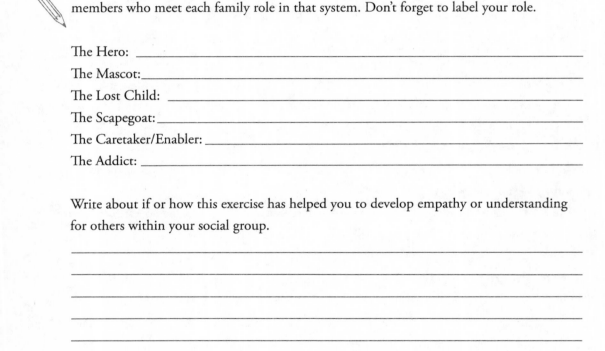

In the spaces below, consider one family system (work, home, school, etc.) and identify the members who meet each family role in that system. Don't forget to label your role.

The Hero: _____

The Mascot:_____

The Lost Child: _____

The Scapegoat:_____

The Caretaker/Enabler: _____

The Addict: _____

Write about if or how this exercise has helped you to develop empathy or understanding for others within your social group.

_____

_____

_____

_____

_____

_____

_____

You will have many opportunities during your treatment to explore relationships and family dynamics. Sometimes looking at these situations can be uncomfortable. The end result, however, can move you closer to creating a solid foundation for your recovery.

Life Skills

Life skills are sometimes referred to as psychosocial abilities and can include both day-to-day living, as well as emotional skills. These skill sets can be defined and learned, and they may be related to many areas of life, such as personal, interpersonal, social, cognitive (thinking), affective (dealing with emotion), or universal (day-to-day) skills.[134]

Day-to-Day Living

Life skills, as they relate to recovery from addiction and mental health challenges, generally are about basic day-to-day living skills. These practical skills often pertain to food, shelter, health, and financial income. Tackling these needs may lead to the individual's ability to identify and promote internal change. This ability involves the emotional side, including self-esteem, socializing, tolerance, self-awareness, problem-solving, and hope. Sometimes, individuals who struggle with long-term addiction lose the ability to provide and maintain for their basic needs. The loss of this skill can create numerous problems, including poor health, low self-worth, a failure syndrome, isolation, depression, legal concerns, and homelessness.

Developing life-skill sets in early recovery can sometimes feel childlike. And for many, this perspective is often true. Let's take a look at someone's history to get an idea of their challenges in recovery:

Sam is a twenty-eight year old, single male who started drinking alcohol and experimenting with other drugs around sixteen years old. He finished high school and some college. He held numerous jobs; however, most of the time his income was insufficient and required assistance from others to meet his basic needs. As the years passed, his ability to manage his life had declined. Most of the time, he would sit and drink or use other drugs. His daily use of practical skills was limited.

His friends and family were concerned; however, nothing really changed. At twenty-eight, he found himself in jail and alone. There was no one to help him out of that situation. The court sent him to treatment. He completed their recovery program and was placed on probation.

Sam decided to live on his own believing that completing a recovery program restored previous skills and prepared him for what he would need. He later reported an immense amount of fear and anxiety. He stated he struggled just to leave his apartment to get food. The idea of getting a job was out of the question. He said his personal hygiene was poor. Sam had not anticipated that he would struggle to re-enter life as a sober/drug-free, productive, and contributing member of the community. His lack of confidence and shame in not having the skills to manage his life led to months of isolation and eventually to drink and use drugs again. He sought some help. Confused about the situation, he shared his fears and embarrassment about not having the skills to manage his basic needs. Sam was reassured that many people, after years of being under the influence, have struggled with the same challenges. A plan was initiated to help him develop a few basic living skills that would assist him in maintaining his recovery.

Please take a moment to reflect on Sam's situation and review some of the life skills categories below. Do you think Sam would relate to any of these? Can you identify with any of these?

Housing (shelter):

Has adequate housing that is financially supported by the individual who maintains the house with utilities and cleanliness.

_____

_____

Food:

Selects, purchases, prepares, and eats nutritional meals.

_____

_____

Clothing:

Maintains good hygiene: bathing, dental, vision, clothing.

_____

_____

Employment:

Secures and maintains adequate employment to meet present needs.

_____

_____

Communication and interpersonal skills:

Gathers and expresses thoughts and ideas with others.

_____

_____

Sociability:

Initiates new relations and has the ability to maintain these.

_____

_____

Coping skills:

Manages various degrees of stress.

_____

_____

Problem-solving and decision-making:

Manages numerous tasks comfortably and makes decisions based on evaluations.

_____

_____

Creative thinking:

Considers options comfortably, thinks without fear.

_____

_____

Self-awareness:

Has the ability to see oneself in the context of relations, thought, actions, and outcomes.

_____

_____

Sometimes we think of a life skill as a tool or practice we engage in that helps manage our lives. For example: opening and managing a bank account; buying and maintaining a car (insurance, registration, maintenance, gas, etc.); washing, drying, and ironing clothes; obtaining housing and utilities; cleaning your teeth or going to the dentist; having a physical; cleaning the house; opening the mail; taking care of legal concerns; and so forth. These are all basic living skills. Without acquiring and maintaining these, life can become challenging.

Emotional Skills

There are also other types of life skills that can support your recovery. These are called emotional skills. These skills are often lost or suffer a significant decline during addiction or mental health challenges.

The following emotional skills, suggested to contribute to the quality of one's life, were discussed during the United Nations Inter-Agency meeting in Geneva, Switzerland, which included the World Health Organization and the Department of Mental Health. We have offered this list simply to recognize that numerous organizations in the world highly value the education of both basic and emotional skill sets.

Dealing with Conflict that Cannot Be Resolved	Sociability	Self-Esteem
Dealing with authority	Solving problems	Making and keeping friends/relationships
Cooperation	Self-awareness	Clarification of values
Creative thinking	Dealing with stress	Negotiation
Decision-making	Resisting pressure	Coping with disappointment
Critical thinking	Planning ahead	Tolerance
Time management	Empathy	Trust
Assertiveness	Dealing with emotions	Sharing
Respect	Active listening	Self-advocacy

Adapted from the work of the WHO Partners in Life Skills Education

You may see the term "skill set" used extensively throughout this book. The term usually reflects the evidence that there is a solution to a problem. A skill set is simply a tool waiting to be understood and practiced.

Throughout your treatment experience, you will begin to explore the actions, ideas, and abilities that can increase the quality of life through skill sets. The benefits of considering, learning, and developing basic day-to-day and emotional skills supports recovery and can improve the overall quality of your life.

CHAPTER ELEVEN
Preventing Relapse

With co-occurring disorders, you have two or more separate, but highly interwoven disorders, resulting in several potential relapse dynamics.

How a relapse may present itself and the symptoms or warning signs you experience differ from individual to individual, as well as from diagnosis to diagnosis. It is important to be mindful that you may be further along in the recovery process with one diagnosis than the other. And, because of the interwoven nature of your disorders, relapse risk is based on the *whole* of you, not just *part*. For example, you may not have used alcohol or other drugs for a significant time and may be in the active stage of change in your recovery; however, you may have avoided addressing your mental health symptoms (such as anxiety or depression), hoping these feelings would fix themselves by you staying abstinent and in recovery. The ongoing discouragement concerning the persistence of these symptoms may be a potential stumbling block to recovery.[135] Relapse prevention, and early intervention if relapse does occur, focuses on every aspect of your recovery.

The beginning of a relapse often involves the return of symptoms, like slipping into old, negative thought patterns or unhealthy coping skills. It can also include a full-fledged return to previous levels of the use of alcohol and/or other drugs, or the experience of significant mental health symptoms.

If a relapse does occur, it is important to get help immediately and to avoid giving up on recovery and yourself. When a relapse is immediately addressed, it is easier to review your recovery plan in order to recognize what happened and how to strengthen your recovery process.[136]

It is imperative that you guard against dynamics that worsen the relapse and immediately reconnect with your support system. Some people who experience the onset of relapse may think, *Well, I've had one drink. I might as well just keep drinking*, or *I'm feeling better now. I don't need my medication anymore.*

Don't fall into this trap. Here, relapse is not addressed with recovery, but with continued relapse. Here, the relapse is justified. In this trap, you surrender to your old pre-recovery patterns.

Relapse, and/or signs of relapse, can be a learning tool. Having a relapse does not mean you have failed or that you will never be successful in your recovery. You may have already experienced several relapses and, as a result, are now ready to learn how to recognize and address your triggers and symptoms. At this stage, you can use your relapse experience to develop and apply effective coping skills, tools, and supports. You may be more aware that you need to develop a maintenance routine and have an awareness of warning signs. It does not mean relapse is inevitable, but if it occurs, it can strengthen your wisdom and willingness to take action to protect your recovery. It is a *normal* part of the process of recovery to experience warning signs of a relapse and potentially a relapse.[137]

Warning Signs

Warning signs in recovery are symptoms or clues that let you know something is about to be dangerous. If you can learn to recognize a warning sign early, then you can make a U-turn or take a detour before any serious damage has been done. As you become adept at recognizing your warning signs and taking actions to stop them, you will be able to focus on the things in your life that you wish to accomplish.

Consider this: You are driving and see a sign stating, "Road Closed 100 Feet." You may be frustrated by the inconvenience or annoyed that you can't go that way or that your favorite drive is not available; yet, you still may be grateful for the warning. The sign gives you the opportunity to slow down and not injure yourself or damage your car. You can make a U-turn or take a detour and find another way to get where you are going, or go somewhere else altogether.

Some days may seem worse than others because of these warning signs. Some days it may feel like your addiction or mental health issues control your thoughts, emotions, and behaviors. As you learn how to recognize and address your warning signs, this can change. Each time you successfully read and navigate through a warning sign, you are making progress that can help you along the way; each day can get better than the last one. You most likely will experience fewer and fewer dangerous roads as you establish a safe, recovery-focused lifestyle. And, you can continue to develop your skills to work and gain more control of your life.

Recognizing Warning Signs

There is an old saying that "every *problem* is actually an *opportunity*." If you apply this to your recovery, then every warning sign is actually an opportunity for you to prevent relapse, make progress, strengthen your recovery, and feel better about yourself. The earlier you recognize a warning sign, the easier it is to take action.

One important thing you can do to prevent relapse is to recognize a warning sign for what it is, an *opportunity* to do the following:

- Stop your relapse in its tracks
- Ask for help
- Enhance your recovery
- Understand your symptoms better

Subtle Warning Signs

Subtle warning signs range from a change in attitude to a change in behavior that might seem minor or unimportant, but could lead to more obvious warnings or high-risk situations.[138] Subtle warning signs are not easily detected so it is important to really know and understand your own subtle warning signs. If subtle warning signs are monitored in your daily journal and caught early, the chance of preventing relapse can be very good.

Some examples of subtle warning signs appear in the following statements:

"When my sponsor asked what I did today, I left out the part where I visited a friend who still uses."

"Even though I take my meds every day, I keep thinking, 'Why do I have to take this stuff? It isn't even working.'"

"I hate my job. I don't really try to get fired, but I am not trying to do it well. I don't care whether or not I get fired from my job."

"I find myself avoiding people I used to be comfortable with."

"Often, I wake up in the middle of the night and can't get back to sleep. My mind just won't be quiet."

Checklist of Subtle Warning Signs

Personal Thoughts and Behaviors

- ☐ Experiencing confusing and disorienting thoughts
- ☐ Having more negative and depressing thoughts
- ☐ Missing your "former" life of using drugs and/or alcohol

225

☐ An overactive mind or racing thoughts

☐ Thinking you cannot change

☐ Feeling more sad and depressed than usual

☐ Feeling more anxious, afraid, nervous, or fearful than usual

☐ Feeling more bored, restless, and listless than usual

☐ Shifts in mood from one extreme to another

☐ Experiencing manic tendencies; feeling indestructible, and on top of the world

Medication and Treatment

☐ Losing interest in your recovery plan

☐ Not asking for help when you are sick regarding medication management

☐ Missing scheduled appointments with your counselor, doctor, or sponsor

☐ Complaining about having to take your medication

☐ Forgetting or skipping medication doses

☐ Complaining about side effects even though medication hasn't changed

☐ Refusing to take medication

Family and Friends

☐ Being dishonest to family and friends

☐ Arguing and getting angry with others more than usual

☐ Being more irritated or frustrated than usual

☐ Yelling, screaming, or cursing more than usual

☐ Losing interest in associating with other people

☐ Losing contact with sober friends

☐ Continuing to spend time with people who are using

☐ Isolating yourself

Daily Activities

☐ Missing work

☐ Losing interest in your hobbies or fun activities

☐ Losing interest in what happens in your life

☐ Sudden changes in job or living arrangement

☐ Going back to your old stomping grounds

☐ Not going to meetings

☐ Not calling or seeing your sponsor

☐ Allowing yourself to get bored and lonely

☐ Going to clubs, bars, or other places that promote risky behaviors such as drinking alcohol and/or using other drugs

Eating and Sleeping

☐ Eating more or less than usual

☐ Smoking more than usual

☐ Drinking more caffeine or eating more sweets/sugar than usual

☐ Having trouble sleeping or getting to sleep

☐ Having trouble getting back to sleep if awakened

☐ Sleeping more or less than usual

☐ Sleeping during the day

Subtle warning signs are difficult to spot because they have little or no noticeable consequence in the moment. They can and might build to create relapse, but in the moment, they can be easy for you to dismiss as harmless. By utilizing a daily recovery plan, sharing openly with other people in recovery, and surrounding yourself with support, you can minimize the confusion caused by these subtle warning signs.

Obvious Warning Signs

Obvious warning signs are those that can easily be detected and may lead to high-risk situations where you are likely to relapse. It is critical to recognize these warning signs and take immediate action to prevent a relapse from happening. The more obvious the warning sign, the more at risk for relapse you are.

Here are some examples of thoughts or statements that contain obvious warning signs.

"When I get off work, I drive around the old neighborhood park to see if my friends are still using and hanging out."

"I like the way I feel without my medication, so I stopped taking it."

"I can't relate to the people in my meetings. What can they do for me anyway? I haven't been in a few weeks, and I'm not going back."

"I am getting so much more done because I haven't slept in three days."

"I'm going to a party on Saturday, and there'll be drinking and drugs there, but I'm going anyway. I have been to the club three times and been fine."

Checklist of Obvious Warning Signs

Personal Thoughts and Behaviors

- ☐ Thoughts of harming yourself or suicide
- ☐ Talking with slurred speech or much faster or slower than usual
- ☐ Changing the way you dress that is out of character for you or meant to convince others you are doing better or worse than you are feeling
- ☐ Mood shifts from depression to frantic energy for no apparent reason
- ☐ Extremely depressed; feeling doomed and without hope
- ☐ Feelings of worthlessness and hopelessness
- ☐ Physical symptoms, such as severe headaches, nausea, vomiting, etc.
- ☐ Thinking that having "just one" (of whatever substance you have used in the past) is not a problem
- ☐ Glorifying days of using substances or telling "war stories" about alcohol or other drug experiences

Medication and Treatment

- ☐ Discontinuing meeting with your counselor, doctor, or sponsor
- ☐ Not refilling or taking your medications
- ☐ Missing support group meetings or mental health group meetings
- ☐ Using over-the-counter drugs irresponsibly
- ☐ Not taking your medications as prescribed or adjusting your dose

Family and Friends

- ☐ Deceiving others regularly
- ☐ Experiencing high levels of anger and frustration for no apparent reason
- ☐ Threatening to hurt others
- ☐ Physically inducing pain or discomfort to yourself or another person
- ☐ Isolating yourself, avoiding people
- ☐ Avoiding people in your recovery network

Daily Activities

☐ Stealing or breaking the law

☐ Changing jobs, living arrangements, relationships, etc., all at once

☐ Having extreme increase or decrease in energy level

☐ Not going to work or school

☐ Obvious change in hygiene, such as not bathing or changing clothes each day

☐ Ignoring your responsibilities, such as childcare, pets, or commitments you made to others

☐ Difficulty taking care of yourself

Eating and Sleeping

☐ Interrupted sleep habits

☐ Unusual increase or decrease in eating habits

☐ Nausea or vomiting after eating

If you find yourself experiencing any of these obvious warning signs, it indicates that you were unable to respond to the more subtle signals and could be in danger of relapse. It is strongly suggested that you return to your recovery plan, including informing your support network of your struggles.

Pop-Up Triggers and Warning Signs

Unexpected events are not predictable, but the warning signs they will trigger, or cause, can be very predictable. You may be taking good care of yourself, taking your medications regularly, and your symptoms may be stabilized, but something unexpected may trigger a craving or a return of symptoms.

Many unpredictable events can occur and cause you to feel disconnected from your recovery. *These events do not have to be big or traumatic to be unsettling.* With practice, your recovery skills, as well as the support of others, can be the solution. Here are some examples of pop-up triggers and warning signs:

- If you used to smoke marijuana while listening to a particular song, you may have a craving when you hear that song again. After a long period of abstaining, you may be taken aback by the intensity of the craving.

- If you used to drink beer with a group of friends and watch football games, simply watching a football game may make you crave beer again.

- You are called upon by a teacher or supervisor to speak in front of peers. Your heart races, your palms sweat, and you feel everyone staring at you. In this type of situation, the setting and the public attention are the triggers for feelings of panic and can also trigger a craving for isolation or alcohol or other drugs as a way to escape or make these feelings "go away."

- You run across a photograph of an old girlfriend and a flood of memories overwhelm you. You begin to feel like you are losing control and are sinking into depression. In this case, you already may have been feeling vulnerable, and the photograph was a trigger for worsening depressive symptoms.
- If you used to buy drugs at the neighborhood park, then driving or walking near that or *any* park may trigger your craving for drugs. If you used to have manic episodes that resulted in expensive shopping sprees at a particular mall, then going shopping may trigger anxiety, fear, lack of control, negative thinking, or mania.

Here is an exercise that may offer you further insight.

Describe your pattern of feeling overwhelmed (this can help you identify people or things that could trigger a warning sign):

_____

_____

_____

Describe your pattern of using alcohol or other drugs (this may help you identify people or things that could trigger a warning sign):

_____

_____

_____

Describe any pop-up triggers or warning signs that you've encountered in the past:

_____

_____

_____

How can using alcohol or other drugs trigger your symptoms of mental illness?

_____

_____

_____

How can symptoms of your mental illness trigger an alcohol or other drug relapse?

_____

_____

_____

Can you add any subtle warning signs that you've experienced before?

_____

_____

_____

Ask your sponsor, therapist, sober friend, or family member to help you identify warning signs, since you may not always be able to recognize them yourself.

_____

_____

_____

Taking Action

Any time you think you are experiencing a warning sign, you can immediately take one or more of these actions to help you put some space between yourself and the risk. These are just a few suggestions.

- **Ask for help.** Call your sponsor or a friend to help you overcome your craving and stay abstinent; process your symptoms of anxiety with your counselor.
- **Find a safe place.** Rather than isolating, go to a safe place—a meeting, your sponsor's or a supportive friend's house, church/temple/ashram/etc., or even a movie—a place where you can reconnect with the truth about your recovery.
- **Do the next right thing.** Sometimes the best way out of a confusing situation is to stop and consider what the next right thing is. It could be simply finishing a task that's in front of you, going for a walk, eating, or calling your sponsor.
- **Remind yourself.** My desire to drink or use (or not taking my medications) is a symptom of my disease and not an indication that I have to participate in that behavior.

The first few times you take action may be the most difficult because you are trying new things, as well as preventing yourself from acting on old behaviors. This will take a lot of practice and mindful effort. A valued skill to keep in mind is to ask for guidance from your counselor, sponsor, or a person on your support team. They are there to help you in times like these.

High-Risk Situations: Stress, Anxiety, or Mania

Experiencing stress, anxiety, or mania may increase and compromise your recovery.[139] This could happen as a result of expected or unexpected events, even associated with your life getting better. It is important to understand how to recognize what these look like for yourself, as they are experienced differently by people. When these occur, be prepared to take action.

Situations that May Lead to Relapse

You will find that certain high-risk situations may tempt you to relapse. Identify these situations so that you can avoid them or take action to combat them the next time they happen to you. Here are some common situations that you might encounter and ways you can handle them:

High-Risk Situations	Solutions
You can't sleep and haven't had a good night's rest for a week.	Talk to your doctor or therapist about relaxation strategies or figure out why you are not sleeping and seek solutions to the problem.
You drive by a store or bar where you used to drink or a street corner where you used to buy drugs.	Walk away or turn your car around. Get away from those places and immediately call your sponsor, supportive friend, or family member who is in recovery. Then, pat yourself on the back since you resisted. It will get easier each time.
Your girlfriend or boyfriend wants you to drink or get high.	Insist that your partner be supportive of your recovery. If he or she can't, then it is probably best to end the relationship.
Your friends tell you, "You're no fun anymore" because you don't get drunk and high with them.	It is important to have friends who don't drink alcohol or use other drugs in recovery. This may mean leaving your using friends behind for friendships that are healthier and more rewarding.
You feel lonely.	Loneliness is a big relapse trap. It takes work to find new, recovery-oriented social contacts. Go to a meeting, call your sponsor, go to church, go to the gym, or go to the library. Keep working at finding healthy alternatives to staying home alone.
You feel angry at yourself, angry at the world, and angry at people in your life.	Anger is common in recovery, particularly early recovery. Get help dealing with anger from your therapist or sponsor. Step back from whatever is making you angry. Learn to accept that there will be difficult times along the road to recovery.
You're bored and have too much time on your hands.	Get active. Do something different. At the beginning of each day, schedule healthy activities. Go to a support group/twelve-step meeting or call your sponsor.

High-Risk Situations	Solutions
You feel your depressive symptoms returning, feel that your medication isn't working, and believe that things won't get better.	Talk to your doctor. Be patient with yourself; recovery takes time and relapse happens. It is sometimes a part of the process. Try to stop your negative thoughts. Look at how far you've come already.
You get hurt in a relationship.	Ask for support; call your sponsor or therapist. Learn to cope with disappointments without using.
You get fired from a job.	Be positive about it. Learn from your mistakes, look for a new job right away, and move on. Ask for help and keep busy.

Isolation, Withdrawal

Isolation and withdrawal are indications that you are re-experiencing dangerous aspects of your disease. You may find yourself pulling away from others, not being honest, romanticizing the past, or withdrawing from your recovery by avoiding meetings and your sponsor. During this time, you may notice an increase in judgmental thoughts, an increase in irritability, and a desire to be alone. You may find that you have decided not to tell your counselor or doctor, for example, that you have been having thoughts that others are talking about you or trying to hurt you. And, you may have decided that your medication's side effects are intolerable.

Distressing Feelings

It can be helpful to recognize that negative feelings, such as anger, depression, sadness, and anxiety, may affect your stability and your commitment to your recovery. Feelings, distress, triggers, or cravings will pass, and you will begin to learn that you can get through them without using or changing the course of your recovery and mental health. This is when the skills you've learned, such as Dialectical Behavior Therapy (DBT),[140] can help. People in recovery often experience intrusive and negative thoughts at different times. Stress, distressing thoughts, and situations create an opportunity for relapse. Being mindful of these kinds of thoughts can be helpful.

"It's not worth it. I'm just going to go back to my old life."

"I can't stand feeling this bad. I have to have a drink or get high."

"I'm at the end of my rope! I give up."

"I'll always be like this. Why bother trying to change?"

"The side effects of these medications aren't worth it."

It is important to interrupt negative thinking and gain distance from those thoughts and feelings. Being intentionally positive, confident, and hopeful about your recovery is a good practice. You may have heard the saying, "Fake it till you make it." Even if you don't think you can be successful, behave as if you can. "Fake it till you make it" does not mean to cover up negative feelings, thoughts, or unhealthy behaviors by "faking" recovery; it means taking the action for your recovery, even if you do not feel like it or believe it possible at the time.

Intentional Statements

"I am feeling a little better every day."

"I have seen others succeed, and I believe I can, too."

"I can do anything as long as I continue to work the program."

"I know I can do this, just for today."

"I am not alone; there are people who want to help me through this."

The Experience of Grief

Grief is a normal part of life, but can sometimes leave you feeling unbalanced and fearful for your recovery. Until recovery, you may not have been able to fully experience the feelings associated with loss and, so in early recovery, you may sometimes find yourself reliving past losses as you encounter powerful emotions. You may also experience grief associated with giving up your "old life" and the losses you may have incurred due to your illness. You may be struggling through a divorce, a loss of a career, newly diagnosed health concerns, or financial issues. These emotions may ignite a desire to abandon recovery, but they are an important part of the recovery process and will ultimately lead to a greater understanding of who you are. Allowing yourself to experience and move through grief will create an unshakeable foundation in the development of your character.

Caring for Yourself

It is vital in recovery that you develop an understanding of what it means to truly care about yourself and to acknowledge the progress you have made and the challenges you have faced. You are still learning to value yourself and the process of recovery. As such, you sometimes may fail to acknowledge milestones and the ability to make positive choices when faced with things that have been stumbling blocks in the past.

It can be easy to become impatient with yourself and your recovery. As you successfully navigate challenges that come your way, it is important that you acknowledge your successes and recognize the gifts recovery offers. Having a touchstone of success will allow you to develop a confidence in recovery during difficult times. Some ways you can acknowledge your successes may be sharing with your aftercare group; writing a list of ways you have grown and changed; sharing your experience, strength, and hope with someone who is struggling with similar issues; and doing something that makes you feel joyful.

Downtime

Nights and weekends are the times when the majority of people have free or unstructured downtime. Many people report feeling more acutely aware of mental health symptoms or addictive cravings during downtime. Schedule items in your daily plan that will help you fill your downtime with healthy activities, like sleep, reading, or meeting with a friend.

Fighting Boredom

When you were drinking alcohol or using other drugs, you may have spent a lot of time getting high or finding money to buy more. Or, if symptoms of your mental illness kept you from being active, you may not have developed healthy interests or hobbies. Now that you are healthier, you'll have more time to fill with activities you enjoy. You should replace your old habits with new activities that make you feel good.

People Who Don't Understand Recovery

In recovery, you will not be living in isolation. A common challenge for people in recovery is associating with people who use alcohol and/or other drugs, or those who were in recovery and have relapsed, or those who don't understand the recovery process.

Sometimes people who have no alcohol and/or other drug or mental health issues simply do not understand the pitfalls of relapse and the impact their conversations or well-intended offers can have. Still others are well aware of addiction and/or mental health relapse concerns, but may be resistant to changing the dynamics of the relationship. Consciously or unconsciously, they may want you to stay active in your illness.

Relapse prevention is *your* responsibility. You are the ultimate guardian of your recovery. It is important to remember that regardless of the circumstance of the situation or the relapse trigger you are experiencing, you can find a recovery-focused solution.

Here is an exercise that may increase your understanding of the people in your life. On a piece of paper, list the names of your friends and family. Then write a sentence on each: How might they be supportive? How might they be a relapse trigger?

Example:

Steve   *Is a friend who has offered to help in any way.*

John   *Continues to tell me that it is okay to use just marijuana.*

Note: "What Family and Friends Should Know about Relapse" in Chapter Twelve is a useful tool provided for you to photocopy and give to family and supportive friends.

Cravings and Impulsive Thoughts

Cravings are defined as "intense, urgent, and abnormal desires or longings." Cravings can be powerful and overwhelming, and you can manage cravings by expecting, recognizing, and planning for them. One of the reasons why many people find it helpful to attend meetings is that they hear the stories of others who have successfully walked through these cravings. They often describe a very different relationship with their thoughts today. The intensity and frequency of cravings you might experience in early recovery can change dramatically as you apply the solutions and skills you have learned. As you grow in recovery, you teach your body, mind, and spirit a new way of handling these feelings. With mindful practice, the cravings will become more recognizable and less scary; and it will be easier to take positive actions to avoid a relapse.

Active mindfulness is simply being mentally present and acutely aware of your surroundings and situation, including your emotional responses to them.[141] Impulsive thoughts and behaviors are a sure way to sabotage recovery. A way to short circuit impulsive thoughts is to practice active mindfulness. Active mindfulness is simply being mentally present and acutely aware of your surroundings and situation, including your emotional responses to them. This mindfulness can be difficult and seem nearly impossible to maintain when relapse triggers are rapidly firing and automatic thoughts are pulling your attention or influencing your perspective. With practice, you can move toward mastering this skill.

The end goal is to become more capable of recognizing negative situations and their impact on your recovery.

Here are two examples of experiences that could happen to you or someone you know. Practice learning to identify warning signs and figure out what you could do to stop warning signs from leading to a relapse.

Example #1: Making New Friends

Since you have been in recovery, you have been trying to make new friends. You've always had difficulty making friends and are tired of feeling "different" from everyone else. You're finally in a situation where no one knows you are in recovery.

A new acquaintance, Jessica, invites you to a party, and you automatically say yes. You hear that several people from work will be going, and there might be drinking and drugs available. You think this would be a good way to finally begin to "fit in" and make some new friends. The party is on the same night as your twelve-step meeting, but you haven't told your sponsor that you are considering going to the party.

- Describe three warning signs:

  _____

  _____

  _____

- What actions would you take to stop the above warning signs from leading to relapse?

  _____

  _____

  _____

Example #2: Bad Day

You haven't been sleeping well. You have an argument with a family member in the morning and leave home angry. You are under a lot of pressure at work. When you turn in a project, your boss tells you that you haven't done what she asked you to do. You get overly frustrated, very upset, walk out, and consider quitting. You get in the car and drive through your old neighborhood where you used to buy drugs. When you check in with your sponsor the next day, you don't tell him what you did.

- Describe three warning signs:

  _____

  _____

  _____

- What actions would you take to stop the above warning signs from leading to something worse?

  _____

  _____

  _____

What Happens	Warning Signs	Take Action!
A friend brings alcohol over to your house and starts to drink. You've had a hard couple of days and are feeling more anxious than usual.	You crave drinking again and don't know how to tell your friend to not bring alcohol over again. You don't know how to socialize without drinking and have been experiencing more intense symptoms of anxiety. Your thought pattern is: *I always drink with my friends; I can't change that*, or *I'm just going to drink this once.*	**Remove the booze**: Tell your friend you're not drinking, and ask him not to drink and to remove the alcohol. **Avoid contact**: Ask your friend to leave and take the alcohol with him. **Do something else**: Ask your friend if you can hang out without drinking alcohol. Or, find a healthy activity like taking a walk or joining a friend for dinner. **Ask for help**: Call a friend or sponsor to help overcome your cravings and to stay in recovery and process your symptoms of anxiety with your counselor. **Find a safe place**: Go to a safe place other than your house—a supportive friend's house, a movie, or a meeting. **Stick with your recovery plan**: Your plan is not to drink, so don't make an exception. One drink leads to another.
You don't want to keep going to your support group any longer and don't care about other people's opinions. You are looking for a new job and a new apartment. Your mind is racing and you can't concentrate or fall asleep at night.	You are suddenly withdrawing from friends and others who are supportive. You are experiencing racing thoughts. Too many big changes are happening in your life at the same time. These may be related to increasing stress and symptoms of manic behavior.	**Ask for help**: Keep going to meetings and tell your counselor and doctor or psychiatrist how you feel. **Check in with yourself**: Hold off on making changes all at once. Wait a while, then make one change at a time, if still needed. **Stick with your plan**: Your support group is an important part of your relapse prevention plan. Keep going to meetings. **Manage your feelings**: Stress related to life changes can trigger cravings. Be sure to relieve stress in healthy ways, such as exercising or therapy. **Find a safe place**: Go to a safe place other than your house—a supportive friend's house, a movie, or a meeting. **Practice relaxation**: Decrease your anxiety in a healthy way with meditation or breathing or other techniques, not by drinking.

What Happens	Warning Signs	Take Action!
You've deceived your sponsor—you didn't tell him about visiting an old friend who used to supply you with drugs. You haven't told your sponsor that you have been missing your "former" life of using. You've been getting angry with your spouse. You haven't told your counselor or doctor that you have been having unusual thoughts that others are talking about you or trying to hurt you.	You have been cutting yourself off from your spouse, sponsor, and others. You are experiencing paranoia or unusual thinking. You are romanticizing your using days. You've missed some appointments with your sponsor. You've been fighting with your spouse.	**Ask for help:** Talk with your counselor about your unusual thoughts and admit what happened with your sponsor. **Avoid contact**: Don't see your old friend again and don't return phone calls until you and your counselor think you can handle it. **Ask for help:** Tell your spouse how you've been feeling and ask for understanding and support. **Check-in with yourself**: Do something healthy that makes you feel good, like join a gym, make dinner for your spouse, or rent a movie to watch together. **Find a safe place**: If you are having thoughts about using, go some place where you are unlikely to use, like a meeting or a (sober/non-using) friend's house. **Remember that you want to change**: Your old life may have been fun, but don't forget the pain and suffering you also experienced. **Manage your feelings**: Talk with your therapist about your paranoid fears and increased anger.

Reward Yourself

You deserve a reward. Each time you recognize a warning sign and take action to stop it, reward yourself by doing something that makes you feel good. Some rewards could be:

Eat an ice cream cone	Invite someone over	Read a favorite book
Take a scenic walk	Buy yourself flowers	Buy a new magazine
Call a sober friend	Play a favorite sport	Take a hot bath
Watch a comedy	Start a diary or journal	Visit the library
Listen to music	Spend time with a pet	Visit the zoo
Cook a meal		

Are there any rewards you'd like to add to the list?

_____

_____

_____

_____

Since all of these are healthy activities that make you feel good and many that you can share with another person, do them as often as you want! If you have lots of rewarding and healthy activities to occupy your time, then you will be less likely to experience cravings and more likely to develop positive relationships.

Street Smart Skills

After you've been in recovery for a little while, you will build confidence that you can stay abstinent and in recovery and lead a healthy life. Even if you've been in recovery a long time, it is useful to review some common sense skills that will help you on your recovery journey.

- *Accept disappointment with patience.*

    Nobody is perfect and life isn't fair. Be kind to yourself and others. Be patient and give yourself time. When things go wrong, remember that everybody has to accept disappointment. Learn to cope without using alcohol or other drugs, withdrawing, or reacting in unhealthy ways.

- *Learn how to handle stressful situations.*

    If something is bothering you, don't keep it to yourself, talk to a trusted friend and accept support. Sometimes stress causes increased symptoms or an intense desire to use, and it will take some work to develop new skills.

- *Learn the skills you need.*

    You may never have learned certain skills that are helpful in life, such as managing money, parenting, social skills, job skills, or stress management. Ask your case manager for a referral to a group that can help you learn the skills you need.

- *Get a support network and use it.*

    You are not alone. Develop a network of friends, family, support groups, an active sponsor, a counselor or therapist, or a case manager. Call them when you need them. If you don't know where to start, go to a twelve-step meeting and ask for help.

- *Learn who your real friends are.*

    People who aren't supportive of your recovery have no place in your life. It may be difficult to give up family or friends who are still using or who are physically or emotionally harmful to you, but it is vital to your recovery.

- *There's no such thing as easy money.*

    You've worked too hard to give in to making quick money by dealing drugs or other illegal means. Make your money honestly and legitimately. You'll feel better about yourself and stay out of legal trouble, too.

- *Avoid all alcohol and/or other drugs.*

  You may think you can handle getting high just once, but this won't work because once you start, you will be more likely to do it again and again. It is also faulty thinking if you tell yourself that you can use other substances as long as you don't return to your drug of choice. For example, "Beer is okay as long as I don't smoke a joint." Resist the temptation and it will get easier each time you say no and walk away.

How will you keep yourself from giving in to your next craving and/or impulsive thought?

_____

_____

Medication

Taking your medicines exactly as prescribed by your doctor is an especially important part of what you can do to help yourself get better.[142] Communicating openly with your doctors can allow them to monitor your progress and make any changes that might be necessary. Be sure to check with your doctor before making any changes in your medicine. This includes stopping your medication or taking over-the-counter medications. A change in your medication could alter the balance in your brain chemistry resulting in negative symptoms.

> **Note:** Alcohol and/or other drugs, including street drugs, can have an adverse reaction with your medication.

Prevention Check-In

- ☐ I am taking my medication at the same time every day.
- ☐ I am not changing my medication or dosages without first calling my doctor.
- ☐ I am maintaining a healthy sleeping and eating routine.
- ☐ I am developing rewarding activities and habits.
- ☐ I am managing my stress levels and avoiding overly distressful people, places, and things.
- ☐ I am staying away from alcohol and/or other drugs.
- ☐ I ask myself daily if I am experiencing any warning signs.

☐ I invite my support people to watch for warning signs and to help me to be mindful of relapse.

☐ I am regularly meetings with my sponsor.

☐ I have a home group and am attending twelve-step meetings regularly.

☐ If I notice any warning signs at all, I use my alternative coping responses (ACRs) and ask for help when needed.

☐ I *can* do this; this is my life!

Relapse Prevention Plan

It is a good idea to make plans while your symptoms are stable and things are quiet and calm. You may also find it helpful to practice your plan. Rehearse it with support people, review it in your mind, and display the written plans so you can read them every day. Be ready to do whatever it takes so you'll be prepared when you are faced with a potential relapse situation.

A "Relapse Prevention and Safety Plan" can include many different types of information, including your mental health, addiction and medical diagnosis, and your current medication routine. The plan can also include a list of your professional support team members and your supportive community and their contact information. There may also be written insights into your relapse-risk situations and warning signs, as well as what you can do about them. Note that the end of your "Relapse Prevention and Safety Plan" gives you a place to keep track of people you can call for help. Most people in recovery agree that having the list of positive people handy (and calling them) has been effective.

You may refer to this plan any time you feel vulnerable to relapse, when warning signs are becoming a serious problem. Having a solid relapse prevention and safety plan will help prevent any type of relapse.

Relapse Prevention and Safety Plan

This section is provided for you to photocopy to edit and change as you are in recovery and to give to supportive family members and friends.

My Relapse Prevention and Safety Plan
My mental health diagnosis:
My addiction diagnosis:
My medical diagnosis:
My medication routine (prescription name/dose/time each day):

My Professional Team
My Psychiatrist Name: Address: Phone:
My Primary Care Physician Name: Address: Phone:
My Therapist Name: Address: Phone:
Other Name: Address: Phone:
If I can't call my doctor, counselor, case manager, sponsor, or support team leader, then this person will call them for me. Name: Phone:

My Relapse-Risk Warning Signs Are		
Subtle Signs	Obvious Signs	Pop-up Signs

When I experience a relapse warning sign, I will do the following to keep my symptoms from worsening.

If I need support, I will ask for help from
Name: Phone: Alt. #
Name: Phone: Alt. #
Name: Phone: Alt. #

If I use alcohol and/or other drugs, stop taking my medicine, or don't follow through with treatment, I want my therapist, peers, family, or other supportive people to help me by:

1.

2.

3.

In a crisis situation, I find the following three things unhelpful, and I encourage the support team to not help in the areas of:

1.

2.

3.

If I am a danger to myself, to others, or unable to care for myself, I would prefer the following steps to be taken:

If I am a danger to myself, to others, or unable to care for myself and have to be hospitalized, I would prefer to be taken to:

Care Management Services

The role of the care manager is to work with you in assessing your needs, goals, and resources. After your initial assessment, you and the care manager will have the opportunity to work together to formulate a plan to meet your goals and needs with the resources available.

Transitions and Managing Care

A transition of care takes place when you move between care settings or levels of care, such as

- Leaving a treatment center and returning home;
- Transferring to an outpatient setting;
- Moving to a sober living house;
- Transferring to a long-term recovery program.

Lack of coordination during transitions is, unfortunately, quite frequent and can be problematic for everyone involved. Common problems that occur during transitions include unexpected emotions such as fear, anxiety, confusion, or depression; housing problems; cravings; missed medical appointments; appetite changes; personal hygiene; and possibly relapse.

Your care manager not only helps develop a transition plan with you, he or she also helps to facilitate communication among everyone involved, including physicians, psychiatrists, counselors, family, friends, and those involved in your housing, legal, and employment situations. Care managers also help you find community resources, like sober living support, educational opportunities, occupational opportunities, and twelve-step meetings. They are trained to identify needs and connect you to resources, as well as educate you on how to use resources to attain a more independent lifestyle.

Aftercare Plans

As you move forward with your treatment, you may be meeting with your care manager to discuss your aftercare plans. Some of the areas discussed may include the following: your social relationships (family and friends), community living, home maintenance, transportation, budget, as well as school, volunteer, and leisure activities.

Social Relationships

Social relationships are a cornerstone of healthy recovery. Relationships teach the ability to interact effectively, provide a primary source of support, and allow for accurate, direct feedback for growth and accountability. As you review this section, consider your own relationships, the types of relationships, and how these may affect your recovery.

Intimate Relationships. Intimacy is a close interpersonal relationship in which both parties give and receive emotional support, as well as share mutual respect and attraction of ideas, character, and possibly physical or sexual attraction. The desire to belong in intimate relationships with people whom you find to be attractive is a shared universal human need, as is forming emotional attachments, fulfilling the needs of belonging, and of being cared for. These relationships tend to be emotionally charged and can sometimes distract people from their recovery. Identifying these relationships from the past, present, and potential future is helpful in establishing a recovery plan.

Family. Family members are people who are connected to you by marriage, blood relations, or perhaps by association. An **extended** family simply refers to those significant people who are part of the family, but who may have more distant roles, e.g., grandparents, aunts, uncles, cousins, and so forth. Both primary and extended family members play a significant role in recovery.

Friends. A friend is a person you share an interpersonal relationship with that goes beyond casual acquaintance or association. Friendships can share many different levels of emotional intimacy, but generally are based on a mutual desire for what is best for the other person, shared empathy, mutual honesty, understanding, compassion, and trust of the mutual positive regard. Friends play a key role in recovery. These individuals can affect recovery in a positive, as well as negative way.

Coworkers. Maintaining a supportive working relationships with coworkers is important. You may choose to form friendships inside of the workplace or to keep your work separate from your personal life. Either way, there tends to be a strong influence on recovery and how you interrelate at work. This is an area that your care manager may assist you with, especially if your present employer is somehow involved in your treatment goals.

Neighbors. Neighbors are the people whom you live in close proximity to, generally in the same small area or street. The primary relationship is built on the shared location or area. Relationships with neighbors can be beneficial due to the close proximity and availability for support. They can also be stressful at times and affect your recovery.

Community Living

Community living tends to require a few basic life skills in order for you to function successfully. These often include:

- Adequate income
- Health and social services
- Employment
- Educational options
- Recreational programs
- Community activities

Adequate Income. Adequate income simply means to have enough income to support your needs within a community or lifestyle. The cost of living varies from place to place, as does the availability and definition of affordable housing and other necessities. Isolation due to financial differences can be a barrier to recovery.

Health and Social Services. Access to health and social services is a necessity for many in order to manage their co-occurring disorders. Often rural or small communities will lack the resources needed or maybe the resources are not available at all.

Employment. Employment opportunities for some can be a challenge in early recovery. If this is a concern of yours, your care manager can assist you in reviewing your options for employment, as well as future career goals. A lack of employment and social isolation can be a barrier to recovery.

Educational Options. While most communities provide a public school system through the twelfth grade, adult remedial or higher education may be limited in availability due to community size and resources. You can discuss your educational goals with your care manager to see how they can fit into your recovery plan.

Recreational Programs and Community Activities. Recreational programs and community activities are available most everywhere. They can include swimming, yoga, sports, games, computer skills, and so forth. This list is endless. When developing your community care plan, free time tends to be a challenge. Investigating your interests, hobbies, and the availability of activities is suggested.

Home Maintenance

Managing home maintenance, such as doing chores and running errands, takes an ability to predict needs for your home environment before these needs are unmet or reach a crisis state. If keeping a clean and healthy living environment is not a task that you have undertaken, do not assume it is simple. Maintaining a clean and healthy home, stocked with necessities, is a skill that you may want to learn. Managing your daily tasks in a successful way can build confidence and display a sense of self-investment and respect.

Transportation

Having a plan for transportation increases most people's sense of freedom and effectiveness in community independence. Managing transportation for some can be challenging if you are unfamiliar with the details that can include maintenance, gas, insurance, registration, cleaning, safety, and so forth. If the plan includes public transportation, then an understanding of taxi, bus, and train schedules and fees, as well as how to safely navigate public transportation is important.

Budget

The ability to budget money is of critical importance to people new to their recovery. Knowing how much money is needed to pay for monthly necessities, such as electricity, heat, food, and rent, is vital. Managing one's money includes being certain that there is enough for not only monthly bills, but enough left to maintain a bank account and provide for unexpected expenses through savings. Knowing you are capable of meeting your own needs financially is a practical display of your independence. It can also be a frustrating and stressful challenge if finances are compromised. Finances tend to be a large trigger for relapse. Considering this in your recovery plan is advisable. Some have found that taking a class in budgeting supported their recovery goals greatly.

School

School can be a great way to increase your independence and practice structure and time management skills in a somewhat more forgiving environment than the workplace. It allows for independence and achievement through the investment of time and resources.

If you stopped your education prematurely due to the effects of your co-occurring disorder, school can be a practical step. And you are certainly building knowledge and skills by receiving a formal education that will help you in the future.

Volunteer Activities

Volunteer activities can also be a great way to practice independence and have structure in a more flexible environment than school or the paid workplace. Just like school, it allows you to gain responsibility and achieve goals through your time and effort.

If you lack experience or confidence in your ability to go back to work, volunteer work can help you regain your footing. Acquiring real world skills through volunteer work is useful now and can be added to a resume later when you are ready for employment.

Leisure

Being able to balance leisure time in relation to work and life responsibilities is a skill that requires both knowing your limits and maintaining mindful responsiveness to your needs. Reviewing these areas can be helpful in developing and supporting your recovery.

- Relaxation
- Stress reduction
- Managing downtime alone
- Managing downtime socially

Relaxation Skills and Stress Reduction. Relaxation is both physical and mental, and it goes hand in hand with stress reduction. Relaxation is more than peace of mind or enjoying a hobby; it is about decreasing and recuperating from the effects of stress on your mind and body. Relaxation techniques can help you cope with everyday stress, as well as acute or situational stress.

When faced with numerous responsibilities and tasks or the demands of life and recovery, relaxation techniques may take a backseat in your life, and you might miss out on those benefits. Practicing relaxation techniques can reduce stress symptoms in the following ways:

- Slowing your heart rate
- Lowering your blood pressure
- Slowing your breathing rate
- Increasing blood flow to major muscles
- Reducing muscle tension and chronic pain
- Improving concentration
- Reducing anger and frustration
- Boosting confidence to handle problems

Including a variety of relaxation techniques in your recovery plan can help support your long-term goals.

Create a New Life

Part of your relapse prevention plan is an evaluation of your current life and a plan for changing the parts that need to be fixed. Think about what's going on in your life and perform an honest self-assessment.

1. Are there people who are still using in my life? If so, who are they?

_____

_____

_____

2. How might I be setting myself up for relapse?

_____

_____

_____

3. How can I get rid of any potential triggers in my life?

_____

_____

_____

4. What healthy goals have I set in my life?

_____

_____

_____

5. Am I accepting or tolerating a situation that I need to change? Why or why not?

_____

_____

_____

6. Am I participating fully in my recovery plan? Why or why not?

_____

_____

_____

Here is a **Life Chart** that can help you determine where you are now, where you'd like to be, and how to get there in all areas of your life. The one shown here is provided as an example, and a blank one is shown on the next page for you to complete.

Sample Life Chart

Life Area	Where I Am Now	Where I'd Like to Be	How to Get There
Social Life	Still hanging out with Jake and Kim, who use.	Have three friends who are in recovery.	Talk to people at meetings and church; develop friendships slowly.
Work	My job is boring and there is no room for promotion or career growth.	I want to be a nurse	Contact a local junior college with a nursing program and talk with a teacher about the nursing profession.
Education	I have no GED.	I want to have a nursing degree.	Look into nursing programs and financial aid.
Support system	I have a few supportive people in my life.	I'd like to have a bigger, stronger support system.	Develop relationships with people who are in recovery.
Recovery program	My sponsor hasn't been there for me lately.	I want a sponsor who is more stable and has a good recovery program.	Start talking to people in meetings and putting feelers out or talk to my sponsor and see if we can work things out.
Romantic life	I get into relationships too quickly and end up regretting it.	I want to be single for a while, or if anything, date only casually.	Stop seeing my current boyfriend and live alone for a while.
Personal life (hobbies, self-growth)	I don't have a hobby I'm excited about, and I get bored a lot.	I want to start painting.	Call the Parks and Recreation Department for a class schedule.

My Life Chart

Life Area	Where I Am Now	Where I'd Like to Be	How to Get There
Social Life			
Work			
Education			
Support system			
Recovery program			
Romantic life			
Personal life (hobbies, self-growth)			

If You Experience Relapse Symptoms

Refer to this plan any time you feel out of control or are feeling vulnerable to relapse, when warning signs are becoming a serious problem, or you need help but don't know where to turn.

If you are a person in dual recovery, you may experience relapse symptoms for your mental illness, substance/behavioral addiction, or both. Refer to this plan to help prevent any type of relapse.

1. When I experience warning signs, I will perform these routine actions to keep my symptoms from getting worse:

_____

_____

_____

2. I will avoid these high-risk situations:

_____

_____

_____

3. I am more likely to experience particular warning signs, and will be watchful for these:

_____

_____

_____

Exercise: A Cornerstone to Long-Term Recovery

When someone mentions the word "exercise," people may have different ideas of what that means. Many people tend to believe that exercise is important to maintaining and improving physical health. However, not many people understand that exercise has been shown to have significant and important effects on mental health and emotional well-being. Exercise can do the following:

- Reduce the risk of chronic disease
- Improve balance and coordination
- Support healthy weight
- Boost self-esteem
- Improve mood
- Support hormone balance

Generally speaking, exercise is a planned, structured, and often repetitive physical activity. The Department of Health and Human Services issued recommendations for exercise for adults eighteen to sixty-four years of age. Specifically, the recommendations include 150 minutes of moderate aerobic activity per week and strength training at least twice a week

If your first thought is *150 minutes! Plus weights!* you are probably not alone. The good news is that a twenty-minute walk can make a difference, and strength training can be as simple as sit-ups and push-ups. There are many ways to start and maintain a fitness program. In this section, we will explore the following:

1. Physical benefits of exercise
2. Psychological benefits of exercise
3. Types of exercise
4. Recommendations to get started

Physical Benefits of Exercise

Exercise creates physical changes in the body, both during and after the activity. Exercise causes increased cellular metabolism, which means that the chemical processes in the cell cause more glucose (sugar) and oxygen to be used and more energy to be produced and utilized. There are also more waste products produced by the cell as a result of the increased cellular metabolism, which can result in muscle soreness following exercise. In the same way that exercise causes an increase in activity, energy production, and consumption in the body's cells, it can also create increased activities in a number of the body's vital organs.

- Exercise causes cells in muscle tissue to demand more glucose and oxygen, which the circulation system delivers along with other nutrients.
- Stored fat may be broken down to provide additional nutrients for energy as the lungs work to keep up with the oxygen demands.
- The heart acts like a pump in the delivery system, and as demand increases, the pump pushes more oxygen and nutrient-rich blood throughout the body.

The circulation system is also responsible for removing the waste products of energy consumption, such as carbon dioxide and lactic acid. By increasing the demands on these systems, we are encouraging them to operate at higher and more efficient levels.

The stress of exercise, when performed properly, is generally a positive type of stress that is called **eustress**. For example, the stress on the heart during an endurance activity, such as running, actually strengthens the heart by making it work harder. However, if you try to do too much too soon in your fitness program, you can cause **distress**, which is the negative impact of stress. This is why most experts recommend developing and following a fitness plan that includes gradually building strength, endurance, and flexibility.

Medical research indicates that exercise has been demonstrated to have many physical benefits. This is a result of the eustress response. Exercise is also useful in both preventing and treating many types of diseases.

- **Coronary heart disease**: Exercise improves functioning of the heart and the blood vessels that serve the heart.
- **Cardiovascular disease**: Exercise improves circulation and strengthens the muscle fibers found in some blood vessels, which can often prevent hardening of these blood vessels, which can lead to high blood pressure, stroke, and/or heart attack.
- **Osteoporosis**: Exercise builds bone density and strength by increasing the mineral content of bones. This is important in preventing and healing fractures as well.
- **Diabetes**: Exercise improves blood sugar control and reduces insulin resistance. Exercise is also important in maintaining a healthy weight, which is a significant factor in diabetes prevention.
- **Obesity**: Exercise increases energy expenditure. To maintain a healthy weight, energy intake (measured in calories) must be balanced with energy expenditure. In combination with lowering energy intake, exercise is an important part of a weight loss program.

Exercise also plays these important roles.
- **Boosts immunity**: Exercise boosts the body's antibodies and lymphocytes, including T-cells, which fight infections.
- **Preventing chronic inflammation**: Exercise supports the systems responsible for targeting and repairing tissues experiencing inflammation, which helps prevent the inflammation from becoming chronic. Chronic inflammation is associated with the development of many age-related disorders.
- **Reducing arthritis pain**: Some types of exercise, particularly those focusing on flexibility and weight-bearing exercises, can improve joint mobility and reduce the joint pain associated with arthritis.
- **Pain management**: Exercise, particularly aerobic exercise, causes the release of endorphins, which are chemicals in the brain that act as the body's natural morphine. Additionally, exercise speeds up the elimination of hormones, which reduces the cramping associated with menstrual pain.
- **Improve sleep**: Studies have demonstrated that consistent exercise helps people suffering from chronic insomnia to fall asleep faster, stay asleep longer, and achieve a better quality of sleep.

In general, when it comes to physical health, a well-balanced exercise program can improve general health, build endurance, and slow many of the effects of aging as well. Also, exercise in combination with a reduced-calorie diet is the safest and most effective method of weight loss.

Psychological Benefits of Exercise

The benefits of exercise not only improve physical health, but they also enhance emotional and psychological well-being. Studies have shown that exercise, along with other supportive treatments, can significantly improve one's overall mental health, with such conditions and/or disorders as depression, fatigue, thought processes, memory, anxiety, sleep, and cravings. Studies have also shown that exercise can decrease and, in some cases, eliminate the need for medications. Exercise is also associated with increased self-esteem and self-worth. Self-efficacy, or the perception of how likely you are to succeed, is positively impacted by exercise, as is self-confidence. In short, exercise can support shaping positive opinions and feelings about yourself.

Exercise and Stress Management

One way to look at stress is that it is sometimes the body's reaction to a stimulus. We generally think of stress, or distress, in negative terms; however, even positive stimuli can cause stress. For example, learning French is a stressor—the same as getting married or buying a home. The difference is in our reaction to the perceived level of stress. In other words, how we cope with stress is just as important as the stressor itself.

Your perceptions of stress and how you cope with it can be both genetically programmed as well as learned. While you can do little to change your genetic programming, you can override your instincts to some degree by learning new patterns of behavior. Exercise supports this new learning in two major ways. First, exercise allows you to learn new patterns of behavior or new reactions to stress. When you challenge yourself with exercise, you not only provide an outlet for excess stress, but you are given the opportunity to face and overcome stressful situations regularly, thereby creating new patterns. Second, this same system works at the cellular level as well. Exercise generates chemical by-products in the brain and body, but also supports repair mechanisms that leave the repaired and replaced cells stronger and more resilient. Neuroscientists call this form of stress and recovery stress **inoculation**. It is similar to receiving a vaccination.

Exercise, Focus, and Clarity

One of the greatest challenges in early recovery can sometimes be your ability to focus and think clearly. It is interesting to note that two chemicals in the brain that are associated with stressful situations actually allow you to focus more clearly. This sometimes explains why those with Attention Deficit

Disorder (ADD or ADHD) and others in early recovery tend to thrive on excitement, thrill-seeking, and adrenaline. From another perspective, you may simply be trying to activate those chemicals that allow you to stay on task and feel productive.

Ironically, you can naturally activate these same chemicals with regular exercise. Endurance activities or aerobic exercise initiates the release of norepinephrine, which arouses attention, and dopamine, which sharpens your focus. Rather than creating drama before your next test in school or presentation at work, why not try a twenty-minute walk, another form of aerobic exercise, or a swim? You may find you are better able to focus and think more clearly.

Exercise and Anxiety

There are two major ways that exercise can help with anxiety.

- First, exercise can diminish the brain's reaction to the symptoms of anxiety. Research has demonstrated that increased heart rate, sweating, and rapid breathing associated with rigorous exercise can often desensitize sufferers of those symptoms. Basically, the people in the study produced the symptoms of anxiety through exercise; so when they did experience anxiety, they tended not to react to it. This result was noted as early as after the second session of rigorous exercise.

- Secondly, physical activity lowers the amount of tension in the muscles when resting (not exercising), which interrupts the anxiety feedback loop in the brain because when the body is calm, the brain follows suit. Exercise is also associated with the release of GABA, an amino acid, considered to be the body's natural sedative.

Exercise and Depression

Consistent rigorous exercise causes the release of endorphins. Endorphins are the body's natural morphine. The brain does not make any distinction between types of pain when it reacts to pain and stress; it does not matter whether the pain you are experiencing is the result of a stubbed toe or a recent break-up—your brain will tell you that you are in pain. Pain, both emotional and physical, is strongly related to depression. The endorphin-releasing effect of exercise can combat the experience of pain and thus improve mood. Additionally, exercise triggers the chemical processes in the brain that convert tryptophan, an amino acid, to serotonin, which supports feelings of well-being. Serotonin is a chemical in the brain stimulated by Prozac and other selective serotonin reuptake inhibitors (SSRIs), which are used to treat depression.

Exercise and Other Mental Health Issues

Because exercise can cause chemical changes in the brain and body, many studies have been conducted to determine the effect of exercise on a number of mental health issues. For example, studies of aerobic exercise in people with schizophrenia demonstrated positive short-term effects, including a reduction in hallucinations and other negative symptoms. In a study of Japanese workers, participants in a walking program had fewer depressive symptoms and better social adaptive skills than their non-walking counterparts when tested after four weeks. Additional studies are underway investigating exercise as a way to minimize the need for sedatives in nursing home residents in the United Kingdom. Overall, the literature demonstrates that exercise can improve mood and support an individual's feeling of well-being.

Exercise and Addiction

While there is not one accepted cause for addiction, recent research has demonstrated that addiction is a disorder that impacts an area of the brain called the limbic system. The limbic system is responsible for emotions and motivation, and it is sometimes called the reward center of the brain. Addiction can be seen as a malfunction of the reward system in the limbic system, and it is sometimes referred to as reward deficiency syndrome. The National Institute for Drug Abuse (NIDA) defines addiction as a compulsion, which persists in spite of negative health and social consequences. The compulsion is generally caused because the brain's natural reward system does not work properly. That means the person can be compelled to seek relief and rewards through other means. The chemical in the brain most closely associated with a reward is dopamine. Dopamine is related to stress management and the ability to experience pleasure. If an individual is unable to manage stress or experience pleasure normally, this person may drink alcohol and/or use other drugs, gamble, or engage in risky sexual activities in order to experience relief. Exercise has been demonstrated to increase dopamine levels and the number of dopamine receptor sites. Research on addiction and recovery has shown that people who exercise report fewer cravings, experience less severe withdrawal symptoms, and are more likely to maintain abstinence from alcohol and/or other drugs. Exercise is an important part of any recovery program.

Types of Exercise

Aerobic exercise overloads the heart and lungs, causing them to work harder than when they are at rest through continuous use of large muscle groups over extended periods of time. Aerobic activity is also called endurance training or cardiovascular exercise. Examples of aerobic exercise include running, skating, doing jumping jacks, or swimming laps. The word "aerobic" refers to the body's need for more oxygen during this type of exercise. Most of the benefits discussed previously are achievable with aerobic exercise. One hundred and fifty minutes of aerobic exercise are recommended each week. Optimal results are obtained by performing an average of thirty minutes of consecutive aerobic exercise five days per week, but results may be realized by performing intervals as short as ten minutes each, two to three times daily.

Strength training or strengthening exercise is a form of anaerobic exercise. It focuses on increasing muscle strength and mass (size), bone strength, and metabolism. Strengthening exercises work by putting more strain on a muscle than normal stimulation of the growth of proteins inside muscle cells. There is growing evidence that adding strength training to an aerobic exercise program is better than aerobic exercise alone for improving self-esteem and body image and supporting weight loss. Examples of strength training exercise include isometric, isotonic, and isokinetic exercises. **Isometric exercise** contracts the muscle without motion, such as pushing against a wall or holding a position in yoga. **Isotonic exercise** involves the movement of a joint during muscle contraction and includes lifting weights and moving body weight such as sit-ups, pull-ups, and push-ups. **Isokinetic exercises** are generally used in physical therapy. These exercises involve a controlled range of motion, usually at a particular speed and resistance.

Range of motion or flexibility exercise refers to activity aimed at improving movement or use of a particular joint. This type of exercise can be passive, where an outside person or machine moves the joint, or active, where the exercise is performed by the individual.

Martial arts combine several types of exercise with discipline. Studies have shown that practicing martial arts can be an effective way to support improved self-esteem as well as providing physical benefits.

Getting Started

Before beginning any exercise program, it is a good idea to get a physical check-up and confirm you are cleared for all types of exercise. Once the doctor gives you the green light, it is time to get started. Remember, almost everyone can perform some level of exercise. It is important to "run your own race" and try not to do too much too quickly.

Joining a gym is one way to get started, but it is not necessary. Advantages of joining a gym include taking group classes and having access to staff assistance. There is also evidence from studies that show working out in groups supports the positive effect exercise has on mood through social interaction. If you are new in a community, exercising at a gym can also be a way to meet new people. However, not everyone is ready for this type of financial commitment in early recovery.

Walking briskly and running are two of the best ways to get aerobic exercise and are fairly inexpensive. Proper footwear is recommended, but do not get carried away. There are guides to footwear needs online that can be helpful in determining the appropriate shoes for your personal needs and within your financial capability. In the winter months, many communities have walking groups that meet at the mall or other indoor locations to support each other in maintaining fitness levels. Many communities have regular 5K run/walk events that support local charities and causes like breast cancer research, mental health services, and other similar groups.

September is known as National Recovery Month, and a variety of recovery/health-oriented activities take place around the US. You can find and/or participate in any number of events being held in your local community.

It is always more fun to do things with friends. Finding a workout buddy will not only increase the benefits of working out by adding social interaction, but it can also serve as a support to keep you going when you want to give up. Often when life shows up and you need exercise the most, it seems to be the hardest to find the time. Having a workout buddy can help you maintain your fitness commitment.

In summary, exercise will improve the functioning of important physical systems in the body, support positive mood and well-being, and improve your chances of staying in recovery. Exercise will also help you feel good about yourself by improving self-esteem and confidence. Starting an exercise program is a great way to demonstrate not only your commitment to recovery, but also to loving yourself.

The following may give you a few ideas as to the activities you enjoyed in the past, what you are presently participating in, and what you hope to do in the future for your recovery.

Activity	Past	Present	Future
Walking			
Hiking			
Riding a bike			
Aerobic class			
Yoga			
Tai Chi			
Swimming			
Weight training			
Stretching			
Dancing			
Sailing			
Snorkeling			
Skiing			
Surfing			
Rock climbing			

(continued)

Activity	Past	Present	Future
Landscaping			
Roller skating			
Hang gliding			
Ropes course			

What are your roadblocks to exercising?

_____

_____

_____

_____

_____

What are a few personal benefits to exercise?

_____

_____

_____

_____

_____

Who will support your new exercise lifestyle?

_____

_____

_____

_____

_____

Nutrition in Recovery

Proper food and nutrition are an essential component of any recovery program. A nutritious and balanced diet keeps your body strong and functioning properly. Simply changing food habits and food choices can also help diminish common mood swings and withdrawal-like symptoms such as fatigue, depression, and irritability.

Practitioners working with recovering addicts have repeatedly found that people become well much quicker, with far fewer symptoms—and stay drug-free much longer—when they follow good nutrition principles. Most substance abusers need three square meals a day with good quality protein, complex carbohydrates, and fats served at each meal. They often need snacks as well, especially during the early stages of recovery.[143]

> **Note:** As you read through this section, please keep in mind that you have your own unique dietary requirements based on a wide range of factors—genetic background, age, environment, activity level, food choices, and allergies—as well as your ability to absorb, transport, and digest nutrients. That means a diet that is adequate for your neighbor or roommate may not be appropriate for you and your specific nutritional needs.

Many people rely on limited knowledge of nutrition and may not consider the impact of eating habits in their recovery. Consideration of past eating patterns and how individual eating choices are made can increase a sense of well-being in early recovery.

What are your current food choices and eating habits? To find out, keep a food log of everything you eat and drink for a week, including all beverages like water, coffee, and soda. Also jot down the time when you eat/drink and any noteworthy physical feelings at that time.

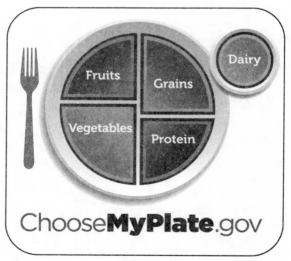

Courtesy of USDA Center for Nutrition
Policy and Promotion (CNPP).

What to Eat in Recovery

Once you have a sense of your own daily food habits, take a look at the plate above. It shows five main food groups—fruits, vegetables, grains, proteins, and dairy—currently recommended by the USDA for a healthy diet.

Fruits/Vegetables

Half of what you eat can consist of fruits and vegetables. Fruits and vegetables are high in vitamins and minerals and low in fat and calories. Unfortunately, many people in recovery are not getting the amounts they need daily. If they are getting some fruits and vegetables, they often consume a large portion of them in forms high in fat and low in nutrients like iceberg lettuce, French fries, and potato chips.[144] Also, many recovering individuals are deficient in a wide range of vitamins and minerals such as Vitamin C, calcium, magnesium, and iron, all of which are found in many fresh fruits and leafy green vegetables.

> **Tip:** Make your plate as colorful as possible by choosing a wide range of fruits and vegetables. This may help you get more of the vitamins and minerals your body needs in recovery.

Grains

Grains such as wheat, rice, oats, cornmeal, or barley can contribute to about one quarter of your daily diet. When choosing grains, consider whole grains rather than refined grains. Whole grains, like oatmeal and brown rice, take longer to digest and help to keep your blood sugar levels from fluctuating. In contrast, refined grains, like white bread and crackers, have been stripped of most nutrients and are quickly absorbed into the body, causing blood sugar levels to skyrocket. An upset in your natural balance can lead to a host of physical and emotional problems—shakiness, mood swings, irritability, sudden fatigue, and mental confusion. It can also exacerbate diet-related health problems like hypoglycemia and adrenal fatigue that are common for many recovering from alcohol and/or other drug abuse.

> **Tip:** Some find it helpful to avoid or eliminate refined grains from their diet. Consider replacing refined grains like cereals (except oatmeal), breads, pies, cakes, spaghetti and other white pasta with whole grain options to help regulate your blood sugar levels.

Protein

Protein is needed for proper functioning of the body and brain. The guidelines suggest that just less than a quarter of your diet can be protein. However, when your body is under stress or chemically imbalanced, as is the case for most in early recovery, your reserves may be so depleted that you might require even more protein than the norm.[145] Protein is especially important for those in recovery as deficiencies can lead to common recovery problems of depression, poor recall, hostile and aggressive behavior, mental confusion, anxiety, and paranoia.

Protein can be found in all foods made from meat, poultry, and seafood, and in beans, peas, eggs, soy, nuts, and seeds. While many people consume a large quantity of their protein from beef (e.g., hamburgers), that particular protein source is not always the best choice because it can be high in fat and not as easily digested as some other protein sources.[146]

Tip: The body doesn't store protein, so it needs a daily supply from a wide range of sources. Try varying your protein choices to include food such as nuts, seeds, and seafood.

Dairy

Each day, you may want to consider consuming about three cups of low-fat dairy products such as milk, cottage cheese, and yogurt. Dairy foods provide nutrients that are important for your health, like calcium, potassium, Vitamin D, and protein. Many people in early recovery have deficiencies in these particular nutrients because of poor dietary choices and the consumption of too much sugar, caffeine, and alcohol and/or other drugs that disrupt how the body might absorb and process vitamins and minerals. Many withdrawal-like symptoms like irritability, fatigue, and pain can also be linked to inadequate vitamins and minerals, many of which can be found in dairy products such as milk, yogurt, and cheese.

Tip: Foods like butter, cream cheese, and cream do not have much calcium so are not included in the dairy group.

Fats

In addition to eating food from the five groups described above, the USDA also recommends you eat small amounts of high-quality fats each day. Fats are an important nutrient needed to absorb vitamins, help to maintain good health, and provide necessary energy for your body. Fats have also been known to help elevate mood and promote good sleep.[147]

Fats are composed of fatty acids, two of which are known to be absolutely necessary to the body—Omega-6 and Omega-3. These two essential fatty acids are not produced in the body and must be obtained solely from the diet.[148] Many doctors have found that those individuals who have abused alcohol and/or other drugs have deficiencies of Omega-3 and Omega-6 fatty acids and that adding them to their program greatly aided recovery.[149]

The best sources of dietary fat for most people in recovery are natural whole grains and seeds, various fish (the best for fats are mackerel, herring, sardines, tuna, anchovy, salmon, and trout), and unsaturated oils like extra virgin olive oil that are as fresh and unprocessed as possible. Fats from dairy and meat can be used sparingly.[150] Some saturated fats like butter and unhydrogenated coconut oil can help keep you feeling full longer and stabilize your blood sugar levels.[151]

> **Tip**: Consider sticking to high-quality saturated and unsaturated fats while avoiding hydrogenated fats.

Food Group	Some Common Examples	USDA Recommended Daily Amounts *(Depends on gender, age, and activity)*	
		Men	**Women**
Fruits	Apples, bananas, cherries, grapefruits, lemons, limes, mangoes, nectarines, oranges, pears, peaches, plums, pineapples, and berries.	2 cups/day	1.5–2 cups/day
Vegetables	Dark green vegetables: spinach, romaine lettuce, broccoli, and collard greens. Beans and peas: black beans, black-eyed peas, garbanzo beans (chickpeas), kidney beans, lentils, pinto beans, and split peas. Starchy vegetables: corn, green peas, and potatoes. Other vegetables: artichokes, asparagus, avocado, beets, cauliflower, cucumbers, green beans, onions, and zucchini. Red/orange vegetables: butternut and acorn squash, carrots, pumpkins, red peppers, and tomatoes.	2.5–3 cups/day	2–2.5 cups/day

(continued)

Food Group	Some Common Examples	USDA Recommended Daily Amounts *(Depends on gender, age, and activity)*	
		Men	**Women**
Grains	Whole grains: bulgur, oatmeal, brown rice, buckwheat, muesli, popcorn, quinoa, whole wheat flour, whole wheat bread, whole wheat crackers, whole wheat pasta, and whole wheat tortillas. Refined grains: white flour, white bread, corn bread, tortillas, crackers, spaghetti, macaroni, pretzels, many breakfast cereals (e.g., corn flakes), and white rice.	6–8 ounces	6–8 ounces
Protein[152]	Grains/legumes: quinoa, brown rice, tofu, corn, chickpeas, and lentils. Fish/meat: tuna, cod, salmon, sardines, and chicken. Nuts/seeds: sunflower and pumpkin seeds and cashew nuts. Eggs/dairy: eggs, natural yogurt, and cottage cheese. Vegetables: peas, other beans, and broccoli. Combinations: lentils and rice, beans and rice	5.5–6.5 ounces of lean and varied proteins	5–5.5 ounces of lean and varied proteins
Dairy	All fluid milk products and foods made from milk like yogurt, cheese, and ice cream. Low calcium foods like butter, cream cheese, and cream are not included in this group.	3 cups/day	3 cups/day
Fats	Saturated: butter, eggs, fish, chicken, and unhydrogenated coconut oil. Unsaturated: high-quality fish oils, vegetable oils like sesame, safflower, corn, olive, and flaxseed. Hydrogenated: margarine, shortening, most processed foods, commercial salad dressings and sandwich spreads.	6–7 teaspoons	5–6 teaspoons

What Foods to Avoid in Recovery

Poor nutrition is one of the critical risk factors for substance abuse. If you ignore your diet, you might put yourself at risk for a relapse.[153] If you eat a diet high in "junk food," you may find it hard to stay abstinent and in recovery. Junk food is highly-processed, containing preservatives, hormones, artificial colorings, and sugar. Below is a list of some items to avoid. Check your food labels and try to avoid these whenever possible.

Sugar

Sugar is one of the common foods that many individuals in early recovery turn to when trying to stay abstinent and not use. That is because sugar is highly addictive and works much like alcohol and other drugs to provide temporary relief from the low blood sugar levels common to recovery. Unfortunately, consuming sugar in the form of candy bars, cake, doughnuts, and soda might also exacerbate a number of health problems and withdrawal-like symptoms.

Refined sugars like sucrose and high fructose corn syrup provide little or no nutritional value. In fact, they do the opposite; they actually deplete the body of essential vitamins and minerals.[154]

Those who are trying to avoid sugar often turn to artificial sweeteners. These can sometimes cause problems with weight gain, increased cravings for sweets, impaired coordination, decreased mental function, diabetes, multiple sclerosis (MS), Parkinson's, seizures, and migraine headaches. Consider replacing artificial and refined sugar with naturally occurring sweeteners like raw cane sugar, pure maple syrup, raw honey, or molasses. It is often suggested to use them sparingly, as natural sweeteners can similarly affect your blood sugar levels and contribute to cravings for sweets. Be sure to consider balancing sugar with good fats and protein to help stabilize blood sugar and reduce cravings for sweets.[155]

> **Tip**: Sugar comes in many forms like sucrose, corn sweeteners, honey, maple syrup, and molasses. It is found in many foods such as flavored yogurts, fruit drinks, ketchup, pizza, hot dogs, bread, and some peanut butters. You can recognize sugars in commercial foods by looking at the labels for ingredients that end in "ose" or "ol."

Processed Foods

A majority of the sugar in our diets generally comes from prepared, processed foods. Processed foods are foods that have been altered from their original natural state—food that has been cut, diced, cooked, puffed, ground, canned, or changed from its initial state. Many processed foods are not as healthy because they have been stripped of many nutrients and can be made with saturated fats, sugar, sodium, artificial flavorings and colors, and other additives.

> **Tip**: Not all processed food is bad. For example, frozen food is processed but is still a good source for fruits and vegetables.

White Flour

White flour is a highly processed food choice. The body breaks down white flour like sugar, and it can lead to many of the same problems described above. When whole wheat flour is processed and turned into white flour, the fiber and many of the vitamins and nutrients are removed. Because it is lacking fiber, it can cause constipation and other bowel problems. Wheat is also a major allergen and may cause reactions like headaches, fatigue, malabsorption, irritability, upper respiratory congestion, nausea, diarrhea, and other bowel disorders like celiac and Crohn's disease.

> **Tip:** White flour is found in most commercial breads, crackers, pasta, bagels, and pancake mixes. Consider replacing these with whole grains.

Additives

A number of additives in food have been associated with changes in the brain and can sometimes contribute to hyperactivity and/or learning difficulties.[156] Some of these additives are monosodium glutamate (MSG), found in commercially processed foods such as stocks, sauces, chips, dips, and processed meats; phenylethylamine, found in chocolate; tyramine, found in aged cheese and Chianti; xanthines, from caffeine; and aspartame, which is the artificial sweetener known as NutraSweet.

Phosphates are another group of additives used in processed foods. These can be found in beverages, oils, baked goods, soft drinks, and fruit products. They have been associated with hyperactivity in certain children whose behavioral problems diminished when the phosphates were removed from their diets.

High Fructose Corn Syrup

High fructose corn syrup is a common ingredient found in many processed and packaged food. Studies have shown that it can lead to obesity and cardiovascular disease. It can also deplete nutrients in the body, raise cholesterol levels in the blood, and possibly accelerate the aging process. High fructose corn syrup is found in a wide range of foods, including bread, cereals, soft drinks, and even in some ketchup and spaghetti sauces.

Hydrogenated Oils

Hydrogenated oils are made by rearranging the chemical composition, which can make them difficult to digest. These can contribute to problems such as heart disease, diabetes, and obesity. Hydrogenated oils are found in almost all processed foods, commercial salad dressings, sandwich spreads, and margarine.

> **Tip**: Consider replacing these oils with real butter, extra-virgin cold-pressed olive oil, flaxseed oil, and coconut oil. All of these are rich sources of saturated fatty acids and vitamins.

Caffeine

Many people turn to caffeine when trying to recover from alcohol and/or other drug abuse. Although widely accepted, caffeine is another type of drug that can alter your chemical balance. It pumps adrenaline into the bloodstream, which temporarily provides energy. Adrenaline also can dump stored sugar into the bloodstream, which can eventually trigger symptoms like fatigue, lack of physical endurance and stamina, impaired ability to deal with stress, depressed immune system, allergic reactions, weight gain, low blood pressure, dizziness and lightheadedness, or blacking out when standing up. Caffeine can also impair calcium absorption and stimulate the liver to release more sugar in the bloodstream, which further stresses the body's delicate sugar-regulating mechanism.

If you choose to quit using caffeine, you may want to start slowly. For example, you may want to begin by cutting your caffeine intake in half each week until you no longer need it. Also, eat protein-based meals with whole grains and good fats to keep your blood sugar stable and reduce your cravings for sugar and caffeine.

List some food items you consume regularly that you may want to avoid. What nutritious food options might you eat instead?

_____

_____

_____

_____

_____

Do you drink a lot of sugary and/or caffeinated beverages each day? If you do, write down a plan for how you can slowly replace some of these beverages with healthier options.

_____

_____

_____

_____

_____

Do you regularly read the labels on the food you buy? _____

Look at the ingredients on your food labels and consider these questions:

- Is there a long list of ingredients (more than five or six)? _____
- Are the ingredients difficult to read/pronounce? _____
- Does it have a lot of sugar and/or sodium (salt)? _____
- Does it have any hydrogenated oils? _____

If you answered "yes" to any of the questions above, then that food is probably highly processed and may not be your most healthy option.

When to Eat in Recovery

Besides eating high-quality foods, eating at the right time is also an important part of the nutritional puzzle. It is important for the body to receive a steady supply of fuel to control blood sugar levels. This can improve mood and self-control and help reduce cravings that can often block your recovery efforts.

Several different eating patterns have been shown to work well, and they can help support your recovery. There are a number of books that you may find helpful as you learn healthy eating behaviors. For example, *Food & Behavior* recommends three main meals along with light snacks every couple of hours so that your blood sugar does not drop to a crisis point. In contrast, *Potatoes Not Prozac* recommends eating only three high-protein meals per day at regular intervals. That program does not recommend the "six-times-a-day" eating plans because of the concern that snacking can lead to grazing for those in recovery who might be sensitive to sugar.

In general, most experts recommend that individuals in recovery consume a diet that consists of high-protein meals at regular intervals to regulate the body and ward off cravings. Listen to your body and see what works best for you. Also, since it is not always possible to time when you are hungry or need a snack, carry healthy snacks with you such as nuts and seeds, dried fruit (if you are not sugar-sensitive), and sliced carrots. In addition, be sure to keep your body well hydrated with water.

Common Vitamin and Mineral Deficiencies

Many people in recovery are often deficient in key minerals such as calcium, magnesium, zinc, and chromium as well as Vitamin C and the B-complex vitamins. Dr. Beasley in *Food for Recovery* notes that he has never taken care of someone who was recovering from addiction who was not deficient in vitamins and minerals—both because of his or her poor diets and because of the addiction-induced damage to the organs that process nutrients.

Vitamins and minerals are needed in small quantities each day in order for the body to function properly. Research shows that the lack of a single vitamin or mineral can cause metabolic imbalances that will create addictive cravings.[157] Below are foods rich in the vitamins and minerals most commonly deficient in recovering people. Consider including some of these foods into your daily diet.

Try Eating Some of These Foods High in Key Vitamins and Minerals	
Zinc	Oysters, ginger root, round steak, lamb, pecans, peas, shrimp, parsley, and potatoes
Chromium	Chromium is widely distributed in food, but most foods contain only small amounts of it. Meats and whole grain products like whole wheat and rye, some fruits, shellfish like oysters and shrimp, vegetables, brewer's yeast, cornmeal, butter, and spices
Magnesium	Leafy green vegetables, kelp, peas, molasses, nuts like almonds and cashews, brown rice, whole grains and seafood
Iron	Liver, oysters, leafy greens, red meat, blackstrap molasses, kelp, brewer's yeast, eggs, and beans
Potassium	Potatoes, bananas, leafy green vegetables, oranges, whole grains, and sunflower seeds
Selenium	Butter, smoked herring, wheat germ, bran, liver, and eggs
Vitamin C	Fresh fruits and vegetables like green peppers, citrus fruits, tomatoes, potatoes, cauliflower, Brussels sprouts, broccoli, and cabbage **Note:** *Many nutritionally based recovery programs also supplement with large doses of Vitamin C; however, it is highly acidic, and when used in moderate or large doses, it can cause ulceration of the digestive tract and further depletion of calcium and magnesium levels in many people. If supplementing with large doses, be sure to consult a physician.*
B-Complex Vitamins	Found in most whole, unprocessed foods such as potatoes, lentils, chili peppers, tempeh, bean, brewer's yeast, and molasses **Note**: *Some supplementation may be required for those who are severely imbalanced; however, severe liver damage and other health factors sometimes associated with alcohol and other drug abuse may make it especially difficult for some people to tolerate supplements of B vitamins such as niacin. This means that a variety of healthy food alternatives is even more important.*

A balanced diet of nutritious food that includes fruits, vegetables, whole grains, protein, dairy, and high-quality fat is integral to your recovery plan. It can supply important nutrients to your depleted body and stabilize both your energy level and mood. The bottom line is that it can lead to a more successful recovery and a heightened feeling of well-being. If overhauling your diet seems too daunting, then begin gradually. Small changes made and sustained over a long period of time will eventually evolve into a habit. One wise choice today can start you on the road to a lifetime of healthy eating.

This nutrition section is in part an abbreviated version of Nutrition in Addiction Recovery *by Rebecca Place Miller, published by Many Hands Sustainability Center. May 2010. (http://mhof.net/sites/default/files/Nutrition%20i%20Addiction%20Recovery.pdf).*

Notes

CHAPTER TWELVE
Helpful Information for Family and Friends About Relapse

As a family member or friend of a person who is in recovery from a mental illness and addiction, here are the most important things you should remember.

Know it's not that person's fault (it's not your fault either). If the person in recovery begins to show relapse symptoms, he or she is not doing it on purpose. Most people in recovery do their best to stabilize their symptoms and prevent relapse, but relapses can still occur, especially in early recovery.

Educate yourself about warning signs. Read this book and other materials to educate yourself about warning signs so that you can help the person in recovery detect those warning signs early and prevent relapse. If you are a designated support person to your friend or family member, it is a good idea to make sure he or she shows you a copy of a relapse prevention plan, and that you keep a copy.

Learn relapse communication skills. Learn how to better communicate with the person in recovery by attending meetings, talking to a counselor, and reading books on this topic. When a problem arises, it is natural for you to feel frustrated and even angry. Avoid any impulses to be critical and blaming of the person in recovery. If you can encourage the person to speak freely, without interruption, and if you can show understanding, encourage discussion, and give constructive feedback, then there is a good chance you can help. If a person in recovery can find solutions to triggers, warning signs, and even initial relapse behaviors, he or she can avoid ongoing relapse. Sometimes all the person needs is a friend to listen and be supportive. It's important to remain caring and supportive, regardless of what happens.

Recognize an emergency and ask for professional help. If you think the person in recovery will hurt him- or herself or another person, or is unable to care for him- or herself in a safe way, then you should call a professional for help. The relapse prevention plan the person shared with you contains a section for this type of emergency situation. The person in recovery has spelled out his or her wishes. Do your best to keep the person calm and safe while waiting for help. Do not try to handle the problem alone. *If there is an emergency, follow the plan.*

Family Recovery

Living with active addiction and mental health challenges can be extremely isolating—for the individual as well as for the family. Recovery can provide opportunities to develop family relationships, friendships, and a sense of feeling connected in a community.

Family recovery is sometimes about acknowledging, or simply considering, that they are not the only ones affected by the confusion and pain of addiction and mental health concerns. The reality may be that other people close to the family may have experienced similar feelings simply by being around the confusion and destruction caused by a loved one's active addiction.

Research suggests that active participation in family treatment programs supports the success of long-term recovery for the individual with an addictive disease and other mental health issues. This also suggests that family members who practice healthy recovery skills can also experience long-term physical and mental health. For this reason, the involvement of your family and "supportive others" in the recovery process can be an important factor in the success and well-being of everyone.

Communication

Have your family or friends ever asked you questions such as, "Why don't you just quit?" or made statements such as, "Just snap out of it," or "Get over it already"? These examples can be a common reaction for people who do not understand the complexities of co-occurring disorders. Once your family and supportive others are educated about the realities of addiction and other challenges, there is an enormous opportunity for a new way to communicate, relate, and connect with others. This can promote a better understanding, more realistic expectations, and a chance to heal and grow.

Healthy communication in relationships can often assist you in building a foundation for long-term recovery. This is sometimes easier said than done. Learning to communicate in a way that is honest, genuine, productive, and effective can take patience and practice. Changing old habits and patterns may not happen overnight. Here are a few key areas that you may want to consider.

What is active listening? Some believe that listening has become a lost art. Most of us will agree that people in general want to be heard. While someone is talking, have you ever caught yourself looking at your watch or thinking about what you plan to do later that day? It's pretty common to get distracted, particularly if the conversation does not interest you. Some people start looking the other way or cross their arms like they are late for something. There are many ways people respond to a conversation, as well as watch how people listen to you.

To practice active listening, try the "mirror technique." After the other person is finished speaking, relay back to him or her in your own words what you heard that person say. This can help alleviate miscommunication while also reinforcing that you were actually listening.

Expressing your needs by setting healthy boundaries. One of the most important functions of boundaries is to help keep you and/or others safe. Sometimes healthy boundaries can be confused with threats or ultimatums. A boundary expresses your need, concern, or issue. An ultimatum is a threat, which creates defenses and is likely ineffective in the long-term.

To practice setting healthy boundaries, try starting the boundary by saying, "I need to . . ." as opposed to "You need to . . ." This helps you to express your own needs without attempting to control another person.

How Family and Support Systems Can Be Impacted by Co-occurring Disorders

Many of the same symptoms and behaviors associated with co-occurring disorders can impact family and friends in a similar manner.

For example: An addictive family relationship may start to show difficulty in the areas of genuine and healthy communications. The result of this can then negatively influence other parts of your lives and how you and your family or loved ones might respond to situations.

A common quote from people in recovery is: "We are as sick as our secrets."

The secrets around addiction and mental health seem to create numerous problems and concerns. Sometimes these are simply too overwhelming to deal with, and keeping secrets or avoiding situations can be easier. For the moment, the easier way may seem to work for a while; however, over time, these small steps in avoiding a situation can develop into a group of responses called "defense mechanisms."

Defense Mechanisms

There are many definitions for what a defense mechanism is. Sigmund Freud, in his development of psychoanalytic theory, proposed that our overly defensive actions may be the brain's way of protecting itself from extreme anxiety or situations that are too difficult for the conscious mind to deal with. Others may tend to view them in a similar fashion, indicating that they are a way for us to cope with difficult or uncomfortable situations.

Most agree that defense mechanisms can protect us in a healthy way for a while. However, over time, these defensive actions can become a habitual way to live and to respond to life situations. Oftentimes we are unable to stop using them without support.

Here are a few responses that you may relate to:

Denial

It is common for people diagnosed with co-occurring disorders to experience denial. Examples may be, "I don't have a drug or alcohol problem," and "I certainly don't have any mental health issues." The best known antidote for denial tends to be education. Your efforts to learn more about yourself and your patterns can help reduce denial and open the door for positive changes in your life.

Since your family and supportive others may also experience denial (sometimes in the form of rationalization, justification, or minimization), any efforts they make to learn about co-occurring disorders will go a long way in the recovery process for all involved.

Intellectualization

To intellectualize means to keep in the mind as opposed to feeling or speaking from the heart. Intellectualizing can impair your ability to heal because feeling facilitates healing and personal growth. An example of intellectualizing would be to say, "My daughter isn't really an addict because her doctor prescribed her pain medication; it's not like she bought it off the street."

Sometimes families do not want to believe there are problems, and they attempt to develop elaborate and believable responses as to why someone is drinking or using drugs.

Rationalization

Rationalization is the mind's attempt to justify reality. To say, "My husband is a great provider and deserves to drink every night to wind down," is an example of rationalization. Another example would be, "She's not clinically depressed, she's just sensitive, emotional, and needs to get some rest."

Acting Out

When you act out you may be taking your feelings out on others (or yourself) in destructive ways. An example of this is when a person has feelings of anger and then drives his or her car (commonly known as "road rage"); perhaps it is not just the traffic or the slow or inconsiderate driver that is the root of the frustration. In other words, acting out may be displaced anger. Anger is a natural human emotion. The key is to find ways of processing feelings of anger without hurting yourself or anyone else in the process. DBT practices can calm the "acting out" impulse and help you to self-soothe in moments of frustration.

Families may tend to take on similar behaviors when untreated addiction or mental health issues exist. This can be in the form of anger as well as simply not saying anything. Some families are quiet and say nothing for years.

Undoing

After saying or doing something that may be hurtful to others in some way, have you ever tried to overcompensate with compliments and kindness? This is an example of "undoing," an effort to repair or balance out any potential damage done. To say something like, "You're just a lazy fool; why don't you get it together already?" followed later by, "You are really good at your job," "You are a great husband," or "I really appreciate all your efforts," are examples of attempts at "undoing."

Sometimes families take the blame for addiction and continue to apologize for being angry or thinking about past behaviors.

Compartmentalization

Compartmentalization is a way to dissociate or separate from difficult thoughts, behaviors, or values. An example might be if someone in active addiction feels content because he is functioning well enough at work but is struggling in all other areas of his personal life. Compartmentalization, in other words, is an attempt to focus only on an area that is less problematic to self-soothe and perhaps turn away from the more challenging areas of life. Compartmentalization is a type of contradiction that can cause inner conflict and discomfort.

Families can also compartmentalize situations, such as how they present themselves in public versus at home. They may pretend to be the perfect family on the outside, but at home it may be a different story.

Repression

Repression is like an unconscious "forgetting" of thoughts, feelings, or events. If an event from the past is too painful or difficult to grasp, repression serves to "erase" it from memory. This is a common defense mechanism for trauma or abuse survivors as it facilitates distance from the emotional and physical responses associated with these painful experiences.

This is also effective for families in forgetting how many times the crisis of addiction and mental health disorders have affected them. Sometimes, families simply want to forget how bad it was or pretend that nothing happened.

Displacement

Sometimes when we experience feelings or emotions, like anger, it might be difficult to address or confront these directly with the persons involved. In displacement, the tendency is to direct the anger at some other source. For example: If a person has a bad day and is feeling frustrated, she may yell or lash out at family, friends, or the dog. The immediate result may be relief. However, this defense mechanism is largely ineffective because it can create more conflict as opposed to lessening it.

Families often blame a number of things in defense of someone using alcohol and/or other drugs, such as peer pressure, one parent's behavior, poor childhood, money, and so forth.

Dissociation

Dissociation is generally disorientation from time, people, and places. Alcohol and/or other drugs, as well as some mental health disorders, can create this separation or "disconnect" from the world, like an escape from reality.

It is also common for people with a history of childhood abuse or trauma to separate themselves from the memories of situations in this way. It can be a short-term solution to disassociate or separate from themselves and the emotional pain they experience.

Sometimes families will disconnect from the person using drugs and alcohol in an attempt to stop the emotional pain. They may simply refuse to be around them and often try to forget they were in their lives.

A Closer Look

Take a look at the table on the next page. As you are going through it, please consider the similarities of those who are addicted to alcohol and/or other drugs and perhaps struggling with mental health concerns, and those who are close to them, such as family and friends. You may find that their behaviors are similar, both in identifying the problem as well as the solution.

The columns to the right may offer you a chance to reflect on defenses that directly relate to your life. You may find that you and your family have a lot in common and that everyone has a part in the recovery process.

Addict/Alcoholic	Family/Friends	How I might respond	How my family/ friends might respond
Denial	**Denial**	**Denial**	**Denial**
I don't have a problem with alcohol or other drugs.	My kids don't take drugs.		
I am not depressed or suicidal.	She is just emotional and needs to rest.		
Rationalization	**Rationalization**	**Rationalization**	**Rationalization**
Everybody drinks and drives.	He made a mistake, and I am sure it won't happen again		
It was just bad luck; wrong place, wrong time.	It was most likely his friends' fault.		
Acting Out	**Acting Out**	**Acting Out**	**Acting Out**
I will usually do what it takes to get what I want.	My anger is growing, and I am fighting more with my mate.		
I am going to drink, and no one can stop me.	I might as well drink too. If you can't beat them, join them.		
Undoing	**Undoing**	**Undoing**	**Undoing**
I'm sorry I was arrested for the third time; it will never happen again.	I was not there for you; I will buy you a car.		
I will never hit you again, I promise.	I should not have said that to make you mad; I will be more careful.		
Compartmentalization	**Compartmentalization**	**Compartmentalization**	**Compartmentalization**
I don't do drugs, I just drink; I use a little pot, but that's not a drug.	Well, he is in college and holds a job, so maybe it's okay.		
I never use at home.	He drinks only at the bar.		
Repression	**Repression**	**Repression**	**Repression**
We were all at the party when he overdosed. I don't want to think about it.	I remember when the police told me. That's all I can recall.		
I am acting like my father when he got drunk. I had forgotten that.	This reminds me of when I was a child growing up with an alcoholic mother.		
Displacement	**Displacement**	**Displacement**	**Displacement**
If I'd had a better childhood ... It is my parents' fault.	If my husband had not left ...		
I was arrested because the police don't like me.	They are always harassing young people.		

Family and Recovery: A Few Key Considerations

Stigma and Shame

There is often a stigma placed on those with a psychiatric diagnosis and those who have a history of addiction that can be reinforced by a lack of awareness, understanding, and education. Many individuals still keep addictive and mental health disorders a secret and rarely discuss them outside the family. With increased awareness and education about co-occurring disorders, the hope is that anyone who faces these challenges will receive welcoming treatment, support, and compassion.

Shame can often sabotage recovery for the dually diagnosed person. How a person views addiction and mental health issues can play a large role in how he or she may overcome and accept that fact and strive for the freedom recovery brings.

The family's response, or willingness to accept the addiction or diagnosis, is equally important. If a family is ashamed of someone with these disorders, then the support—or lack of it, in this case—has the potential to sabotage recovery.

Keep in mind that things will not change overnight. In early recovery, both the individual and his or her family need time to adjust to new ways of thinking and acting. You may want to evaluate these dynamics when developing your aftercare plans. Having a supportive and structured living environment that is open and educated about these challenges is very important for those first three to six months of recovery.

Self-Medication

In an effort to seek relief from emotional or psychiatric symptoms, some individuals turn to alcohol or other drugs as a means to feel better. Some relief may be experienced initially; however, in time, this can turn into dependence and result in more complex challenges.

For example:

- If you are prone to depression, you may seek out drugs like cocaine or amphetamines.
- People suffering from depression may also turn to alcohol, which is a depressant and can ultimately increase the very symptoms you seek to relieve.
- A person experiencing a manic episode (associated with bipolar disorder) may seek out alcohol, benzodiazepines, or sedative hypnotics in an effort to reduce symptoms.
- Recent research hypotheses also suggest that there is a correlation between people suffering from Post-Traumatic Stress Disorder (PTSD) and the abuse of opiates.

There may also be complications with psychopharmacological interventions prescribed by a doctor if an individual is still drinking or using. The medications intended to help with psychiatric symptoms are often compromised due to misuse, lack of reporting symptoms to the physician, or simply missing doses. In essence, balancing addiction and trying to gain relief from psychiatric symptoms is challenging.

Families and friends are encouraged to work together to assist individuals when stabilizing on psychiatric medications. It can be a bit complicated, so having the support from others can make a difference. Just a few examples: Gentle reminders about doctor's appointments or when prescriptions are due, and offering feedback on side effects and symptoms.

Medication Management

It is helpful to open the lines of communication with your family and supportive others on the topic of medication. If you are prescribed a medication for your psychiatric symptoms, it is important for those close to you to be free to address any issues or concerns that may arise. For example, if changes in symptoms or behaviors are identified, an open discussion can facilitate any necessary adjustments that your psychiatrist may need to make to your regimen. Families can also be supportive of medication compliance, helping you to stay on track. An open dialogue about medications also serves to eliminate shame and reduce stigma.

Attempts to Control

One of the ways to identify if someone is addicted to a substance is his or her inability to stop drinking/using, despite increased negative consequences. You may recognize a similarity here with your own history in trying to stop or control a substance. You may also have noticed your family and friends wanting you to stop. These behaviors may have gone on for many years, so it may take a while for families to change this.

One of the focuses of family recovery is to discourage attempts to "micromanage." A familiar phrase in twelve-step meetings is "I am responsible for my own recovery and you are responsible for yours." While it will be important for your family to not keep you "under a microscope" during your recovery, family involvement in identifying psychiatric symptoms and medication management can be helpful.

Inviting Your Family to Participate in the Recovery Process

Allowing your family and supportive others to have some involvement in your treatment and recovery can be helpful and supportive for everyone.

List three ways you can include your family/friends in your recovery:

1. _____
2. _____
3. _____

Resources for Your Family and Supportive Others

Following are some organizations specific for families and loved ones of those suffering with addiction and/or mental health challenges.

- National Alliance for Mental Illness (NAMI): Focuses on support, education, research, and advocacy to help individuals and families affected by mental illness. Website: www.nami.org.
- Al-Anon: A twelve-step fellowship for families and friends of alcoholics that provides a forum for learning, support, and healing. Website: www.alanon.org.
- Nar-Anon: A twelve-step fellowship for families and friends of addicts that provides a forum for learning, support, and healing. Website: www.na.org.
- Family Therapist: A specialist in co-occurring disorders can be beneficial for the entire family. An outside objective view can sometimes assist in guiding people and their families toward a place of recovery.

Community Resources for You

"Community resources are a group of services and/or assistance programs that are provided to the members of a community for free or at an affordable price. Each resource is made available to community members to help them become self-reliant and maintain their human rights and well-being."[158]

Community resources for people in recovery can play a significant role in establishing a foundation for long-term recovery. Support groups such as Alcoholics Anonymous, Narcotics Anonymous, Dual Recovery Anonymous, SMART Recovery, and Al-Anon all share a common interest in supporting an abstinent-based and recovery-oriented lifestyle.

There are also many other organizations that support a healthy recovery-oriented lifestyle. For example, the YMCA offers numerous programs and opportunities. Others include groups and support for employment, exercise, social development, and so forth. In addition, many religious and spiritual organizations offer ongoing support that can include counseling, family, and group support.

Twelve-Step Programs

The twelve-step models or methods have been successfully utilized and adapted over the years by a number of community resource groups. These groups have incorporated the basic concepts of recovery in hundreds of self-help organizations worldwide. Examples include anonymous programs for narcotics, cocaine, crystal meth, pills, sex, gambling, eating disorders, love addiction, work, crime, emotions, and so forth. The original Twelve Steps were founded by Alcoholics Anonymous (AA), with the first twelve-step meeting being held in 1938 in Akron, Ohio.

The Twelve Steps

These are the original Twelve Steps as published by Alcoholics Anonymous:

1. We admitted we were powerless over alcohol—that our lives had become unmanageable.
2. Came to believe that a Power greater than ourselves could restore us to sanity.
3. Made a decision to turn our will and our lives over to the care of God *as we understood Him*.
4. Made a searching and fearless moral inventory of ourselves.
5. Admitted to God, to ourselves, and to another human being the exact nature of our wrongs.
6. Were entirely ready to have God remove all these defects of character.
7. Humbly asked Him to remove our shortcomings.
8. Made a list of all persons we had harmed and became willing to make amends to them all.
9. Made direct amends to such people wherever possible, except when to do so would injure them or others.
10. Continued to take personal inventory, and when we were wrong, promptly admitted it.
11. Sought through prayer and meditation to improve our conscious contact with God *as we understood Him*, praying only for knowledge of His will for us and the power to carry that out.
12. Having had a spiritual awakening as the result of these Steps, we tried to carry this message to alcoholics, and to practice these principles in all our affairs.

The Twelve Traditions

As AA was growing in the 1930s and 1940s, definite guiding principles began to emerge as the Twelve Traditions. The Twelve Traditions followed after the development of the Twelve Steps. The traditions provide guidelines for group governance, as well as public policy.

1. Our common welfare should come first; personal recovery depends upon AA unity.
2. For our group purpose there is but one ultimate authority—a loving God as He may express Himself in our group conscience. Our leaders are but trusted servants; they do not govern.
3. The only requirement for AA membership is a desire to stop drinking.

4. Each group should be autonomous except in matters affecting other groups or AA as a whole.

5. Each group has but one primary purpose—to carry its message to the alcoholic who still suffers.

6. An AA group ought never endorse, finance, or lend the AA name to any related facility or outside enterprise, lest problems of money, property, and prestige divert us from our primary purpose.

7. Every AA group ought to be fully self-supporting, declining outside contributions.

8. AA should remain forever nonprofessional, but our service centers may employ special workers.

9. AA, as such, ought never be organized; but we may create service boards or committees directly responsible to those they serve.

10. AA has no opinion on outside issues; hence the AA name ought never be drawn into public controversy.

11. Our public relations policy is based on attraction rather than promotion; we need always maintain personal anonymity at the level of press, radio, and films.

12. Anonymity is the spiritual foundation of all our traditions, ever reminding us to place principles before personalities.

Recommended Reading

Alcoholics Anonymous, *Alcoholics Anonymous* (Fourth Ed.) (New York: AA World Services, 2001).

Alcoholics Anonymous, *Twelve Steps and Twelve Traditions* (New York: AA World Service, 1981).

Katie Evans and J. Michael Sullivan, *Dual Diagnosis: Counseling the Mentally Ill Substance Abuser* (New York: Random House, 1998).

Gary Fisher and Thomas Harrison, *Substance Abuse: Information for School Counselors, Social Workers, Therapists, and Counselors* (Boston: Allyn & Bacon, 1997).

Craig Nakken, *The Addictive Personality* (Center City: Hazeldon Publishing, 1988).

Narcotics Anonymous, *Narcotics Anonymous* (Fifth Ed.) (Van Nuys: NA World Service, 1988).

Recovery Publications, Inc., *The 12 Steps: A Way Out* (San Diego: Recovery Publications, Inc., 1989).

Substance Abuse and Mental Health Services Administration (SAMHSA), "Substance abuse treatment and domestic violence" (Tip 25) (Rockville: SAMHSA, 1997).

Substance Abuse and Mental Health Services Administration (SAMHSA), "Substance abuse treatment for persons with child abuse and neglect issues" (Tip 36) (Rockville: SAMHSA, 2000).

Amy Beth Taublieb, *A-Z Handbook of Child and Adolescent Issues* (Boston: Allyn & Bacon, 2000).

Sharon Wegshieder-Cruse, *Another Chance: Hope and Health for the Alcoholic Family* (Mountain View: Science and Behavior Books, 1991).

K. J. Wilson, *When Violence Begins at Home: A Comprehensive Guide to Understanding and Ending Domestic Violence* (Alameda: Hunter House Publishers, 1997).

Janet Woititz, *Adult Children of Alcoholics* (Deerfield Beach: Health Communications, Inc., 1990).

Steven Wolin and Sybil Wolin, *The Resilient Self: How Survivors of Troubled Families Rise Above Adversity* (New York: Villard Books, 1993).

Notes

References

Anderson, R.A., Bryden, N.A., and M.M. Polansky. "Dietary Chromium Intake: Freely Chosen Diets, Institutional Diets and Individual Foods." Biological Trace Elements Research; 32:117-21. 1992 as cited in (http://dietary-supplements.info.nih.gov/factsheets/chromium.asp).

Bates, Charles, Ph.D. Essential Fatty Acids and Immunity in Mental Health (Washington: Life Science Press), 1987 as cited in Finnegan and Gray, 1990.

Beasley, Joseph D., M.D. and Susan Knightly. Food for Recovery. (New York, New York: Crown Publishers, Inc.), 1994.

Bennett, Connie, C.H.H.C., and Stephen T. Sinatra, M.D. Sugar Shock! (New York, New York: Penguin Group), 2007.

Braverman, Eric, M.D. et al. The Healing Nutrients Within. (Laguna Beach, California: Basic Health Publications), 1987.

Cass, Hyla, M.D. and Patrick Holford. Natural Highs Feel Good All the Time. (New York, New York: Penguin Putman, Inc.), 2002.

DesMaisons, Kathleen, Ph. D. Potatoes Not Prozac. (New York, New York: Fireside), 1998.

Drake, M.E. "Panic Attacks and Excessive Aspartame Ingestion." Lancet; page 631. September 1986.

Finnegan, John. Addiction: A Nutritional Approach to Recovery. (Mill Valley, California: Elysian Arts), 1989.

Finnegan, John. Understanding Oils and Fats (California: Leysian Arts), 1990 as cited in Finnegan and Gray, 1990.

Finnegan, John and Daphne Gray. Recovery from Addiction. (Berkeley, California: Celestial Arts), 1990.

Fishbein, Diana, Ph.D. and Susan Pease, Ph.D. "The Effects of Diet on Behavior: Implications for Criminology and Corrections." Research in Corrections, Volume 1, Issue 2. June 1988. (http://www.nicic.org/pubs/pre/006777.pdf).

Gant, Charles, M.D., Ph.D. and Greg Lewis, Ph.D. End Your Addiction Now. (NY, NY: Warner Books, Inc.), 2002.

Lappe, Frances Moore. Diet for a Small Planet. (New York: Ballantine), 1975 as cited in Stitt, 2004.

Larson, Joan Mathews, Ph.D. Seven Weeks to Sobriety. (New York: Fawcett Books), 1992.

Larson, Joan Mathews, Ph.D. and Robert A. Parker, M.Sc. "Alcoholism Treatment with Biochemcial Restoration as a Major Component." International Journal of Biosocial Research, Volume 9(1): 92-106. 1997. (http://allianceforaddictionsolutions.org/images/pdfs/HRC_Alc_Study_proofed.pdf).

Lipinski, Lori. "The Kitchen Transition." Wise Traditions in Food, Farming and the Healing Arts, the Quarterly Magazine of the Weston A. Price Foundation. December 5, 2003. (http://www.westonaprice.org/The-Kitchen-Transition.html).

Marsano, L., and C.J. McClain. "Effects of Alcohol on Electrolytes and Minerals." Alcohol Health & Research World; 13(3):255-260. 1989 as cited in Public Health Service, Institute of Health (http://www.seekwellness.com/nutrition/alcohol.htm).

Merck Manuals. Table of Trace Mineral Deficiency and Toxicity." Online Medical Library. (http://www.merck.com/media/mmpe/pdf/Table_005-1.pdf).

Public Health Service, National Institutes of Health. Updated 2000. Accessed on 4/15/10. (http://www.seekwellness.com/nutrition/alcohol.htm).

Putnam, Judy, Allshouse, Jane, and Linda Scot Kantor. "U.S. Per Capita Food Supply Trends: More Calories, Refined Carbohydrates and Fats." FoodReview, Vol. 25, Issue 3. Winter 2002.

Reuben, Carolyn. Cleansing the Body, Mind, and Spirit. (New York: Berkley Books), 1998.

Ross, Julia, M.A. The Diet Cure. (New York, New York: Penguin Group), 1999.

Ross, Julia, M.A. The Mood Cure. (New York, New York: Penguin Group), 2002.

Rudin, Donald O., M.D. and Clara Felix. The Omega 3 Phenomenon (New York: Rawson Associates), 1987 as cited in Finnegan and Gray, 1990.

Smith, Lendon. Feed Yourself Right. (New York, New York: Dell Publishing Co.), 1983.

Stitt, Barbara Reed. Food & Behavior: A Natural Connection. (Manitowoc, Wisconsin: Natural Press), 2004.

United States Department of Agriculture (USDA). Dr. Meira Fields in the Proceedings of the Society of Experimental Biology and Medicine; 175:530-537. 1984.

United States Department of Agriculture (USDA). Choose My Plate.gov. Website accessed 2/25/13. (http://www.choosemyplate.gov/).

United States Select Committee on Nutrition and Human Needs, United States Senate, Dietary Goals for the United States, page 48. (Washington, D.C.: US Government Printing Office), 1977.

Walker, M.M. "Phosphates and Hyperactivity: Is There a Connection?" Academic Therapy; 17(4): 439-446. 1982.

Walton, M.E. "Seizure and mania after high intake of aspartame." Psychosomatics; 27: 218-220. 1986.

Bibliography

Bernard, P., and G. Ninot. "Benefits of exercise for people with schizophrenia: A systematic review." *L'Encephale*. Bethesda: National Institutes of Health, 2011.

Birge S. J., and G. Dalsky. "The role of exercise in preventing osteoporosis." Public Health Report. Bethesda: National Institutes of Health, 1989.

Blum, K., A.L.C. Chen, M. Oscar-Berman, T.J.H. Chen, T. Lubar, N. White, J. Lubar, A. Bowirrat, E. Braverman, J. Schoolfield, R.L. Waite, B.W. Downs, M. Madigan, D.E. Comings, C. Davis, M.M. Kerner, J. Knopf, T. Palomo, J.J. Giordano, S.A. Morse, F. Fornari, D. Barh, J. Femino, and J.A. Bailey. "Generational association studies of dopaminergic genes in Reward Deficiency Syndrome (RDS) subjects: Selecting appropriate phenotypes for reward dependence behaviors." *International Journal of Environmental Research and Public Health*. Bethesda: National Institutes of Health, 2011.

Blum, K., J. Giordano, S. Morse, A. Bowirrat, M. Madigan, W. Downs, R. Waite, M. Kerner, U. Damle, E.R. Braverman, G. Bauer, J. Femino, J. Bailey, N. Dinunile, D. Miller, T. Archer, and T. Simpatico. "Understanding the high mind humans are still evolving genetically." *The Institute of Integrative Omics and Applied Biotechnology Journal*. West Bengal, India, 2010.

Burton, D. A., K. Stokes, and G.M. Hall. "Physiological effects of exercise." *Continuing Education in Anaesthesia, Critical Care & Pain*. Cary: Oxford University Press (USA), 2004.

Current Comment Fact Sheets. American College of Sports Medicine. Retrieved from http://www.acsm.org/access-public-information/brochures-fact-sheets/fact-sheets.

Guilleminault, C., A. Clerk, J. Black, M. Labanowski, R. Pelayo, D. Claman. "Nondrug treatment trials in psychophysiologic insomnia." Archives of Intern Medicine. Bethesda: National Institutes of Health, 1995.

Ikenouchi-Sugita, A., R. Yoshimura, K. Sugita, H. Hori, K. Yamada, M. Sakaue, J. Nakamura. "The effects of a walking intervention on depressive feelings and social adaptation in healthy workers." *Journal of UOEH*. Bethesda: National Institutes of Health, 2013.

In Gale Encyclopedia of Medicine online. Retrieved from http://medical-dictionary.thefreedictionary.com/exercise.

Lam, P. and M. Miller. *Why Tai Chi for Arthritis?* Tai Chi for Health Institute. Retrieved from http://www.taichiforhealthinstitute.org/articles/individual_article.php?id=344.

Mayo Clinic staff. Fitness Basics. Mayo Clinic. Retrieved from http://www.mayoclinic.com/health/fitness/ MY00396.

Mobasheri, A. and A.F. Mendes. "Physiology and pathophysiology of musculoskeletal aging: Current research trends and future priorities." *Frontiers in Physiology*. Columbus: Ohio State University, 2013.

President's Council on Fitness, Sports and Nutrition. *Physical Activity Guidelines for Americans*. Retrieved from http://www.fitness.gov/be-active/physical-activity-guidelines-for-americans, 2008.

Ratey, J.J. and E. Hagerman. *Spark: The Revolutionary New Science of Exercise and the Brain*. New York: Little, Brown and Company, 2008.

Sharma, A., V. Madaan, and F.D. Petty. "Exercise for mental health." *Primary Care Companion/Journal of Clinical Psychiatry*. Memphis: 2006.

Siñol, N., E. Martínez-Sánchez, E. Guillamó, M.J. Campins, F. Larger, and J. Trujols. "Effectiveness of exercise as a complementary intervention in addictions: A review." *Adicciones*. Retrieved from http://www.adicciones.es/ files/071-086%20SINOL.pdf.

Westcott W., J. Varghesse, N. Dinubile, N. Moynih, R.L. Loud, S. Whitehead, S. Brothers, J. Giordano, S. Morse, M. Madigan, and K. Blum. "Exercise and nutrition more effective than exercise alone for increasing lean weight and reducing resting blood pressure." *Journal of Exercise Physiologists*. Beaumont: American Society of Exercise Physiologists, 2011.

End Notes

1 S. Cohen and D. Janicki-Deverts, "Can we improve our physical health by altering our social networks?" *Perspectives on Psychological Science*, volume 4, issue no. 4 (2009): pp. 375–78.

2 S. Rollnick, W.R. Miller, and C.C. Butler, *Motivational Interviewing in Health Care: Helping Patients Change Behavior* (New York: Guilford Press, 2008).

3 M.F. Brunette, K.T. Mueser, and R.E. Drake, "A review of research on residential programs for people with severe mental illness and co-occurring substance use disorders." *Drug and Alcohol Review*, volume 23, issue no. 4 (2004): pp. 471–79.

4 S. Rachman, "The evolution of cognitive behavior therapy." *Science and Practice of Cognitive Behavior Therapy* (New York: Oxford University Press, 1997).

5 M.M. Linehan, K.A. Comtois, A.M. Murray, M.Z. Brown, R.J. Gallop, H.L. Heard, N. Lindenboim, "Two-year randomized trial and follow-up of Dialectical Behavior Therapy vs. therapy by experts for suicidal behaviors and Borderline Personality Disorder." *Archives of General Psychiatry*, volume 63, issue no. 7 (2006): pp. 757–66.

6 A. Ellis, *Reason and Emotion in Psychotherapy* (New York: Carol Publishing Group, 1962).

7 R.D. Zettle, "The evolution of a contextual approach to therapy: From comprehensive distancing to ACT." *International Journal of Behavioral Consultation and Therapy*, volume 1, issue no. 2 (2005): pp. 77–89.

8 G.P. Sholevar, *Textbook of Family and Couples Therapy: Clinical Applications* (Washington, DC: American Psychiatric Publishing Inc., 2003), Chap. 1.

9 M.L. Van Etten, and S. Taylor, "Comparative efficacy of treatments for Post-Traumatic Stress Disorder: A meta-analysis." *Clinical Psychology and Psychotherapy*, volume 5 (1998): pp. 126–44.

10 U.S. Department of Health and Human Services, *Detoxification and Substance Abuse Treatment* (2006): pp. 4–5.

11 F. Brennan, D.B. Carr, and M. Cousins, "Pain management: A fundamental human right." *Pain Medicine*, volume 105, issue no. 1 (2007).

12 B. Dubuc, "The Brain from top to bottom." *Canadian Institutes of Health Research: Institute of Neurosciences, Mental Health and Addiction* (2012). Retrieved May 22, 2012, from www.cihr-irsc.gc.ca.

13 M.S. Micozzi and C. Vlahos, "Yoga." *Fundamentals of Complementary and Integrative Medicine* (3rd ed.) (St. Louis, MO: Elsevier Saunders, 2006), 508–17.

14 E.H. Chudler, "Neuroscience for kids." *University of Washington Engineered Biomaterials* (2012) Retrieved May 22, 2012, from http://faculty.washington.edu/chudler/neurok.html.

15 K.S. Saladin, *Anatomy and physiology: The unity of form and function* (New York: McGraw Hill, 2009).

16 Genetic Science Learning Center, "Mental illness: The challenge of dual diagnosis." *Learn.Genetics* (1996). Retrieved May 22, 2012, from http://learn.genetics.utah.edu/content/addiction/issues/mentalillness.html.

17 Genetic Science Learning Center "Ritalin and cocaine: The connection and the controversy." *Learn.Genetics* (1996). Retrieved May 22, 2012, from http://learn.genetics.utah.edu/content/addiction/issues/ritalin.html.

18 G. Maté, *Scattered: How attention-deficit disorder originates and what you can do about it* (New York: Penguin Group, 2000).

19 T.K. Clarke, M. Laucht, M. Ridinger, N. Wodarz, M. Rietschel, W. Maier, G. Schumann, "KCNJ6 is associated with adult alcohol dependence and involved in gene × early life stress interactions in adolescent alcohol drinking." *Neuropsychopharmacology*, volume 36, issue no. 6, (2011): pp. 1142–48.

20 C.T. Taylor, M.H. Pollack, R.T. LeBeau, and N.M. Simon, "Anxiety disorders: Panic, social anxiety, and generalized anxiety, in *Massachusetts General Hospital Comprehensive Clinical Psychiatry* (Philadelphia, PA: Mosby Elsevier, 2008).

21 G. Maté and P.A. Levine, *In the Realm of Hungry Ghosts: Close Encounters with Addiction* (Berkeley, CA: North Atlantic Books, 2010).

22 National Institute of Mental Health, Science Writing, Press, and Dissemination Branch. *Mental Health Medication* (2012). Retrieved, May 22, 2012, from http://www.nimh.nih.gov/health/publications/mental-health-medications/complete-index.shtml.

23 American Society of Addiction Medicine. "Public policy statement on principles of medical ethics adopted by the ASAM board of directors," Oct. 3, 1992. *American Medical Association*. Retrieved from http://www.ama-assn.org/ama/pub/physician-resources/medical-ethics/about-ethics-group/ethics-resource-center/educational-resources/federation-repository-ethics-documents-online/society-addiction-medicine.page.

24 LiveScience, "Addiction Now Defined As Brain Disorder, Not Behavior Problem." *Live Science.com* (2011). Retrieved from http://www.livescience.com/15563-addiction-defined-brain-disease.html.

25 American Society of Addiction Medicine, "Public policy statement on principles of medical ethics adopted by the ASAM board of directors, Oct. 3, 1992." American Medical Association. Retrieved from http://www.ama-assn.org/ama/pub/physician-resources/medical-ethics/about-ethics-group/ethics-resource-center/educational-resources/federation-repository-ethics-documents-online/society-addiction-medicine.page

26 B. Dubuc, "The brain from top to bottom." *Canadian Institute of Neurosciences, Mental Health, and Addiction* (2002). Retrieved from http://thebrain.mcgill.ca.

27 T.J. Gould, "Addiction and cognition." *Addiction Science and Clinical Practice*, volume 5, issue no. 2 (2010): pp. 4–14.

28 J.S. Meyer and L.F. Quenzer, *Psychopharmacology: Drugs, the brain, and behavior* (Sunderland, MA: Sinauer Associates, 2005).

29 Genetic Science Learning Center. "Mental illness: The challenge of dual diagnosis." *Learn.Genetics* (2011). Retrieved from http://learn.genetics.utah.edu/content/addiction/issues/mentalillness.html.

30 T.D. Gould and H.K. Manji, "DARPP-32: A molecular switch at the nexus of reward pathway plasticity." *Proceedings of the National Academy of Sciences*, volume 102, issue no. 2 (2005): pp. 253–4.

31 J.H. Jaffe, "Drug addiction and drug abuse," in *The Pharmacological Basis of Therapeutics* (5th ed.) (New York: MacMillan, 1975), 284–324.

32 J.D. Barchas, P.A. Berger, R.D. Ciaranello, and G.R. Elliot, *Psychopharmacology: From Theory to Practice.* (New York: Oxford University Press, 1977).

33 National Institutes of Health. *Mental Health Medications.* NIH Publication No. 08-3929 (2008). Retrieved from http://www.nimh.nih.gov/health/publications/mental-health-medications/complete-index.shtml.

34 American Psychiatric Association. *Diagnostic and Statistical Manual of Mental Disorders* (4th ed.) (Washington, DC: American Psychiatric Association, 2000).

35 Genetic Science Learning Center. "Addiction treatments past and present." *Learn.Genetics* (2011). Retrieved from http://learn.genetics.utah.edu/content/addiction/issues/treatments.html.

36 M.S. Micozzi and C. Vlahos, "Yoga," in *Fundamentals of Complementary and Integrative Medicine* (3rd ed.) (St. Louis, MO: Elsevier Saunders, 2006), 508–17.

37 B. Vitiello, "Understanding the risk of using medications for attention-deficit hyperactivity disorder with respect to physical growth and cardiovascular function." *Child Adolescent Psychiatric Clinics of North America*, volume 17, issue no. 2, xi, (2008): pp. 459–74.

38 National Institutes of Health. *Mental Health Medications*. NIH Publication No. 08-3929 (2008). Retrieved from http://www.nimh.nih.gov/health/publications/mental-health-medications/complete-index.shtml.

39 American Psychiatric Association. *Diagnostic and Statistical Manual of Mental Disorders* (4th ed.) (Washington, DC: American Psychiatric Association, 2000).

40 J. Kremer, *How to Live Your Dreams*. (Taos, NM: Open Horizons, 2008).

41 S. Rollnick, W.R. Miller, and C.C. Butler, *Motivational interviewing in health care: Helping patients change behavior* (New York: Guilford Press, 2008).

42 W.R. Miller, A. Zweben, C.C. DiClemente, and R.G. Rychtarik, *Motivational Enhancement Therapy Manual* (Washington, DC: National Institute on Alcohol Abuse and Alcoholism, 1992).

43 K. Sciacca, "Removing barriers: Dual Diagnosis treatment and motivational interviewing." *Professional Counselor*, volume 12, issue no. 1 (1997): pp. 41–46.

44 W.R. Miller, A. Zweben, C.C. DiClemente, and R.G. Rychtarik, *Motivational Enhancement Therapy Manual* (Washington, DC: National Institute on Alcohol Abuse and Alcoholism, 1992).

45 A. Roth and P. Fonagy, *What works for whom? A critical review of psychotherapy research* (2nd ed.) (New York: Guilford Press, 2004).

46 L. Dimeff and M.M. Linehan, "Dialectical Behavior Therapy in a nutshell," *The California Psychologist*, volume 34 (2001): pp. 10–13.

47 W.R. Miller, A. Zweben, C.C. DiClemente, and R.G. Rychtarik, *Motivational enhancement therapy manual* (Washington, DC: National Institute on Alcohol Abuse and Alcoholism, 1992).

48 J. Kremer, *How to Live Your Dreams*. (Taos, NM: Open Horizons, 2008).

49 S.W. Bowen, N. Chawla, S.E. Collins, K. Witkiewitz, S. Hsu, J. Grow, G.A. Marlatt, "Mindfulness-based relapse prevention for substance use disorders: A pilot efficacy trial." *Substance Abuse*, volume 30, (2009): pp. 295–305.

50 G.A. Marlatt, and J.R. Gordon, "Determinants of relapse: Implications for the maintenance of behavior change, in *Behavioral Medicine: Changing Health Lifestyles* (New York: Brunner/Mazel, 1980), 410–52.

51 W.R. Miller, and S. Rollnick, *Motivational interviewing: Preparing people to change addictive behavior* (New York: Guilford Press, 1991).

52 Ibid.

53 W.R. Miller and G.S. Rose, "Toward a theory of motivational interviewing," *American Psychologist*, volume 64, issue no. 6 (2009): pp. 527–37.

54 J. Kremer, *How to Live Your Dreams*. (Taos, NM: Open Horizons, 2008).

55 L. Dimeff and M.M. Linehan, "Dialectical Behavior Therapy in a nutshell." *The California Psychologist*, volume 34 (2001): pp. 10–13.

56 J. Kabat-Zinn, *Full Catastrophe Living: Using the Wisdom of Your Body and Mind to Face Stress, Pain, and Illness* (New York: Dell Publishing, 1990).

57 M.M. Linehan and E.T. Dexter-Mazza, "Dialectical Behavior Therapy for Borderline Personality Disorder," in *Clinical Handbook of Psychological Disorders: A Step-by-Step Treatment Manual* (New York: The Guilford Press, 2008), 365–420.

58 Ibid.

59 Ibid.

60 Alcoholics Anonymous. *Alcoholics Anonymous* (3rd ed.) (New York: A.A. World Services, 1986).

61 A. Furnham and T. Yazdanpanahi, "Personality differences and group versus individual brainstorming." *Personality and Individual Differences*, volume 19 (1995): pp. 73–80.

62 P.C. Amrhein, W.R. Miller, C.E. Yahne, M. Palmer, and L. Fulcher, "Client commitment language during motivational interviewing predicts drug use outcomes." *Journal of Consulting and Clinical Psychology*, volume 71 (2003): pp. 862–68.

63 W.R. Miller, and S. Rollnick, *Motivational interviewing: Preparing people to change addictive behavior* (New York: The Guilford Press, 1991).

64 K. Witkiewitz and S. Bowen, "Depression, craving and substance use following a randomized trial of mindfulness-based relapse prevention." *Journal of Consulting and Clinical Psychology*, volume 78, (2010): pp. 362–74.

65 K. Sciacca, (1997). "Removing barriers: Dual Diagnosis treatment and motivational interviewing." *Professional Counselor*, volume 12, issue no. 1 (1997): pp. 41–46.

66 L. Dimeff and M.M. Linehan, "Dialectical Behavior Therapy in a nutshell." *The California Psychologist*, volume 34 (2001): pp. 10–13.

67 W. Dyer, "Seek out and cherish the silence," in *Dr. Wayne W. Dyer*. Retrieved May 11, 2012, from http://www.drwaynedyer.com/

68 Ibid.

69 G.A. Marlatt and J.R. Gordon, "Determinants of relapse: Implications for the maintenance of behavior change," in *Behavioral Medicine: Changing Health Lifestyles* (New York: Brunner/Mazel, 1980), 410–52.

70 A. Roth and P. Fonagy, *What works for whom? A critical review of psychotherapy research* (2nd ed.) (New York: Guilford Press, 2004).

71 A.S. Bellack, M.E. Bennett, J.S. Gearon, C.H. Brown, and Y. Yang, "A randomized clinical trial of a new behavioral treatment for drug abuse in people with severe and persistent mental illness." *Archives of General Psychiatry*, volume 63, issue no. 4 (2006): pp. 426–32.

72 M.E. Copeland, *Dealing with the Effects of Trauma–A Self-Help Guide* (SMA-3717) (Rockville, MD: Substance Abuse and Mental Health Services Administration (SAMHSA), 2002). Retrieved from http://store.samhsa.gov/product/Dealing-with-the-Effects-of-Trauma-A-Self-Help-Guide/SMA-3717.

73 N. Eisenberg, A. Cumberland, T.L. Spinrad, R.A. Fabes, S.A. Shepard, and I. Guthrie, "The relations of regulation and emotionality to children's externalizing and internalizing problem behavior." *Child Development*, volume 67, issue no. 6 (1996): pp. 1112–34.

74 J. Read, B.D. Perry, A. Moskowitz, and J. Connolly, "The contribution of early traumatic events to schizophrenia in some patients: A traumagenic neurodevelopmental model." *Psychiatry: Interpersonal amd Biological Processes*, volume 64, issue no. 4 (2001): pp. 319–45.

75 A. Bandura, *Self-efficacy: The exercise of control* (New York: W.H. Freeman, 1997).

76 V.M. Follette and J.I. Ruzek, *Cognitive-behavioral therapies for trauma* (2nd ed.) (New York: Guilford Press, 2007).

77 W.G. Parrott, (Ed.), *Emotions in social psychology* (Philadelphia, PA: Psychology Press, 2001).

78 R. Plutchik, "The nature of emotions." *American Scientist*, volume 89, issue no. 4 (2001): pp. 334–50.

79 Ibid.

80 W.G. Parrott, (Ed.). *Emotions in social psychology* (Philadelphia, PA: Psychology Press, 2001).

81 A. Downs, Foundationsrnetwork. "Freedom institute presentation: Overcoming Shame Based Trauma," [Video] (2010). Retrieved from http://www.youtube.com/watch?v=0cboTjvW3KQ&list=PLBF018D859DBA32DE&index =1&feature=plpp_video.

82 A. Bandura, *Aggression: A social learning analysis* (Englewood Cliffs, NJ: Prentice-Hall, 1973).

83 V.M. Follette and J.I. Ruzek, *Cognitive-behavioral therapies for trauma* (2nd ed.) (New York: Guilford Press, 2007).

84 N. Eisenberg, R.A. Fabes, and B.C. Murphy, "Parents' reactions to children's negative emotions: Relations to children's social competence and comforting behavior." *Child Development*, volume 67, issue no. 5 (1996): pp. 2227–47.

85 J. Read, B.D. Perry, A. Moskowitz, and J. Connolly, "The contribution of early traumatic events to schizophrenia in some patients: A traumagenic neurodevelopmental model." *Psychiatry: Interpersonal and Biological Processes*, volume 64, issue no. 4 (2001): pp. 319–45.

86 N. Eisenberg, R.A. Fabes, and B.C. Murphy, "Parents' reactions to children's negative emotions: Relations to children's social competence and comforting behavior." *Child Development*, volume 67, issue no. 5 (1996): pp. 2227–47.

87 M.L. Van Etten and S. Taylor, "Comparative efficacy of treatments for post-traumatic stress disorder: A meta-analysis." *Clinical Psychology Psychotherapy*, volume 5, issue no. 3 (1998): pp. 126–44.

88 Ibid.

89 Ibid.

90 J. Read, B.D. Perry, A. Moskowitz, and J. Connolly, "The contribution of early traumatic events to schizophrenia in some patients: A traumagenic neurodevelopmental model." *Psychiatry: Interpersonal and Biological Processes*, volume 64, issue no. 4 (2001): pp. 319–45.

91 W.G. Parrott, ed., *Emotions in social psychology* (Philadelphia, PA: Psychology Press, 2001).

92 A. Bandura, *Aggression: A social learning analysis* (Englewood Cliffs, NJ: Prentice-Hall, 1973).

93 N. Eisenberg, A. Cumberland, T.L. Spinrad, R.A. Fabes, S.A. Shepard, and I. Guthrie, "The relations of regulation and emotionality to children's externalizing and internalizing problem behavior." *Child Development*, volume 67, issue no. 6 (1996): pp. 1112–34.

94 W.G. Parrott, ed., *Emotions in social psychology* (Philadelphia, PA: Psychology Press, 2001).

95 M.L. Van Etten and S. Taylor, "Comparative efficacy of treatments for post-traumatic stress disorder: A meta-analysis." *Clinical Psychology Psychotherapy*, volume 5, issue no. 3 (1998): pp. 126–44.

96 V.M. Follette and J.I. Ruzek, *Cognitive-behavioral therapies for trauma* (2nd ed.) (New York: Guilford Press, 2007).

97 N. Eisenberg, R.A. Fabes, and B.C. Murphy, "Parents' reactions to children's negative emotions: Relations to children's social competence and comforting behavior." *Child Development*, volume 67, issue no. 5 (1996): pp. 2227–47.

98 E.D. Krause, T. Mendelson, and T.R. Lynch, "Childhood emotional invalidation and adult psychological distress: The mediating role of emotional inhibition." *Child Abuse Neglect*, volume 27, issue no. 2 (2003): pp. 199–213.

99 A. Bandura, *Aggression: A social learning analysis* (Englewood Cliffs, NJ: Prentice-Hall, 1973).

100 V.M. Follette and J.I. Ruzek, *Cognitive-behavioral therapies for trauma* (2nd ed.). (New York: Guilford Press, 2007).

101 E.D. Krause, T. Mendelson, and T.R. Lynch, "Childhood emotional invalidation and adult psychological distress: The mediating role of emotional inhibition." *Child Abuse Neglect*, volume 27, issue no. 2 (2003): pp. 199–213.

102 S. Bloch, "A pioneer in psychotherapy research: Aaron Beck." *Australian and New Zealand Journal of Psychiatry*, volume 38, issue nos. 11–12, (2004): pp. 855–67.

103 E. Tolle, *A new earth: Awakening to your life's purpose* (New York: Dutton/Penguin Group, 2005).

104 A. Bandura, *Self-efficacy: The exercise of control* (New York: W. H. Freeman, 1997).

105 N. Eisenberg, R.A. Fabes, and B.C. Murphy, "Parents' reactions to children's negative emotions: Relations to children's social competence and comforting behavior." *Child Development*, volume 67, issue no. 5 (1996): pp. 2227–47.

106 L. Dimeff and M.M. Linehan, "Dialectical Behavior Therapy in a nutshell." *The California Psychologist*, volume 34, issue no. 3, (2001): pp. 1–3.

107 N. Eisenberg, R.A. Fabes, and B.C. Murphy, "Parents' reactions to children's negative emotions: Relations to children's social competence and comforting behavior. *Child Development*, volume 67, issue no. 5 (1996): pp. 2227–47.

108 A. Bandura, *Self-efficacy: The exercise of control* (New York: W. H. Freeman, 1997).

109 A. Bandura, *Aggression: A social learning analysis*. (Englewood Cliffs, NJ: Prentice-Hall, 1973).

110 L.M.C. Van den Bosch, R. Verheul, G.M. Schippers, and W. Van Den Brink, "Dialectical Behavior Therapy of borderline patients with and without substance use problems: Implementation and long-term effects." *Addictive Behaviors*, volume 27, issue no. 6, (2002): pp. 911–923.

111 L. Dimeff, L. M.M. Linehan, "Dialectical Behavior Therapy in a nutshell." *The California Psychologist*, volume 34, issue no. 3, (2001): pp. 1–3.

112 M.M. Linehan, *Skills training manual for treating borderline personality disorder* (New York: Guilford Press, 1993).

113 L. Dimeff and M.M. Linehan, "Dialectical Behavior Therapy in a nutshell." *The California Psychologist*, volume 34, issue no. 3 (2001): pp. 1–3.

114 M.M. Linehan, K.A. Comtois, A.M. Murray, M.Z. Brown, R.J. Gallop, H.L. Heard, N. Lindenboim "Two-year randomized trial and follow-up of Dialectical Behavior Therapy vs. therapy by experts for suicidal behaviors and Borderline Personality Disorder," *Archives of General Psychiatry*, volume 63, issue no. 7 (2006): pp. 757–66.

115 Spirit, in *Dictionary.com*. Retrieved, Feb 3, 2012, from http://dictionary.reference.com/browse/spirit.

116 Spirituality, in *Dictionary.com*. Retrieved, Feb 3, 2012, from http://dictionary.reference.com/browse/spirituality.

117 Religion, in *Dictionary.com*. Retrieved, Feb 3, 2012, from http://dictionary.reference.com/browse/religion.

118 Alcoholics Anonymous. *Alcoholics Anonymous* (4th ed.) (New York: A.A. World Services, 1986).

119 Alcoholics Anonymous. *Twelve Steps and Twelve Traditions* (New York: A.A. World Services, 1981).

120 S.C. Hayes, V.M. Follette, and M.M. Linehan, (Eds.), (2005). *Mindfulness and acceptance: Expanding the cognitive-behavioral tradition* (New York: Guilford Press, 2005).

121 R.J. Donatelle, *Health: The Basics* (6th ed.) (San Francisco, CA: Pearson Education, Inc., 2005).

122 S.B.S. Khalsa, G.S. Khalsa, H.K. Khalsa, and M.K. Khalsa, "Evaluation of a residential Kundalini yoga lifestyle pilot program for addiction in India." *Journal of Ethnicity in Substance Abuse*, volume 7, issue no. 1, (2008): pp. 67–79.

123 J. Kabat-Zinn, E. Wheeler, T. Light, A. Skillings, M.J. Scharf, T.G. Cropley, and J.D. Bernhard, "Influence of a mindfulness meditation-based stress reduction intervention on rates of skin clearing in patients with moderate to severe psoriasis undergoing phototherapy (UVB) and photochemotherapy (PUVA)." *Psychosomatic Medicine*, volume 6, issue no. 5 (1998): 625–32.

124 J. Kabat-Zinn, (2003). "Mindfulness-Based Interventions in context: Past, present, and future." *Clinical Psychology Science and Practice*, volume 10, issue no. 2 (2003): pp. 144–56.

125 J.R. Griffith and M.E. Griffith, *Encountering the sacred in psychotherapy: How to talk with people about their spiritual lives.* (New York: Guilford Press, 2002).

126 B.H. Mccorkle, C. Bohn, T. Hughes, and D. Kim, "'Sacred Moments': Social anxiety in a larger perspective." *Mental Health Religion Culture*, volume 8, issue no. 3 (2005): pp. 227–38.

127 K.I. Pargament, *Spiritually integrated psychotherapy*. (New York: Guilford Press, 2007).

128 P.C. Hill and K.I. Pargament, "Advances in the conceptualization and measurement of religion and spirituality: Implications for physical and mental health research." *American Psychologist*, volume 58 (2003): pp. 64–74.

129 K.R. Scherer, "What are emotions? And how can they be measured?" *Social Science Information*, volume 44, issue no. 4 (2005): pp. 695–729.

130 D.W. Goodwin, "Genetic determinants of alcohol addiction." *Advances in Experimental Medicine and Biology*, volume 56 (1975): pp. 339–55.

131 L.A. Prest, M.J. Benson, and H.O. Protinsky, "Family of origin and current relationship influences on codependency." *Family Process*, volume 37, issue no. 4, (1998) pp. 513–28.

132 M.P. Johnson, "Conflict and control: Gender symmetry and asymmetry in domestic violence." *Violence against Women*, volume 12, issue no. 11, (2006): pp. 1003–18.

133 C. Black, "Family Roles." Retrieved January 16, 2012, from http://claudiablack.com/documents/toD_docLib/13.pdf.

134 World Health Organization. "Proceedings from Inter-Agency meeting on Life Skills Education." World Health Organization Headquarters, April 6–7, 1998, Geneva, Switzerland.

135 K. Witkiewitz and S. Bowen, "Depression, craving, and substance use following a randomized trial of mindfulness-based relapse prevention." *Journal of Consulting and Clinical Psychology*, volume 78 (2010): pp. 362–74.

136 J.E. Irvin, C.A. Bowers, M.E. Dunn, and M.C. Andwang, "Efficacy of relapse prevention: A meta-analytic review," *Journal of Consulting and Clinical Psychology*, volume 67, (1999): pp. 563–70.

137 S.W. Bowen, N. Chawla, S.E. Collins, K. Witkiewitz, S. Hsu, J. Grow, and G. A. Marlatt, "Mindfulness-based relapse prevention for substance use disorders: A pilot efficacy trial." *Substance Abuse*, volume 30 (2009): pp. 295–305.

138.G.A. Marlatt and J.R. Gordon, "Determinants of relapse: Implications for the maintenance of behavior change, in *Behavioral Medicine: Changing Health Lifestyles* (New York: Brunner/Mazel, 1980), 410–52.

139 S.W. Bowen, N. Chawla, S.E. Collins, K. Witkiewitz, S. Hsu, J. Grow, G.A. Marlatt, "Mindfulness-based relapse prevention for substance use disorders: A pilot efficacy trial." *Substance Abuse*, volume 30 (2009): 295–305.

140 M.M. Linehan, H. Schmidt, L.A. Dimeff, J.C. Craft, J. Kanter, and K.A. Comtois, "Dialectical behavior therapy for patients with borderline personality disorder and drug-dependence." *American Journal on Addiction*, volume 8, issue no. 4 (1999): pp. 279–92.

141 T. Bhikkhu, *Access to Insight*. (2010). Retrieved from http://www.accesstoinsight.org/lib/authors/thanissaro/mindfulnessdefined.html.

142 A.S. Bellack, M.E. Bennett, J.S. Gearon, C.H. Brown, and Y. Yang, "A randomized clinical trial of a new behavioral treatment for drug abuse in people with severe and persistent mental illness." *Archives of General Psychiatry*, volume 63, issue no. 4 (2006): pp. 426–32.

143 J. Finnegan and D. Gray, *Recovery from Addiction* (Berkeley, CA: Celestial Arts, 1990).

144 J. Putnam, J. Allshouse, and L.S. Kantor, "US per Capita Food Supply Trends: More Calories, Refined Carbohydrates, and Fats." *FoodReview*, volume 25, issue no. 3. Winter 2002.

145 J.M. Larson, *Seven Weeks to Sobriety* (New York: Fawcett Books, 1992).

146 B.R. Stitt, *Food and Behavior: A Natural Connection* (Manitowoc, Wisconsin: Natural Press, 2004).

147 J. Ross, *The Diet Cure* (New York: Penguin Group, 1999).

148 J. Finnegan and D. Gray, *Recovery from Addiction*. (Berkeley, CA: Celestial Arts, 1990).

149 Ibid.

150 H. Cass and P. Holford, *Natural Highs Feel Good All the Time* (New York: Penguin Group, 2002).

151 J. Ross, *The Diet Cure* (New York: Penguin Group, 1999).

152 H. Cass and P. Holford, *Natural Highs Feel Good All the Time* (New York: Penguin Group, 2002).

153 C. Gant and G. Lewis, *End Your Addiction Now* (New York: Warner Books, Inc., 2002).

154 L. Lipinski, "The Kitchen Transition." *Wise Traditions in Food, Farming, and the Healing Arts, the Quarterly Magazine of the Weston A. Price Foundation*. Retrieved June 2013 from http://www.westonaprice.org/The-Kitchen-Transition.html.

155 Ibid.

156 D. Fishbein and S. Pease, "The Effects of Diet on Behavior: Implications for Criminology and Corrections." *Research in Corrections*, volume 1, issue no. 2. June 1988. Retrieved August 2014 from http://www.nicic.org/pubs/pre/006777.pdf.

157 B.R. Stitt, *Food and Behavior: A Natural Connection* (Manitowoc, WI: Natural Press, 2004).

158 http://www.ehow.com/facts.

Notes